INTERCESSION
YOUR POWER TO
POSSESS NATIONS

(and Everything Else Around You!)

MICHAEL HOWARD

DESTINY IMAGE EUROPE
Via Maiella, 1
66020 San Giovanni Teatino (Ch) - Italy

ISBN: 88-89127-15-5

For Worldwide Distribution
Printed in the U.S.A.

1 2 3 4 5 6 7 8/10 09 08 07 06

This book and all other Destiny Image Europe books are available at Christian bookstores and distributors worldwide.

To order products, or for any other correspondence:

DESTINY IMAGE EUROPE
Via Acquacorrente, 6
65123 - Pescara - Italy
Tel. +39 085 4716623 - Fax: +39 085 4716622
E-mail: info@eurodestinyimage.com

Or reach us on the Internet:

www.eurodestinyimage.com

❧ *Dedication* ❧

I would like to dedicate this work to my friend and fellow intercessor, Samuel Howells, and his noble staff of warriors at the Bible College of Wales in Swansea.

I have had the supreme privilege of fellowship with Rev. Howells and his staff for many years and am so honored to be associated with such men and women. They practice the highest, most admirable qualities of Hebrews 11 and demonstrate Christianity as Jesus ordained it to be. Such warriors have changed the face of nations and the course of history.

❧Contents❧

✎ *Foreword* ✎

One of the key objectives of the Holy Spirit in our day is to see the restoration of apostolic standards in the Church throughout the world. This will herald a release of power which will see the fulfillment of Joel's prophecy, *"In the last days I will pour out of my Spirit upon all flesh."*

This was a particular intercession which the late Rev. Rees Howells carried when he was called to leave a powerful revival ministry in Southern Africa to found the Bible College in Swansea.

It has been our privilege in recent years to see God's hand resting upon individuals from different countries. Each of these carries a distinct anointing. Through the indwelling Holy Spirit the Name of Jesus is being uplifted in their ministries.

One such is our dear friend Michael Howard whom we have known for many years and whose recent visits have greatly encouraged us. The Lord has trained and used him mainly in Africa.

In this book he refers to the spiritual principles which the Holy Spirit applies in the ministry of intercession. Michael shares his own personal experiences of this in real situations, showing how the death and resurrection principles have proved very effective in breaking satan's power and bringing blessing to many.

At the College we have never taken intercession lightly since we witnessed it operating at its deepest level through our founder. It is encouraging, therefore, through this latest of Michael's books, to be reminded of what God can do once He finds a man to stand in the gap.

Our prayer is that the message of this book will prove to be a blessing and challenge many.

Samuel Howells
Honorary Director,
Bible College of Wales

᭞ *Introduction* ᭞

Many people wonder what intercession really is and, once they know, they often ask, "Does it actually work today?" The Holy Spirit led me down the path of intercession before I ever met the "Intercessor" and came to know the Holy Ghost saints of the Bible College of Wales.

The Holy Spirit's dealings are the same in Africa with an African boy as they are in Wales with a Welsh coal miner. Whether one is an African villager in the remote bush of that vast continent or a young man in a Welsh coal mining village, God is able to explode either and both into a vast ministry for the purpose of taking the gospel to the ends of the earth through the methodology of the Holy Spirit. That methodology does not change. It is the same for all and for every age: The vessel must be utterly empty so that the Holy Spirit might fill him or her and therefore work through that person. For such to happen, there must be a process of death. Whilst situations and people may be different, the process remains the same: Death works in me that life might flow in you. It is called the process of the cross and is not a popular message today.

The Holy Spirit is the one who has come to convince people of sin, righteousness, and judgment. This is true in the life of both the believer and the unsaved. It is only the Holy Spirit who knows the mind and will of the Father and is able to translate such onto us. Without His glorious

Person there can be no intercession. He intercedes both through us and in us to reach a lost and dying world.

Every account in the following pages is true. Some people who have a tendency toward diagnostic legalism may raise their eyebrows at "conversations with the Spirit." These readers may split theological hairs and, in so doing, miss the greater purpose of *Intercession*—which is to demonstrate that the Holy Spirit is a distinct Person of the Triune God and has His own characteristics.

This book was written under the most severe conditions. Time and again the enemy sought to prevent the completion of the work. I would like to say a special thanks to my beloved sister and co-director, Roz Heyns, who has worked so hard in typesetting, completing the format, and having this work published. It is an end-time book, and I pray that it will provoke many to seek and work towards obtaining a mantle of intercession.

There have been many confirmations from God about the importance of publishing this book. One that was especially unique came through my sister. Roz was at intercession in the home of some friends in California. A complete stranger who knows nothing of us or our situation or ministry walked directly up to her and declared, "The Lord says to tell your brother to get the book on intercession completed with urgency."

In this book I have endeavored to recount events, emotions, and outcomes accurately, and I pray that many may be mightily inspired and quickened to take hold of God in intercession. Nowhere have I sought to present any kind of doctrinal stand, though I have not failed to clearly present the Lord's feelings toward some traditions exactly as He spoke to me concerning them.

I pray that you, the reader, will find something for yourself as you read.

CHAPTER ONE

Holy Ghost Invasion

THE BREAKTHROUGH CAME in an unprecedented wave upon wave of the presence of the Lord. Suddenly I was carried up in ever-increasing spirals, higher and higher, higher and higher to be immersed in the very heart of God. He was everywhere—so real, so present, so thick as to be almost tangible. The very atmosphere was electrified, alive, quickened, dynamic and fearful. He pervaded every part of my being, and I was exposed and naked before Him. Like Adam in the Garden, I had no place to hide; there could be no pretense and nothing profane in His holy, awesome presence. I felt excited and thrilled, yet terrified and overawed at the same time. Great heaving sobs welled up from deep within—so deep that I did not know from whence they came. He was the Holy Spirit. His light was zeroing in on the recesses of my life, and I was undone, utterly undone. Suddenly the tears began to flow. It was not a trickle but a copious torrent, as if someone had opened the floodgates of a vast dam to release the pent-up waters.

I wept and wept until I felt there was not a drop more that could be shed, and then I wept some more, unable to stop the flow. My body was not my own. I was in the hands of One so holy and divine, One who had come in and taken complete control. He was clearly and distinctly saying, "There can be nothing of you, Michael, nothing of you."

I realized in a flash that this was the infinite invading the finite, the unlimited meeting the limited, the timeless squeezing into time that was too small to contain His vastness. The Holy Spirit had indeed come and catapulted me into the very presence of God, into the throne room of

Heaven, into the heartbeat of the Father. I saw the blessed Holy Spirit as a person for the first time. I had known He was, but now the reality exploded upon me. He was requiring surrender—unconditional surrender—and made it quite clear that there could be no progress until He had my assurance that I was ready and willing. It was frightening. I had wanted to meet God, had cried, agonized, and travailed for years for this moment, but when it came it was too holy. My only thought was, "But what if I fail?"

"There is no failure with Me," came the instant and firm reply. "No failure if there is full surrender. I cannot and will not work on any other terms. It is all of Me or not at all."

My whole being shook, and the weeping that began that hour continued for days as the Holy Spirit made Himself more and more real. At the same time, He introduced me to more of the nature of the Father and the Son. Yet it was the Spirit Himself who was working and seeking to take up permanent residence, though it had to be all on His terms. He was ever so gentle yet absolutely firm, and He conveyed the distinct understanding that there was no room for trifling. Everything is crystal clear with Him because He is the Spirit of Truth. He will tolerate no mixture, no shades of gray, no overlapping areas. He zeros in on the important things and discards the peripheral issues that we find so important because we really do not want to get down to business.

I found out that the Holy Spirit is a tough businessman, for He will never lose a deal; bargaining and compromise—NEVER! He had come to utterly convince me of sin and iniquity, and in the following days He acted like a heavenly dentist prodding and poking, scraping and polishing, digging and drilling until He had gone through my entire life. It was not so much sin with which He had to deal, but the abiding motives of the self-life. He began to prod at the "whys" and, in so doing, shook everything I had ever done or wanted to do in the Kingdom.

I detested those who were always trying to impress people by drawing attention to themselves. I had seen far too much jostling for power in the church and hated the selfishness of church politics. The Spirit showed me, however, just how prominent a role people's opinions played in my life, not so much from the point of view of impressing them but of hurting them.

"You can never be fully Mine until you are dead to people's opinions. You cannot be afraid of disappointing, hurting, or offending people because of your obedience to Me," He emphasized.

In a moment He showed me the many times I had compromised for the sake of people; I had, in fact, been a people-pleaser and that had to stop. He was going to deal with *relationships* and get to the "nitty-gritty" honesty of the reason for all and any relationship, including those whom I deeply loved. He distinctly emphasized and showed in a new light, *"He that loveth father or mother more than Me is not worthy of Me.... And he that taketh not his cross and followeth after Me, is not worthy of Me"* (Matt. 10:37-38).

I saw for the first time that taking up the cross in this realm would be just as painful and heart-wrenching, more so in fact, than giving up "things" and "activities." They were all alike to the Spirit and they had to go.

Part of the ministry of the Spirit is to convince one of sin, righteousness, and judgment. As He took me into the very presence of the glorious Triune God, I saw Jesus, the Son of Righteousness. He is righteousness personified, so pure, so holy, so awesomely lovely that words absolutely fail to adequately describe the smallest portion of His vast perfection. In a moment I saw His different natures: He is love; He is judge; He is righteousness and peace, mercy and truth, all in one, and I heard Him distinctly say, *"He that hath seen Me hath seen the Father"* (John 14:9).

I had stepped beyond the veil to experience all of God and discovered that the Father is frightening, yet awesomely magnificent and lovely. Each member of the Triune God was distinctly different yet distinctly ONE, and what so totally overwhelmed me is how each of the Three gave such total honor to the other Two. There was no conscious effort; they simply lived it, and I clearly understood for the first time the frighteningly enormous price the whole Godhead had paid in my very own redemption. In seeing Their sacrifice, I saw my own wretchedness and realized that without the Godhead I was utterly, miserably, horribly lost and fit only for eternal separation.

In a split moment, I saw everything I was, measured against the utter perfection and purity of the Heavenly Three, and I abhorred myself. In that process of utter abhorrence, I saw the Glory of the Righteousness personified suddenly become *"the Lamb slain from the foundation of the world*" (Rev. 13:8). I looked into eternity and saw Him with His out-poured blood, the Father's wrath upon Him, and I knew—knew above any doubt—that I was thoroughly cleansed of everything past, present, and future right into eternity.

Suddenly, I was not a stranger, but fully "at home." I had a right to be there, not because of anything I was—for the Holy Spirit was exposing just how rotten and corrupt I was—but all because of Him and Him alone. I was clothed with His light beyond that veil and have lived there ever since.

Ever so reassuringly but emphatically the Spirit demanded, "Your will must go," and I knew that if I was going to abide in the Father there was only one place to go: to the Garden of Gethsemane where He sweat His precious blood. It was there that Jesus, in the severest of agony, cried out, *"Father, if Thou be willing, remove this cup from Me: nevertheless, not My will, but Thine be done"* (see Matt. 26:39).

Through His blood is conquest over our will, which stands as an affront to God. As I pondered that fact, the words of the great hymn, "When I Survey the Wondrous Cross," burned into my soul, and I could hear clearly the slightly changed words of the final stanza:

> Were the whole realm of nature mine,
> That were an offering far too small;
> Love so amazing, so divine,
> Demands my WILL, my life, my all!

I saw clearly just how strong my will was and how many times it had stood firmly in the way of what God had wanted in my life, for my life, and through my life. The root of it all was selfishness, which would have to be dealt with at every level. Before this point, I had looked at the utter selfishness in other believers and marveled at their sin. Now the Holy Spirit showed me the cancer of my own.

"You realize," He insisted, "that everything you are and everything you have must be surrendered: your time, your money, your freedom, your enjoyments."

I began to argue. Imagine the audacity of it? I began to argue that I *had* given up these things, but deep within I knew I was fighting a losing battle because He *is* the Spirit of Truth. He did not have to say anything because I could feel His discernment piercing into the depths of my being, chiseling out all that was dark. I understood just how much He is the *"discerner of the thoughts and intents of the heart"* (Heb. 4:12), and He dealt with me as if I were the only individual in the world. He is not interested in comparisons.

A fear shot through me as I marveled that I stood before One who had eaten in Abraham's tent, and as I was thinking the very thought, He knew what I was thinking. Without any indication whatsoever—for He is such a Gentleman—He allowed the Truth to convict me. I have found out *that*, indeed, is His *modus operandi*. He says very little. He does not need to because His Truth is everywhere and pervades everything. The problem was that, hitherto, I had been blinded to Him and deafened to Him because there was so much of self and so much activity and noise from the world that had forced Him out.

The Holy Spirit works through choice: He manifested the Truth and allowed me to choose—though really it was not a choice at all. How could it be when I was dealing with things eternal? As I just lay before Him, I learned how temporal I had been and how much I had limited God and His ministry in my life.

The hours were ticking away as I was prostrate before the Throne. I saw no apparitions, no blinding light, though my whole body quivered with the fear that if I actually looked up I might see something and I was too afraid! But I distinctly knew that I was in the Throne Room of Heaven sobbing and overawed by all. My whole being was undone. I could not have crawled, let alone stood, and walking was totally out of the question. It was perhaps a good thing as, in my natural, I was more than ready to flee that presence. I understood why Jacob anointed the rock "Bethel" and then fled (see Gen. 28); it was too holy for one so corrupt, and His real dealings are serious, so completely serious.

There is absolutely nothing blasé or casual in the Holy Presence of the Holy Triune God. I could hear the sound of multitudes upon multitudes of voices crying, "Holy! Holy! Holy!" in ever-increasing volume, but it never once drowned out the intimacy of Their dealings with me.

Oh, the ability of the Godhead to give Their whole attention to me was utterly overwhelming.

The surrender that the Spirit was demanding of me was something altogether different from salvation. My life would never really be my own again. At that time, I did not fully comprehend the fruit of such surrender, but I knew that I was dealing with issues vastly greater than my own little world. For the first time, I saw the enormity of the heart of God. I saw, too, that God the Holy Spirit could pour Himself into a single life that is utterly yielded to Him and, through that person, impact the whole world.

A war was raging inside me between my spirit, which was in full agreement with God, and my soul. My mind was trying to bargain, though deep down I knew it was useless. My emotions were over-whelmed, and my will was deeply resisting because it was listening to the loud protestations of the flesh. From deep within echoed the victorious words of that grand hymn:

> My *stubborn will* at last hath yielded;
> I would be Thine and Thine alone;
> And this the prayer my lips are bringing,
> Lord, let in me *Thy will* be done.

> Sweet will of God, still fold me closer,
> Till I am wholly lost in Thee;
> Sweet will of God, still fold me closer,
> Till I am wholly lost in Thee.

As my spirit sang within, I repeated the chorus over and over, over and over, until finally the last verse seemed to clinch the deal:

> Shut in with *Thee, O Lord, forever,*
> My wayward feet no more to roam;
> What power from Thee my soul can sever?
> *The Center of God's Will* my home.

"Yes, Lord, yes, yes, yes," I cried out, not knowing the full consequences of what I was doing, but the deed was sealed and there was no turning back. The tears that had continued to pour throughout this whole experience turned to tears of joy, and I had the distinct feeling that victory was flowing over me in boundless, billowing waves of Holy love. I was immersed in God. He was around me, in me, over me, and through me.

Suddenly, God was speaking and was quoting directly from His Word: *"Ask of Me,"* He said, *"and I shall give thee the heathen for thine inheritance and the uttermost parts of the earth for thy possession"* (Ps. 2:8).

It was too big to even begin to comprehend, but it was God, of that I had not the slightest doubt. The Spirit had zeroed in on the very heartbeat of God, had manifested the deepest desire of God's heart, and had offered me the overwhelming privilege of being a part of His frighteningly enormous program. He showed me in a split second the vast sea of endless humanity and then suddenly declared as He read my very thoughts: *"Behold,* [to Me] *the nations are as a drop of a bucket, and are counted as the small dust of the balance"* (Isa. 40:15).

That settled it. God had spoken. There was nothing else to be said. It was final. Nothing was more important. Nothing was more vital. Nothing was more pressing than that the nations and multitudes who were marching to a Christless eternity should be saved. I saw the agendas of men—so many and varied and all of such vital importance to them—but there was only one paramount agenda to God: **Reach the Nations.** I instantly realized that the entire task of the glorious Triune God was completely and utterly devoted to this one supreme purpose for which Jesus had so freely given His life. All else was rather trivial in comparison, yet we *all* (all humankind) had majored on the trivial.

God showed me that as I devoted my life to His heartbeat, I would have the whole resources of Heaven at my disposal. However, the work would be entirely His, done His way, with His resources, at His command, or not at all. "For," He revealed, "I have a battle plan and a strategy and I will brook no interference. *'My thoughts are not your thoughts, neither are your ways My ways. For, as the heavens are higher than the earth, so are My ways higher than your ways, and My thoughts than your thoughts'"* (Isa. 55:8-9).

That settled the matter; there was no argument. There could be no argument; He is God. His methodology was evident and His command was simple: "Die!" And that was to be the ministry of the Spirit:

> *Always bearing about in the body the dying of the Lord Jesus, that the life also of Jesus might be made manifest in our body. For we which live are always delivered unto death for Jesus' sake, that the life also of Jesus might be made manifest in our mortal flesh. So then death worketh in us, but life in you* (2 Corinthians 4:10-12).

The victorious ministry of the Spirit would henceforth take me over and over to the Cross that "self" might be crucified in order for Jesus to reach out through me to a lost and dying world. In that moment, God's burden became my burden; God's concerns became my concerns; and God's heartbeat became my heartbeat. I had always had a desire to reach the lost and had spent most of my spare time crusading, evangelizing, and witnessing. But to carry the burden of the matter as keenly as God did made it so much bigger, and oh so much more urgent. I have carried it ever since and have very little time for the Western church, which is so cold, indifferent to the cries of the lost, and materialistic in its effort to help.

I marveled at just how God was going to take a young African preacher from an African village, use him, and give him nations. I did not doubt; I could not doubt because the Holy Spirit had taken up residence and He is the Spirit of Truth. That's the most wonderful thing about a true intercessor: He is *always* assured of victory because he carries the purpose of Heaven.

Some five or so hours had passed since the Holy Spirit had come upon me. It seemed only as minutes. When I "came to," I was fully prostrate before the Lord under the great canopy of the glorious African sky. The night was so clear and the stars so close that I felt I could simply reach up and pluck them from their place. The splendor and majesty was awesome. A great stillness blanketed the bush. Only the sound of a small mountain stream could be heard as it gurgled its way downwards. This was the 18th day of a 21-day, water-only fast, and God had assuredly visited me as He had promised He would when I embarked upon the separation. My tent stood a little way off, silhouetted against some thick bushes. I was far away from all people, all disturbances, and all activity. I had a lock-in with God to hear His voice and know His finite purposes. All I had was my bedding, a barrel of water, and my Bible. I slept when I was tired—which was not very often—and spent my waking hours in prayer, praise, meditation, and reading His Word. That night seemed no different from any other except that I had gone outside to marvel at His divine handiwork. Whilst in the midst of adoration, the Holy Spirit had come upon me and, without my realization, He had forced me to the ground, humbled before the very presence of God.

Now His work of molding me to conform me into the likeness of Jesus would begin in earnest so that He might work *through* me to the multitudes who did not know Him. It was going to be all of Him for all of His Glory. This was my trysting place with God, and whenever, in the future, I needed to really wrestle things out before the Lord, I would always resort to the seclusion of that idyllic spot where I could wrestle out matters with the Lord.

CHAPTER TWO

Love Them

G ROWING UP IN colonial Africa with very much of a colonial attitude toward the natives, we had been taught to have the
utmost respect for our elders no matter what their color or persuasion.
That was all very fine if there was a master/servant relationship or one
that could be experienced at arm's length. I had enjoyed numerous
native friends in ever-growing numbers, especially with the expansion of
the mission work, and had a vast outreach to the native villages, but I
was always the "Boss," the one firmly in charge.

This was the first thing that the Holy Spirit saw very necessary to
touch and, oh my, did it hurt. I was rather proud of my influence and
relationship with the natives and especially the native pastors, but it was
all on a wrong foundation. The Holy Spirit clearly spoke to me that
"authority does not come because of birth, color or race, breeding or
education, or anything else that is important to and important in the
world. Authority must come because men recognize My residency and
anointing in your life. Men must follow you, not because of your natural talents, but because they see Me and My wisdom and My fruit."

At that juncture I lived in Chipinge, a farming community in the
eastern border area of the country that had just become "Zimbabwe"
(formerly called "Rhodesia"). It was a magnificent region of rich rolling
hills cultivated with tea and coffee on large estates. The vast district also
abounded with dairy and maize (corn) farms and was altogether
substantially wealthy. The people were, in the main, very traditional. They
came from true Afrikaans trekker (settler) stock and were a "no-nonsense"

breed who had fought the relentless terrorist war in which many beloved friends and family members had died, mainly from land mine explosions on the farm roads. Farmers' wives had stood alone to protect their homesteads and property while their husbands were away fighting in the military. Quite naturally and understandably there was much ill-feeling and some very pent-up emotions. The culture of the Afrikaners was heavily supported by their Dutch Reformed Calvinism, which basically taught that the black man was a lower breed and should be treated as such.

Into this very, very conservative community came I, who was immediately termed a "liberal Englesman." However, I was far from being liberal, let alone English. I embraced their culture, their dress, and their food and visited their farms sharing the love of Jesus. I worked and worked. I tilled the soil, sowed the seed, watered it, and finally saw increase. My ratings were up. I enjoyed the support and popularity of the district, and that was no mean achievement. Many even came to the meetings, despite their Dutch Reformed "Dominee" and his threatening tone towards what he called the *"Secta Kerk."*

Things went so well that the extremist breakaway wing of the Dutch Reformed—known as *"Die Hervormde"* (Reformed)—actually granted permission for me to occupy their church building on a regular basis. Their congregation was small in number and only used the building four times a year for their *"Nagmaal"* or communion. On those occasions, the church building was emptied of everything that identified our congregation and all Hervormde trappings were put back exactly in their place so that the six people might have church without being offended.

As is common in such a close-knit village and farming community, everybody knew everybody else's business. There were no secrets and, much sooner than later, news spread like a brush fire.

The local church flourished, but one thing was greatly troubling: There were no native pastors in the whole district, where there were hundreds of thousands of farm and plantation workers who needed to be reached. Indeed they were *"sheep with no shepherd"* (see Mark 6:34), and the weight I felt from that knowledge became intense.

One of the things that the Holy Spirit had me do was to finance a group of young black men through Bible school. I had watched a few in particular and felt the Holy Spirit clearly direct that, upon their graduation, they should come over to this "Macedonia" and assist in the work. Little did I know what was about to take place. (Thank God that He alone knows *"the end from the beginning"* [Isa. 46:10]; otherwise, we would not embark upon many a journey.)

If I would have understood or realized the humiliation, defeat, and utter death that my "foolhardy" design was about to bring, I would not have laid myself open. And yet, the blessed Holy Spirit was fully in the whole affair and led me on as a sheep to the slaughter. My natural love was going to change for His love, and my choices to His choices. As with most people, my choices of friends, acquaintances, and workers had previously been determined from purely natural characteristics and observations. But the Holy Spirit said, "I am going to teach you a new set of principles that have nothing to do with the way *you* look at people. If you are going to be My vessel, then you have to be filled with My love. And My love is quite unconditional."

The flesh began screaming out before anything even started to happen. I knew I was under warrant of death. It reminded me of my childhood days; whenever we misbehaved, Mother would merely say, "Wait until your Father comes home." That was all it took. We lived in agony until Father came home at lunchtime. However, if nothing was said or done about our infractions at lunch, we would secretly rejoice that we had "escaped"—but Mother never forgot. Rather, she knew Father's lunchtime was short and preferred not to interrupt it with discussions of discipline. As soon as Father came home in the evening, he was greeted—and we kids welcomed him with the greatest enthusiasm—then immediately told: "The kids have misbehaved." There was no argument, no discussion, and no questioning. The order was instantly dispatched, "To the bedroom!" Before we even received our stripes, we began kicking and shouting, bawling and crying. I guess we hoped that if we performed loud enough we might get a lighter sentence of "death." It never worked. On the contrary, we usually got more! And harder!

In the Kingdom, if we quietly and quickly bear the full sentence of death, we rapidly learn the principle and never need repeat lessons. The sentence of death in any area is absolutely final. The Lord clearly showed that if I was to be an instrument in His hands to the ends of the earth, then He would be giving me *"an hundredfold now in this time, houses, and brethren, and sisters, and mothers, and children, and lands, with persecutions"* (Mark 10:30).

In other words, I would not be allowed to choose these peoples; they would be chosen for me, and some of them would be very unlovely and would persecute me. How was I going to react to such? I could respond either with the love of Christ who, even upon the cross, could cry out, "Father forgive them," or with the viciousness of Paul's serpent on the Island of Melita in Acts 28:1-5. The Spirit showed me that the sticks that Paul gathered in that account speak of humanity. It was a *bundle* of sticks, which means many, varied, and each of little or no stature. As soon as the "humanity" was applied to the fire, prophetically speaking, the viper or lower flesh nature came out and attached itself to the man of God. There was no drama from Paul. He simply shook off the serpent back into the fire and never allowed the poison to affect him.

An opportunity to choose my response to trials came when Jemu, a young black pastor, arrived in Chipinge. The problem was that he had absolutely no place to stay. The rural council was building houses, one of which we had bought for him, but somehow they had delayed in completing them. In my mind, there was only one answer: Jemu must move in with me. That decision seemed quite natural to me, *but not in that community!* Although it was perfectly acceptable to have a "Kaffir" *work* for you, it was quite another story to have him *live* with you!

The first and most offended was my own black domo (domestic). He felt absolutely scandalized that he had to serve and wait upon one of his own color!

Meanwhile, Jemu, who was young and just out of Bible school, thought that he had already died and gone to Heaven. He was going to make the very most of such free luxury! And he did—to the hilt. Jemu was very energetic, and together we quickly set up a native work. Jemu decided that it was quite within his jurisdiction to invite all and sundry to *my* home for *my* tea and to enjoy everything else that was *mine*.

"Wrong," said the Spirit, "nothing is yours; it's Mine. If they were *your* chosen friends, you would not mind one bit, would you?"

To fully understand the situation, one has to understand that natives are very carefree. Their staple food is maize (corn), which they make into a very stiff porridge, roll into little balls with their fingers, dip into a gravy of vegetables or meat, and swallow in great amounts. The gravy is only to give flavor, and all is eaten with much smacking of lips—this stimulates the taste buds so that they obtain maximum flavor from the little relish, but is not proper etiquette in our white society. The stiff porridge is simple to make and very cheap; thus, natives usually make great quantities because at any time a relative, friend, or even stranger might walk in and must be fed. Our culture, however, demands to know who is coming for a meal and when and how many, so we can receive guests "properly."

Another personal challenge I faced because of cultural differences was that because of their diet, the smoke from their fires, and their sweat from walking in the heat and humidity, many natives had a very sour body odor that would linger long after their departure. It simply "is not done" in their culture to speak about such things. Well, dear Jemu thought that he should freely invite all and sundry to my home and my table, and many times they would leave their lingering "calling card," as well as the bones from their meal, all over the dining room floor..

The domo, Paul, would slap the plate down in front of Jemu at dinner and utterly refuse to serve him. He would throw Jemu's laundry out the back and refuse to wash it indoors, let alone iron it. Jemu brought his friends to the house, but Paul would not offer them tea; and as soon as they left, Paul would vacuum the whole room and spray everything with air freshener. "They stink!" he would say.

Every day I would march down to the council to inquire when the house was to be complete, and every day there would be another typical African delay: "The cement did not come," "The mixer is bloke," "No water," "Forgot to order the flames for windows," and on and on and on!

"You don't get it," whispered the Holy Spirit. "It's not Jemu in school, but you!"

Each and every time that I determined to speak to Jemu about everything—and it was at least a dozen times a day—the Holy Spirit would quietly say, "You are to say nothing."

Little did I know, the worst, the very worst, was still to come! How I supposed that I was going to keep secret the fact that a black man was living in my home, I do not know. I had really thought that it would be for only a few days! But the days *dragged* into weeks, and the weeks elasticized into months. My flesh screamed. I loved to entertain, and everybody wondered why I had ceased to do so. I would try to chase Jemu out of the house before nine in the morning when any visitors might arrive. I schemed and manipulated and cried and died a thousand deaths, all to no avail. Things got worse and worse.

Then horror of horrors struck! It was Sunday morning, and the chapel was full. Everybody was standing and worshipping. Suddenly I opened my eyes. There was Jemu with the first ten members of his new congregation. I broke out into an instant sweat, which trickled right down my whole body and drenched my socks. I was sure that there was at least an instant ten-degree increase in temperature.

The natives have an amazing way of being able to squeeze in any-where, and on this particular day, while the congregation was worship-ping, they distributed themselves amongst the members. I groaned. I was done for. Jemu had not mentioned a word about his plan. He grinned from ear to ear in victory. He was so proud of his achievement. I fumed. This was the *Hervormde Kerk*, and they had clearly said, "NO *Kaffirs*" in the building.

"Oh God," I whispered. "I'm dead. It's over...."

"I wish it were," replied the Spirit, "so that we could get on with the ministry. It's you who is holding up the program...."

How was I going to explain to the congregation just who these peo-ple were? Of course, the elders knew that Jemu was with me but not on what basis. I had been so concerned about reaching out to the natives, but not in my wildest imagination had I realized on what terms I would have to do it. What a mess I was in! While I tried to smile sweetly, I was so miserable and simply wanted to run away. The congregation always mingled for tea after the service—however, was I going to cancel tea that morning and save face? I could not; the ladies had already pre-pared! How was I going to introduce Jemu while at the same time let everyone know that he had "gate-crashed" the church service and his presence there was not my responsibility? I was leading the worship but felt so hollow, so empty. Of course I was!

"You're a sham," said the Holy Spirit. "It's all pretense. How dare you stand to worship God when you're more concerned about *people's* opinions than *His* opinion?"

But…but…but You don't understand, I blurted inaudibly as I tried to sing the next chorus. Just then I saw Jemu's people edge their way in amongst the very traditional farmers. *Oh I hope none of them stink,* I thought.

"The greatest thing in all my life is knowing You…," the song declared.

"Hypocrite," whispered the Holy Spirit. "Die!"

"Send revival, Lord…," we sang on.

"How can I? You don't really love them!" interrupted the Spirit.

The fight was on. I was ugly, and the Spirit was being tough. "Enough is enough," I clearly heard Him say. "This has gone on too long!" During the entire song service He wiped the floor with me until there was nothing left. "You have until tonight to decide (to die to self), or I will remove your candlestick, and it's over. Tonight at sunset I will come for your answer." With that, He was gone, leaving me to my misery.

Somehow I got through the service, tea, and lunch before fleeing in terror to do battle with myself. When the Lord showed me that I really had not kept my feelings and attitudes secret—that they were obvious to all—and such would actually keep someone out of the Kingdom, I finally broke. To think that a man might reject Christ because of me was absolutely unpardonable. I felt utterly wretched as I thoroughly examined my own corrupt nature for the first time.

"If you really wish to win these people and to work amongst them, you have to love them unconditionally."

"But I can't," I finally wailed, "we're really worlds apart."

"Ah," replied the Spirit, "now you're being honest for the first time. If you will surrender to Me, I will love them through you. It is the only way that I can reach the lost—through you! Are you willing?" He questioned.

"Yes, Lord, I really am, but very helpless." At that moment I yielded; and as I did, I felt the liquid love of God begin to pour through my whole being. The misery and agony of the last couple of months, which had climaxed that morning, suddenly rolled away and I was free. I was so free and excited that I leapt up from under the bush where I had been wrestling and began to rejoice and dance and shout and jump. And, as

I did, I saw the sun finally sink below the horizon. That night I went home to face Jemu as a new man.

The most incredible thing, then, was that I could lay down requirements and standards not from a harsh, dominating attitude and point of view, but with a love and compassion that made what I had to say both understandable and acceptable. And, most amazing of all, I found that Jemu instantly changed. Hitherto, he had dug in his heels and had acted in a confrontational way. Now he became as a meek lamb.

Most amazing of all was that suddenly everything at the Council started to fall into place, and Jemu's house began to be built with the greatest of speed. It was completed within the month. My attitude had changed, however, and it did not matter to me if Jemu stayed permanently. The Spirit had gained a victory, a very important victory. The words of Jesus, *"By this shall all men know that ye are My disciples, if ye have love one to another"* (John 13:35), had to be put into action in my life to be real.

The reality of the victory became evident the very next Friday after Jemu's group had attended church. Jemu arose early—which he had never done before. He then took some gardening tools—which he had never done before—and went off to work at his new plot. Because I was a bachelor, my home was free and open to visitors, and many of the farming parents who had children at the local boarding school would simply drop in for tea whilst waiting to collect their children for the weekend. That particular morning I was out, and the wife of a very influential deacon and very precious friend dropped by the house. She had never before met Jemu nor, up to that time, knew anything about the native work. As she sat in the living room drinking her tea, Jemu arrived. He put the garden equipment neatly on the porch and entered the house. He was covered with dirt and looked like the gardener. He moved towards the lady to greet her but obviously thought better because of his condition. Oh my, how things had changed in five short days! Turning without a word he walked off down the passage and went to the bathroom and ran a bath.

Now, this very proper Afrikaans lady was absolutely scandalized. *The pastor's gardener was bathing in his bath!*

(Sometime later I told her, "It's all right, honey, *your* maid uses your *toothbrush* when you're not around! What the eye doesn't see, the heart does not grieve about.")

She immediately fled the house and rushed to report what she had seen to the church secretary, who explained that it must be Jemu, whereupon she was all the more scandalized. She returned to my house after collecting her children and blurted out, "Pastor, oh Pastor, I won't tell my husband. It will ruin the ministry. What will the community say?"

"You know, Maureen," I said, "I don't care what the community says. We want revival for everyone and will never have it until we, ourselves, get revived deep down. That will only come when I repent of my rotten religious spirit."

Well, Jemu and his *"Kaffirs"* kept coming to the Hervormde Kerk and squeezing themselves in amongst the people. I watched as the Holy Spirit dealt with the attitude of others but *I* really was the key. The fact that I would not agree with them, nor take their side, nor quench the dealings of the Holy Spirit as He took the congregation through death, made them realize where I stood. I *never* demanded anything of anyone that I had not surrendered myself or demanded of myself.

As the congregation struggled with the changes, their carnal nature would express itself in many ways: explosions of anger, resignation from the Church (but they *always* came back), tirades, and accusations. Remember that many of the members had lost loved ones to black terrorists who had been mostly young malcontents, and now here was a young black pastor right in their midst!

One farmer in particular—whose lovely home had been burned to the ground, his cattle massacred, and himself shot—dug in his heels. I marveled every Sunday as one native or another always managed to edge himself or herself next to Donald. No matter how he tried, he could not prevent it from happening. Finally one day he exploded, and out poured all the resentment, bitterness, anger, and unforgiveness. Donald was a tough Afrikaaner, and it was extremely rare for such men to weep, but there he was under the dealings of the Holy Spirit. He sobbed his way through to victory, and when Donald came through, a spirit was broken over all the others!

God was preparing His people for that which was to come and from thereafter the race/color factor was never more an issue. Love indeed became the order of the day as homes were opened, tea was taken together and, above all, people could pray and fast together and for each other. Though we all had our different houses, cultures, and lifestyles, we became a united community and were really ready to lay down our lives for one another. This indeed was the *"Lord's doing, and it* [was] *marvelous in our eyes"* (Matt. 21:42).

The final incident that ended the matter, once and for all, involved one couple—wife Joey, husband Huey—who just never seemed to break through. A certain colored (mulatto) pastor and his team were invited to preach at our church, and people from our congregation agreed to provide lodging for them. His very name denoted his racial heritage—or so I thought! Apparently I was mistaken, however, and Joey and Huey *insisted* on having not one, but two people to stay with them. As often happens, the old jalopy that the pastor and his team were riding in broke down, so they arrived very late at night. Everyone was billeted out and, since it was so late, Joey was already in bed asleep. Her husband, Huey, was a lovely, naïve man, who never even thought about the race issue, nor even recognized his guests as colored. The next morning, as "hostess with the mostest," Joey marched into the room in a proper servant role to get the shock of her life upon seeing two coloreds occupying *her* beds!

These two guests, however, soon disarmed Joey with their charm and love. Coloreds were step one for her but a "Kaffir;" never! Some months later a very fine Zulu pastor was coming to preach; and, lo and behold, who should volunteer to have him? Joey and Huey. As they collected him and were driving off, Joey said in Afrikaans, "He may sleep in my bed and do thus and thus, but he's not going to do thus and thus." After arriving at their home, Joey showed him to his room. In the most polite manner and in fluent Afrikaans, the Zulu pastor said, *"Goeie nag, lekker slaap en mag Die Here oer u sein terwyl u slaap"* (which means, "Good night, sleep well, and may God watch over you while you sleep"). Joey was done for. The Spirit broke through! She and her husband became strong crusaders, living with the natives, eating with them, and taxiing them all over the country.

A great victory had been gained, not only with myself, but also with a whole congregation. Never again would such issues be a problem, and the Holy Spirit could release us to the work whereto He had called us (see Acts 13:2).

CHAPTER THREE

War With the Enemy

T HE LORD CLEARLY began to reveal to us that victory over the enemy had to be gained through intercession, not mere words. All too often, people fail to obtain victory because the "sin" and "self" in their lives actually give an open door to the devil to rout them in battle. The Holy Spirit clearly revealed that multitudes across Africa were blinded to the light of His glorious Gospels because their minds and lives were bound by the strongman, the prince of darkness.

As the Holy Spirit consistently gave us victory over "self," besetting habits and sins *within*, so He gave more and more authority *without* to deal with the devil. I clearly saw the devil as the prince of this world, a fact that even Jesus did not dispute. His kingdom was everywhere. I also saw him as *"prince of the power of the air"* (Eph. 2:2) and knew that he had established large spheres of influence in heavenly places (the atmosphere), which led to his domination of whole natural territories, nations, and continents.

The Holy Spirit distinctly showed me that the "prince of Persia"— with whom Michael, the archangel of war, had to battle in order for the messenger to get to Daniel (see Dan. 10)—was still in control of Persia. Evidence of this could be seen in the endless wars and revolutions in the Middle East, notably Iran and Iraq at that time. In particular, God wanted us to deal with home territory before casting the net further afield. He spoke distinctly from His Word that *"if I cast out devils by the Spirit of God, then the Kingdom of God is come unto you"* (Matt. 12:28).

We wanted that power so we could show the native villagers that there was something greater than their witch doctors, greater than their fears and bondages, greater than their medicines and traditions, and greater than the devil. The Holy Spirit assured us that when we gained a position over the enemy we would see the devil cast down just as Jesus declared: *"I beheld satan as lightning fall from heaven. Behold, I give unto you power to tread on serpents and scorpions, and over all the power of the enemy: and nothing shall by any means hurt you"* (Luke 10:18-19). The Holy Spirit quickly taught that such power was not an automatic right but had to be obtained through positioning. He showed us that we should not seek the power but, rather, should seek Him and that of ourselves we could do absolutely nothing, for *"it is the spirit that quickeneth; the flesh profiteth nothing..."* (John 6:63).

I marveled as I saw the Holy Spirit take us through boot camp and basic training, mold us into a fighting force, and issue us God's battle orders—all just as He had told me that night He had come upon me. And the ultimate purpose was to shine His light and show His love to the nations. *"The people that walked in darkness have seen a great light: they that dwell in the land of the shadow of death, upon them hath the light shined"* (Isa. 9:2).

As I looked with the eye of the Spirit I saw the eastern border area of Zimbabwe stretching for endless miles; I saw the neighboring countries, and I saw the whole African continent languishing under the heavy weight of centuries of oppression by the enemy of our souls—the devil. In an instant I saw all the wickedness that had been perpetrated on the African continent: civil wars; hatred; slavery; poverty; fear; human sacrifices; oppression of natives by natives, natives by whites, and natives by Arabs; and I saw with anguish the victory of the enemy, victory upon victory. I felt the Holy Spirit course through me with anger and indignation and declare:

> *The people of the land have used oppression, and exercised robbery, and have vexed the poor and needy: yea, they have oppressed the stranger wrongfully. And I sought for a man among them, that should make up the hedge, and stand in the gap before Me for the land, that I should not destroy it: but I found none* (Ezekiel 22:29-30).

The Holy Spirit was calling me to action and saying that numbers did not matter in the least to Him. *"After all,"* He said, *"it's not by man's might nor by man's power but by Me"* (see Zech. 4:6).

I knew that the sentence of death was upon me and it was useless to argue, though the enormity of the task was frightening. We were up against centuries-old strongholds, against the devil so deeply ingrained that he and his minions were part—a deep part—of the very native culture. To smash that—utterly smash it—was not going to be easy.

"I have the time," emphasized the Spirit. "I've waited a long time. Are you willing?" He questioned as He always seemed to do. This was to be a test case for much greater things of which, at that point, I had not the slightest inkling.

Living in our district were three key witch doctors: one man and two women.

"Like a stone thrown into a pond and causing ever-increasing concentric circles of ripples is how we will work," the Spirit revealed. "We'll start with home ground and move out until we engulf the entire sub-continent and then move on from there."

The three witch doctors had a vast and powerful network that covered many countries. One of the women was very powerful in calling up spirits and causing them to manifest as animals. She terrorized whole areas by calling up spirits that would take on the form of elephants and then stampede through the bush. It was not imagination. This demonic herd had actually been seen and heard by many natives on many occasions. Even national soldiers, armed with AK-47 automatic rifles, refused to go out against such awesomely fearful manifestations of the supernatural. This was 1982, not the Dark Ages, yet no matter what the Age, the devil is at work, for he knows he has but a short time.

Another of the witch doctors—the man—was very famous for his healing potions. Many influential natives came from all over the African sub-continent to consult with him.

"He is robbing the Glory that is rightfully the Lord's," said the Holy Spirit, "and it must stop."

The multitudes that were worshipping this devil because of his diabolic healing power had to see the great power of the Holy Spirit—only then would they be set free, when they saw the strongman bound.

"Do not go out against the enemy until you are fully equipped," warned the Holy Spirit, "or he will jump all over you and utterly defeat you and derail *My* program."

I was instantly reminded of the demoniac in Acts who beat up the sons of Sceva, with the spirit in him crying out, *"Jesus I know, and Paul I know; but who are ye?"* (Acts 19:15). When the devil sees the real thing, he knows he is defeated. There was to be no "hit and miss," no "doubts," and no "maybe." When the arrow was fired, it had to fly true with the first shot. There would be no second chance. The Spirit revealed that we were up against a real Goliath, and we needed to be like David: The first stone had to land fairly and squarely between the eyes of the giant. Therefore, we had to have the whole power and accuracy of Heaven behind us.

Apart from the normal activities of the fellowship there was intercession on a nightly basis in times of crisis. Such seemed almost permanent! It was pointless to go out campaigning and winning the lost until the battle was won in the heavens. In intercession there is a key that will finally unlock the strongest door. The secret is to find that key. In the meantime the Holy Spirit deals with the intercessor as well, taking him or her to the depths of death in each and every matter so that all the Glory might go to Jesus. We wept, we fought, we agonized, we fasted. At times the burden was heavy, so heavy that we felt as if the very life was being pressed out of us. Before us lay the enormity of the price of failure, and we knew that we were drinking of the cup as He had done in Gethsemane; and it had to be to the bitter dregs.

It was obvious that we were dealing with some very strong princes of darkness who had, like granite, been *in situ* for centuries, and they were very obstinate. They were not going to be dislodged without a major fight. Within the natural man, there was the part that said, "This is hopeless"; the arm of flesh will always speak defeat whilst the eye of the Spirit declares victory. Each week, the blessed Holy Spirit would take us a little higher in Himself. Of course the enemy would raise up dissenters, even from amongst our own ranks, who would oppose the work. The Holy Spirit took us to Nehemiah and showed us the Sanballats and Tobiahs who *"laughed us to scorn, and despised us, and said, 'What is this thing that ye do?'"* (Neh. 2:19).

Through the eye of faith we were able to shout Nehemiah's answer, *"The God of heaven, He will prosper us…. But ye shall have no portion, nor right, nor memorial in* [the victory]" (Neh. 2:20). And indeed, it was true. The dissenters never prospered nor really had a part of what the Holy Spirit did in the following years; like Sanballat and Tobiah they became ene- mies of the work, some even to this day. It profits little to discuss the details nor is it edifying. Perhaps if I had seen the full picture through the eye of faith, I might have better explained it, but we were young and learning. Today, in retrospect of course, we have a clearer, richer, fuller comprehension as the Holy Spirit has pieced together the jigsaw, but back then we felt as Abraham must have, as if we were wandering in a strange land not knowing where we were going.

The Holy Spirit was our only Teacher and Guide and He would do nothing more than take us step by step so that we trusted and abided in Him *and* so that all the Glory went to Jesus. Should it have been any other way, we might have made our own plans, fought our own fight, and perhaps even designed our own victories. Such is the work of "self," which would seek preeminence, but this was His work. He would have it no other way. What a tribute to the workings and faithfulness of the blessed Holy Spirit that those who persevered and "stayed with the stuff" are leaders in many works today across Africa and the nations!

It was the Holy Spirit, speaking through His intercessor, Paul the Apostle, who declared:

> *Giving no offense in anything, that the ministry be not blamed: But in all things approving ourselves as the ministers of God, in much patience, in afflictions, in necessities, in distresses, in stripes, in imprisonments, in tumults, in labors, in watchings, in fastings; by pureness by knowledge, by longsuffering, by kindness, by the Holy Ghost, by love unfeigned, by the word of truth, by the power of God, by the armor of righteousness on the right hand and on the left, by honor and dishonor, by evil report and good report: as deceivers, and yet true; as unknown and yet well known; as dying, and, behold, we live; as chastened and not killed; as sorrowful, yet always rejoicing; as poor, yet making many rich; as having nothing, and yet possessing all things* (2 Corinthians 6:3-10).

Such is the life of the true intercessor locked in with God whose life, purpose, and ministry is so often misunderstood.

Every one of our members passed through the fire. Some even became despised by their own families who would no longer have anything to do with them. People walking down the street would deliberately cross to the other side of the road when an intercessor came along, treating us almost as if we had leprosy.

The battle raged on relentlessly. What seemed to give the devil even more legitimacy was that the black terrorist army had taken over the nation. They had not however won the war fairly on the battlefield but because of interference from the globalists in the Western Hemisphere, primarily England and America. Very significantly, the terrorists of the bush war had made blood covenants with the devil through their witch doctors.

The greatest demonic spirit in Zimbabwe manifested itself through a woman named Mbuya Nehanda. She was a witch in Southern Rhodesia during the 1898-99 Shona and Matabele rebellions against the white settlers. So evil was she that she was hanged, and as she went to the gallows, she declared that her spirit would never die and that she would return to lead the black people in a great uprising to expel all the whites from the land.

In the new Zimbabwe, Mbuya Nehanda was receiving the widest acclaim. She had kept her word. She had returned. Witch doctors were suddenly elevated to equal status with medical doctors and given equal access to all hospitals. Mbuya-mania hit the nation, and the devil reveled. Needless to say, there were multitudes of demon-possessed ex-terrorists who had made blood covenants; they had killed and eaten all kinds of wild animals—drinking their blood and eating their sexual organs—that they might take on that particular animal spirit so as to be aggressive and fearless in battle. The greatest victory was to kill a white soldier and, if possible, to drink his blood and eat his heart or sexual organs, which, they were told by the spirit of Mbuya, would give them all power over the white man and his weapons. The depravity of their war could be seen in the atrocities that they committed, even against the black population.

The witch doctors were riding high on the crest of a very popular wave. Their wealth and status had increased. Formerly they would have been imprisoned or even hanged for their activities; now they were heroes and enjoying it immensely. After all, they let it be known widely that because of their power and their spirits they had enabled the terrorists to overcome and win. The devil was parading arrogantly through the arm of flesh. It was humiliating as darkness was seen to be triumphing over light, the devil over God, evil over good.

They were exceptionally tough days and seemed to get bleaker all the time. The Spirit reminded me over again that:

> *We wrestle not against flesh and blood, but against principalities, against powers, against the rulers of darkness of this world, against spiritual wickedness in high places…. Praying always with all prayer and supplication in the Spirit, and watching thereunto with all perseverance* (Ephesians 6:12,18).

It was during this time that the Holy Spirit revealed to me the power of praise in intercession. He showed how the devil had once been the archangel who led the worship of Heaven and since his fall has hated true, pure praise and worship offered to God. With his knowledge of praise and worship he has corrupted and debased the *true* and created a counterfeit, a profane, the soulish. The Spirit took me to the Word and the account of Jehoshaphat who was told:

> *Be not afraid nor dismayed by reason of the great multitude; for the battle is not yours, but God's….And when they began to sing and to praise, the Lord set ambushments against the children of Ammon, Moab, and mount Seir, which were come against Judah; and they were smitten* (2 Chronicles 20:15,22).

The Holy Spirit also showed through the account of Jericho how the devil is both intimidated by silent action and defeated by the victory shout:

> *So the people shouted when the priests blew with the trumpets; and it came to pass, when the people heard the sound of the trumpet, and the people shouted with a great shout, that the wall fell down flat, so that the people went up into the city, every man straight before him, and they took the city* (Joshua 6:20).

There is no doubt that songs of victory and praise have a real impact in both natural and spiritual realms. The Spirit took me to the account of the great defeat of Pharaoh in the waters of the Red Sea. It was here, through the whole account of Pharaoh, his magicians, and their final defeat, that the Spirit gave us the key to the witch doctors. Just as long as the magicians of Egypt could perform by diabolic enchantment the counterfeit miracles, the devil remained firmly entrenched and Goshen remained enslaved. We read: *"And the magicians did so with their enchantments…and the magicians did so…"* (Exod. 8:7,18).

It was as if we were reading the exact same accounts concerning our own witch doctors who were calling up spirits, sending sickness upon the people, causing weather changes, and encouraging the new government in their arrogance and desire to overthrow the name of Jesus, bring down the church, and establish their wickedness as absolutely legitimate. Moses was not merely confronting Pharaoh in the natural, but also the prince of devils who gave Pharaoh his authority and power.

Hitler, centuries later, had the same backing as Pharaoh and therefore the same authority and power. Both were very strong tools in the hands of satan. The document entitled the "Final Solution" and signed, ironically, in a Jewish mansion in Berlin by Hitler and 36 of his high command was subtitled, "The Extermination of the Jews and the God of the Jews for All Time."

The machinations of the devil have no bounds. If satan, through Pharaoh, could destroy the Jews in Egypt, he thought he could prevent the coming of the Messiah. If satan, through Hitler, could destroy the Jews throughout the world, he thought he could prevent the Second Coming. Both Pharaoh and Hitler were powerful anti-Christs before the real one! But behind both was the devil's hatred of God, of all humanity made in God's likeness, and particularly, for all who named themselves by the Lord's name. Just as King Herod did in later years, Pharaoh slaughtered multitudes of Hebrew boys by feeding them to the Nile gods.

The Spirit was showing the key. There was going to be a dislodging. The new communist government in Zimbabwe had clearly laid out their policy of one state church under the president. The president was a Methodist minister who had rewritten themes of the Bible, in the most blasphemous terms, through the eyes of what he termed a "freedom fighter." He was an affront to God. The new system was an affront to God, and the witch doctors and their enchantments were an affront to God. It was time for the prince over Southern Africa to be removed. We were not involved in a little game or petty prayer, but of real war, thick battle, a win-or-lose situation. The lives of untold multitudes depended upon the outcome; nations depended upon the outcome; the whole future of Christianity in southern Africa depended upon the outcome.

The Holy Spirit kept emphasizing to us that it is "your responsibility and I will brook no failure. No failure!"

The turn in Egypt came when *"the magicians did so with their enchantments to bring forth lice, but they could not: so there were lice upon man, and upon beast. Then the magicians said unto Pharaoh, This is the finger of God..."* (Exod. 8:18-19).

The very next day there was to be the plague of flies, but God said, *"I will sever in that day the land of Goshen, in which My people dwell, that no swarms of flies shall be there....And I will put a division between My people and thy people..."* (Exod. 8:22-23).

The magicians had been able to call down their diabolic plagues over the Hebrews in Goshen—just as the witch doctors were doing in Zimbabwe—but when they could no longer perform and their powers were broken, Goshen was free.

It was not the mere defeat of Pharaoh at the Red Sea, but the routing of the devil himself. It was no wonder that the army of Israel, soon to become the Church in the wilderness, rejoiced and danced. It was not merely a few choruses or hymns but a celebration of unparalleled proportions.

The Spirit showed me, "I was able to show them the greater promise: the deliverance from the enemy once and for all at the cross. I was able to show them 'captivity being led captive' by Jesus and the nation, which the Father had promised Abraham, leaving Abraham's bosom and ascending to paradise. I was able to show them what the victory song and dance could accomplish."

I marveled as the Holy Spirit opened up the revelation of truth of God's Word that in their great rejoicing, Israel had gone into the singing of the new song, the song of the Lamb. And when they began to sing the new song of the Lamb, the enemy fled in every direction. The Holy Spirit showed me that this was powerfully prophetic. In fact, so great was the victory at the Red Sea and so great the rejoicing that,

> *Then the dukes of Edom shall be amazed; the mighty men of Moab, trembling shall take hold upon them; all the inhabitants of Canaan shall melt away. Fear and dread shall fall upon them; by the greatness of Thine arm they shall be as still as a stone; till Thy people pass over, O Lord, till the people pass over, which Thou hast purchased.*

Thou shalt bring them in, and plant them in the mountain of Thine inheritance, in the place, O Lord, which Thou hast made for Thee to dwell in, in the Sanctuary, O Lord, which Thy hands have established (Exodus 15:15-17).

The Spirit expressly revealed that as Israel worshipped, praised, and danced at the Red Sea, they opened up a highway, a clear route all the way to Canaan, and that all the tribes of Canaan were already terrorized. Why? Because their magicians, their astrologers, and their satanic princes revealed that Pharaoh and his army were utterly defeated, drowned, and that all the demonic forces had been utterly routed and lost their legitimacy and power. Canaan in a mere ten days was going to experience the same annihilation.

To fully confirm the role of the victory dance, the praise and worship, and the new song, the Holy Spirit—oh what a divine Teacher of Truth—took me into Revelation and showed me where He had linked together the Song of Moses and the Lamb: *"And they sing the song of Moses the servant of God and the song of the Lamb, saying, Great and marvelous are Thy works, Lord God Almighty; just and true are Thy ways, Thou King of saints"* (Rev. 15:3).

"Nowhere else," said the Spirit, "have I recorded the actual title of an earthly song in Heaven. And it was I who inspired Israel to sing the Song of the Lamb at the Red Sea. You see, it has always been in the Father's heart, a heart I know and long to reveal to the sons of men. You do not know just how much the Father is blessed by worship, especially when it glorifies His Son," continued the Holy Spirit. "No mortal can fully grasp the significance of the Red Sea victory. It was an earthly defeat for the enemy and set a precedent. All of Heaven stood still and watched and then celebrated the event. The next time all of Heaven marveled was when Jesus led captivity captive. I recorded that prophetically in Psalm 24."

The awesomeness of the reality of the very Person of the Holy Spirit talking to me and leading me through the Word that He had penned from the heart of the Father was staggering. With His light upon the Word, it became so alive, so meaningful, and so practical. Finally the Spirit led us through Psalm 149 and taught us the real significance of praise and worship and the new song. He said, "You see, when the high praises of God are in your mouth then a two-edged sword will be in your hand."

The high praises are a new song. The new song is the victory the Father has already purposed in His heart expressed in earthly words. The reason men so seldom express the new song is because they have limited understanding, and secondly, because they lack the boldness required to do so. Of course to even start you have to be one with the Father's will. That's a problem to most. Only then, when the high praises are in your mouth will you have the sword in your hand: "I will so anoint the Word that as you speak it under My direction and authority you will see supernatural manifestations: *'To execute vengeance upon the heathen, and punishments upon the people; to bind their kings with chains, and their nobles with fetters of iron; to execute upon them the judgment written: this honor have all His saints'* (Ps. 149:7-9)."

The Spirit clearly revealed that the kings and nobles were ruling princes of darkness who were already defeated *"by the blood of the Lamb and the word of our testimony"* (see Rev. 12:11). But He further explained that where men deliberately and willfully aligned themselves with the enemy and were used as his instruments in the natural realm, they would reap God's swift judgment if they did not repent. The Spirit said, "When I begin to move in revival, it is a more holy event than men could ever imagine. Therefore revival is not something with which to trifle. It is for this reason that Ananias and Sapphira died and others have dropped dead as they mocked and ridiculed my revivalists. I never tolerate the holy being made profane."

The Holy Spirit had fully revealed the key to dealing with the strongman. We had taken months to reach that point in the battle. We began to put into practice the principles He had enunciated and we began to see a dramatic change in our intercession. With the full armor of God and the high praises, we noticed the enemy losing his grip. This manifested itself in the natural realm by a decrease in hostility and a freer atmosphere (for many times it had felt as if the very skies were bound), as well as the sentence of death upon waves of sickness that hit the district. The most noticeable change was in the hard-line attitude of the communist governor and his aides. They softened their stance and became far more amicable in all their dealings.

Suddenly one day there was a significant breakthrough. We rejoiced, danced, and sang as if we, like Miriam, had just gained a victory equal to hers. The celebration lasted several hours. We could see the enemy "thrashed" and his tentacles lose complete grip. Then the Holy Spirit clearly said, "Confront."

We spent the next few weeks marching into the territory of every witch doctor to triumphantly tell them they were a spent force. Oh my, did they cast their bones, shake their charms, lancet themselves, prepare their enchantments, and kill their sacrificial animals to try to terrorize us. They threatened us with all kinds of death, the government, loss of loved one, sickness, and disease. Everything, I mean *everything* they tried, totally failed. We were under the anointing and unction of God, and nothing by any means could harm us. Oh what joy in victory! District after district waited to see the outcome with bated breath. The whole province was electrified as news rapidly spread about our "arrogance," and the witch doctors held their secret councils to discuss how they were going to deal with the situation. They saw, should they lose, the loss of their power and influence and, consequently, their wealth. That made them very angry.

The victorious turning point came when the leading witch doctor, who had influence all across the subcontinent, suddenly and unexplainably dropped dead. His assistant rapidly packed up and moved from the province declaring that "there is no more power" and that his master had died in the process of "witching" the missionaries with death. Then, in light of the news, the leading witch sent for some of the women. She declared that she had lost her power and it was hopeless to come against us because she knew this "was God, and His power is greater than mine." She wailed. "I want Jesus! I want Jesus!" She was gloriously saved as she repented and was delivered of all of her demons. Then, like falling dominoes in a line, the witch doctors and witches either fled or surrendered to the power of Jesus.

I felt veritably as Elijah must have on Mount Carmel. The fruit of victory would not always be visible to us, but this time the Lord allowed us to taste victory. Oh how we rejoiced and gave Glory to Him. It was all for Him. We knew without doubt that we would have messed up a long time back, but the blessed Holy Spirit had kept us steadfastly on the road that led to victory. It was all His work, His methods, and His fruit. We were so humbled to think that we had played a role in a nation-shattering event. Just how significant the victory was, did not become clear for many years. In the interim we continued with the ministry, enjoying the fruit of what had been a tough fight for over 15 long months.

CHAPTER FOUR

Revival Fires

THE HOLY SPIRIT gave us a clear picture of the native lands as they were languishing under a huge glass canopy of demonic bondage. He showed that same glass dome begin to crack and then shatter as the high praises ascended and the Glory of the Lord came down. The devil, in the image of a terror-stricken dog looking back over its shoulder, was fleeing in great haste with his tail between his legs. The Word of the Lord was to *"pull down strongholds and cast down imaginations and every high thing that exalteth itself against the knowledge of God, and bring into captivity every thought to the obedience of Christ"* (see 2 Cor. 10:4-5).

There can be no revival without deep, soul-searching repentance and meltedness or brokenness at the cross. Only then will the blessings flow. The principle will never change: brokenness before blessing. It is the entire picture of God's Word. To think that true Holy Ghost revival can be obtained in any other way is pure delusion.

The blessed Holy Spirit had come to the remote rural regions of Eastern Zimbabwe because some people had touched Heaven in deep contrition. There was no hype, there were no audiences to impress, and there were no video cameras, television stations, or even cassette recorders to capture what happened. The Lord came down over vast areas of territory and the Lord received all the Glory. It was all of Him anyway. No records were ever kept, but it was the Holy Spirit visiting in response to the heart-wrenching sobs of God's people.

I shall never forget the first outpouring. It happened at a very big, rural secondary school. The hall was filled that evening, a Friday as I recall. The students were there more out of curiosity than to show interest in anything spiritual. As we arrived, I distinctly felt His brooding presence and I knew that He, the Enabler, the Holy Paraclete, was there to glorify Jesus. We had no microphones, not even a musical instrument. Such would have been useless anyway for there was no electricity. The hall was lit by lanterns, which were rather dim, but such things are trivial when God appears.

Jemu led the singing, for the Africans love to sing, but this was altogether different. After order was established during the first song, the Holy Spirit seemed to literally latch on to the next and He became the Divine Worship Leader. The fourth or fifth song was a native chorus of worship to God. It was so simple but under Holy Spirit anointing became so very profound. The more we sang the song, the higher and higher the Spirit was taking us, finally spiraling right up into the very heart of the Father. We were not looking for manifestations because we were largely ignorant of such things. All we desired was that Heaven would come down and touch earth, the divine would infuse the mortal, the holy would touch the profane and change it.

After perhaps an hour of singing that same worship song to the Lord, the atmosphere was so drenched with His holy presence that I was beside myself. My natural man wanted to cry out, "Enough, Lord, or I die," and yet another part of me was desiring more and more of Him. Jesus had indeed come and was being glorified by the Holy Spirit.

The breaking began with a junior teacher whose name was Esther. She was near the platform and had been worshipping with hands uplifted and tears coursing down her face. Without warning, she suddenly collapsed under the full power of the anointing, as great, heaving sobs came from deep within. Then the same manifestation began to happen with one and then another all across the hall. There was no hysteria but the true outworkings of the Holy Spirit revealing the divine person of Jesus. Before long, there were bodies lying everywhere, and such a cry was ascending to God that it sounded like a thousand native funerals all taking place at once. In a sense, it *was* a great funeral: the death and burial of the old man. There was no need to lay hands on anybody or pray for any. The Holy Spirit was at work, and it was His doing, all for the Glory of God. This was something out of the Book of Acts; this was Joel's prophecy coming to pass before our very eyes that *"it shall come to pass afterward, that I will pour out My spirit upon all flesh; and your sons and your daughters shall prophesy...* " (Joel 2:28).

At one stage, after many hours, I went outside the crudely built hall to have a breath of fresh air. The crowd outside was greater than that inside. The news of God's visitation had already been carried to the neighboring villagers. "Come and see! Come and see! God has come to our land," they were crying.

People were on their faces, prostrate before God, others lying on their backs. Some were kneeling, others standing, but God was working. I realized that only God could do such a work. Every now and then a wail would ascend that would soon be caught up by many. The noise was deafening, but the Spirit was touching the deepest recesses of the lives of the natives, many of whom had been badly affected by the war. They were being delivered and healed as they were brought into living reality with the cross. Many testified later of how they had experienced visions of the cross, such visions that they were absolutely broken to see the enormous price that Jesus had paid for their salvation.

In the following days, God continued to pour out Himself upon both students and teachers as well as the surrounding villages. We did not need to be there, but each time we called a meeting, we experienced the same outpouring—for the abiding presence of God had tabernacled on a remote tribal area, transforming the whole area into a Holy Haven.

The vast numbers of people who were being saved needed to be baptized. We chose a Saturday morning for the service, and it was a day that I shall never forget. There must have been, as I recall, about 15 people baptizing in the nearby river that came from the mountains. The people began to come from every area, walking down the bush paths, singing and rejoicing as they came. There was no time to examine each candidate, nor was there really any need to do so; the Holy Spirit was awesomely present and sifting each and every heart. Anybody who had not fully come through to salvation would soon find himself face to face with the Heavenly Orchestrator. Groups of students and villagers were gathered everywhere; some singing, some praying, some weeping, and others shouting, but all were ordered under the control of His mighty hand. As the baptisms proceeded hour after hour, the Holy Spirit descended in heavenly waves and baptized hundreds in Himself so that many came up out of the water speaking in tongues and glorifying God.

There were demoniacs too. Perhaps they were traditionalists, perhaps they were from sects and cults, but it did not matter, nor were we concerned as it was His work. One thing was abundantly clear: Not a single demon-possessed person could pass through the waters without the demons manifesting themselves in the most demonstrative ways. They would cause the people to kick and cavort and twist and slither and thrash the water. Many demoniacs were so strong that they literally pulled those who were baptizing under the water with them.

The Holy Spirit whispered to me so clearly and distinctly, "The devil hates water, for he always remembers what happened in the great flood as well as his defeat at the Red Sea."

I have never baptized a demoniac that I have not seen violent manifestation followed by complete deliverance. I told the demons in one person as they were fighting and thrashing, "I'll drown you, you foul spirits!"

"No! No! No!" they screamed out frantically. "We'll go! We'll go! Let us go," they pleaded, and with horrible shrieks they fled. The Lord was fulfilling His Word as He had promised, and the Kingdom of God had truly come to the dry, dusty, remote tribal regions of Africa. *"But if I cast out devils by the Spirit of God, then the kingdom of God is come unto you"* (Matt. 12:28).

As soon as demoniacs were delivered, the people were baptized again and handed over to others for counseling. The wonder of seeing people set free was so thrilling and uplifting that words totally fail. Oh the power of God is a marvel. To see people who had been bound for years suddenly liberated and transformed was enough to cause anyone to fall at His feet and worship Him. That should be our everyday experience and not something unusual.

The baptizing went on for so long that by the time we were finished standing in that icy river we were totally frozen despite the hot African conditions. What did that really matter when we were dealing with eternal souls? We were so thrilled and excited at being part of such an incredible move of God that we would have given anything to be a part of such. And, it had only just begun. So much more was to happen.

Any true revival must breed a passion for the lost. If it does not, then the claim of such to be *true* revival is very questionable. Revival happens when a holy, infinite God comes down to touch mortal man and, in the process, infects men with the Divine Heartbeat. That Divine Heartbeat was made abundantly clear by Jesus: *"[This] is life eternal, that they might know Thee, the only true God, and Jesus Christ, whom Thou hast sent"* (John 17:3).

It is for this reason that He commanded, *"Go ye into all the world and preach the gospel to every creature"* (Mark 16:15).

Revival demands, absolutely *demands*, our fullest attention to this urgent agenda of God. The best resources of Christendom—people, money, and machinery—must be commissioned for this supreme task and such is precisely what we did. It was amazing how people longed to sacrifice both themselves and their entire resources in order that the lost might be saved. Part of the genuineness of the whole move of the Spirit was that those to whom we were giving could never give back anything in return for they had nothing. But the more God poured Himself into us, the more that we gave out to the "whoever."

In particular, however, God was wanting the unreached to be reached and such were mostly the natives in remote rural areas. Thus the Lord manifested Himself and His particular will as well as His *modus operandi* to us. The latter naturally varies slightly according to people, place, and time, but mostly He revealed in the Acts of His Holy Spirit how the lost were to be reached and by whom. His overall plan has not failed and cannot ever fail. To be a part of that divine program was awesomely honoring and humbling. There was also a distinct feeling that there was an urgency. I realized that we were called to reach our generation *and* to train up the next generation to reach theirs. Without the two operations dovetailing to work together, there would be a major bottleneck of God's purpose.

The next place to which God directed us was an area that had been badly affected by the war. That was the Rusitu Valley. It was overlooking this valley that I later discovered the mission station where Mr. Rees Howells had led revival and the Holy Spirit had fallen in 1910. Of course in those days of 1980, which was soon after the war had ended, the mission station was not operating and most of the buildings had been destroyed by the activities of the terrorists. Nevertheless, there was such a presence of God *brooding* over the place. The Holy Spirit distinctly spoke, "I never forget a place where I have moved. My presence always hovers in places of previous revivals, and I always look for a vessel that will be an instrument whereby I will be enabled to pour out Myself again even in the same place."

I was immediately reminded of God's Word, which says, *"For the eyes of the Lord run to and fro throughout the whole earth, to show Himself strong in the behalf of them whose heart is perfect towards Him…"* (2 Chron. 16:9).

We began to work both the valley and the surrounding mountains. I marveled at how the natives had built their villages high up on the mountainsides and appreciated their fitness after I had made a few climbs. We sent out teams that crisscrossed the whole area, speaking to the natives and sharing with them the glorious message of salvation. They were also informed of a week of evangelistic meetings that were to be held at the old, derelict community center at the head of the valley.

I well remember the place. It was ever so magnificent. The views from mountaintop to mountaintop were spectacular and one always felt deep within as if one would be carried away, transformed straight into Heaven from there. In winter, however, it was bitterly cold, and when the drizzle fell the roads and paths became treacherous. The whole district consisted of thick, red clay, which was very fertile, but oh so heavy. When light rain fell it turned the compacted soils smooth and slippery like ice. Many times we had to dig out our vehicles, which were sunken to their axles in mud; many times did we end up like some mud-plastered savages after we'd been caught in the rain and mud; many times we had to sleep on a lonely mountain road because the way became impassable or treacherous in the dark.

Then again, in summer it was hot and very humid, but we tilled and worked the land, sowed the seed, and wept and wept for the hundreds of thousands of souls. We were under divine direction, and through the eye of faith knew that there would be no failure. Whilst we interceded daily at home, the teams continued to move out. The local witch doctor was very stubborn and could not be persuaded to change his ways. He had heard what happened in other areas and decided that he could stand against the Lord and win.

We stood on God's Word, which says: *"They that sow in tears shall reap in joy. He that goeth forth and weepeth, bearing precious seed, shall doubtless come again with rejoicing, bringing his sheaves with him"* (Ps. 126:5-6).

We were *doubtless* because we were under divine direction. We knew we could not fail; there were no "possibles" or "probables," only absolute certainty that we were going to reap a harvest. God was establishing some principles by which we were to work, and they still hold true to this day. There is never a failure because it is all of God. Intercession is an absolute, no hit-and-miss, no wavering, no uncertainties. When we zeroed in to God's heart it was victory all the way, and Rusitu was all victory.

"Isn't that arrogant?" some might ask.

No, it's confidence and security in Him whilst I fully know that without Him I can do nothing.

God fulfilled His Word. We challenged the demoniacs to come and get delivered and healed. They came, and we cast out devils in the name of Jesus and by the power of the Spirit. It was so wonderful to see the enemy routed. The she-witch over Rusitu could do absolutely nothing as she watched her powers waning in face of the greater power of God. The Kingdom of Heaven had come. It was just like living in Bible times and simply has to be when the Holy Spirit takes control and begins to move.

From the outset of the meetings, the unction and Glory rested so heavily upon the whole place that the Word literally distilled in the hearts of the many hundred who came the first night. The increase swelled into thousands, and with the African "telegraph" the news quickly spread from village to village. Multitudes were getting saved and many healed of diverse sicknesses and diseases. We were waiting on the Lord for spectacular miracles. What we did not realize at the time was that God was taking us through Holy Spirit College, one step at a time, as He instilled within us the principles of intercession. Of course with hindsight we can more clearly see and understand the "why" and "wherefores." The most important thing is that it is all His work and all His Glory.

It was here that the Lord taught such a valuable lesson regarding His Glory. The whole crusade had gone incredibly well, and people began to praise me for the success. I had worked so hard at mobilizing both the crusade team and the people. A wealthy local farmer, whose wife was a drunkard, had seen her delivered and set free. He was so filled with gratitude that he offered his six-seater airplane to fly over the whole area and drop tracts. We literally dropped hundreds of thousands of tracts over different weekends and began a project that led to tracts being systematically dropped over the whole nation. The natives loved those little tracts, and to see them falling from the sky was absolutely thrilling. They were read and re-read and digested over and over. There will be no excuse for this generation of Zimbabweans when they stand before the Lord.

"So," said the Holy Spirit, "you think that you can do it without me?"

As I began to protest He continued, "Remember, I am reading your heart."

Suddenly I saw so very clearly that from the outset He was the enabler and without Him there would be nothing. I was about to learn that God will share His Glory with nobody. That truth has remained with me ever since. I was not going to get away without a punishment. Who says God does not do such a thing? *"For whom the Lord loveth He chasteneth, and scourgeth every son whom He receiveth"* (Heb. 12:6).

"It's not because people are praising you," went on the Holy Spirit, "but because you have received such and are secretly pleased about it, whilst outwardly protesting. That's hypocrisy. Well, I'm leaving you and will rest on your friend."

With that, He was gone and I died. There is absolutely nothing in this world that can compare to feeling the departure of the Holy Spirit yet knowing He is there, within reach. I was convicted that day, utterly convicted, that the worst part of hell is going to be the absolute agony of those who are going there being within reach of God but never able to reach Him.

I instantly entered into a hopeless wilderness and felt sick to the depths of my being. He was around but gone, and for the first time I fully understood David's cry: *"Cast me not away from Thy presence; and take not Thy Holy Spirit from me"* (Ps. 51:11).

I saw Him, the Divine Comforter and Paraclete, rest upon one of my deacons whose preaching simply exploded. Souls poured to the front. Instead of being happy for him and at the results, I became envious. And in a flash the Spirit was back—not as Comforter, mind you, but as Judge!

"Now you're jealous," He accused. "So you've added one sin upon another. That's exactly what Cain did. Soon you'll be angry with Me too."

"No, no," I tried to protest lamely, but I was not even sure myself.

"You're utterly corrupt," went on the Holy Spirit. "Selfish! It is all self."

He then proceeded to give me a sound whipping and absolutely cleaned the floor at my expense. "If I choose to rest on somebody, that's My business, and I'm choosing to rest on Simon," He said.

With that, He was gone again.

My bowels turned to water, and I really felt my tongue cleave to the roof of my mouth. I stumbled off leaving Simon in charge. I disappeared into the bush to have what I later coined as a "pity party with the pigs." You know the kind; it's a "feel sorry for me, nobody loves me" type of affair, which we think is going to get us some human sympathy. That was the last thing I needed or actually wanted. I wanted God, the Holy Spirit, back. He would come only when I *repented*.

Alone in the bush, I began, after a season of self-pity, to examine myself and to realize just how corrupt and rotten self really was. I saw that without the Spirit moving step by step, I was nothing. It was being brought to me in a very practical way that the Spirit may rest on "whomsoever" and that if He once departed we were totally lost. I saw, for the first time, that when the Spirit utterly departed Nebuchadnezzar, he took on the lower nature of the animal kingdom, was a reprobate when left to his own devices because of his pride, and that I was no different.

I looked at the African bush of the Rusitu Valley and did not relish the thought of wandering there eating grass for seven years. Quickly I snapped out of my situation and began to weep and plead before the Lord for my corrupt estate. Sleep was gone from me, food did not interest me, and I did not want to see people. I realized that this was an open door for the enemy, and since I wanted to be "all God's," it hurt deeply that I had allowed an avenue for satan. The real change came when I took my eyes off of what I had lost and put them rather on what I *am*, to the full understanding that He is the *enabler* and it is all of God and nothing of ourselves. I thought, *How indeed dare I receive one fraction of Glory because it is nothing of me.* I was made to see that it was a supreme honor and privilege simply to be used of God, nothing more.

After a couple of days I was thoroughly chastened and I rejoiced for Simon, for the team, and above all that His Kingdom was being established. From that time on, it would never matter again to me whom God was to use. If He chose to remove me from the circuit and place me in a hidden life, was I not His vessel and had I not agreed to die? Now I was in the school of "practical outworking" and the flesh did not enjoy it. There would be other lessons in this area but they would merely build on what had already been established.

I became really excited for members of the teams when they excelled on the field, whether I was with them or not. I saw how the disciples in the Bible jostled each other and competed for first place with the Lord. The others were furious with James and John because of the request of their mother. Why? Because they themselves had not thought of such a request and what if Jesus might grant it? Then there was Matthew the tax collector versus Peter the ex-taxpayer, but by the day of Pentecost they were *one* in the Upper Room with one purpose: to glorify Him, no matter whom He chose to use. Death had come on them all—the sentence of the Holy Spirit—so that henceforth they might live only for the King first and His Kingdom.

The last two days of the crusade were all victory. The Holy Spirit returned on His terms of nothing less than absolute surrender and lifted me into Heaven. I saw His power come down in such reality that one and another native was picked off the ground and seemed suspended in mid-air. Others were literally propelled down the length of that old community hall and lay crumpled in His presence. Heaven came down and saturated us all. God was altogether too vast to cram Himself into us though He *had* inhabited a human body. But we were not knowing Jesus after the flesh, and we saw the resurrected Lord as infinite. Souls came pouring into the meetings so hungry for a touch from God. The powers of darkness and the witch doctors were once again smashed as the power of His Gospels broke through to yet again establish His personage and Kingdom supreme in the Rusitu Valley and surrounding mountains. The Word was going forth with amazing power, and I enjoyed, after the Spirit's dealings, exceptional liberty. It was not the miracles and healings that were sought; it was the brokenness of soul, tears of contrition, voices crying out, "What must we do to be saved?"

Once again the Holy Spirit would come down upon the singing and establish Jesus upon the throne created by the high praises that ascended. His directing was perfectly clear, and all we had to do was follow after. All across the districts, God was breaking through the powers of darkness to manifest the amazing love of Jesus, His beloved, to those who had never heard. Of course there were always baptisms to follow as well as the establishment of churches. Now, while this work continued and the Holy Spirit raised up competent teams of men and women, both black and white, God was leading progressively to higher levels of intercession.

In the early days He graciously gave us those tastes of victory, and this continued for some time. How God molded the black workers and white workers together was marvelous. Such love invaded all, and each was truly ready to lay down his life for his friend. A gardener would stand alongside his master as they prayed for the sick or led one and then another through to salvation. They were one in God, one in the work, and one in vision while the one was yet servant to the other.

How I remember Batsie, what a woman of God! Her husband had been killed in the terrorist war and she had dug in her heels against anything to do with God. But the day came when the Holy Spirit gained the foothold, and oh, what a surrender! She became a mighty warrior. There was nowhere she would not go, nothing she would not do, and she gave everything for the preaching of the Gospels. Above all, she wept and travailed for her servants, especially her gardener, John, who was resistant to God's love just as she had been. We always had to "remember John," and her travails for John went on for about five years. Suddenly, and in a most unexpected way, John yielded, and the fullness of God's love and power broke in upon him. Today, he remains a mighty vessel in the work, for John's surrender was complete, just like that of his mistress.

The last night at Rusitu was the crowning stamp of God's authority and approval. Amidst the incredible praise and the excitement of thousands of natives who had been delivered, healed, and brought into an exciting relationship with the Lord, the Holy Spirit came down and filled the crowd in like fashion to that of the day of Pentecost. Hundreds fell under His awesome power, and all began to speak in other tongues as the Spirit gave them utterance. What a crowning victory for the Lord! It was all His doing and very wonderful in our sight.

For several years, He continued to direct in this fashion and gave a powerful revelation of the Glory of His presence flowing down those eastern border mountains to touch the surrounding nations, the African continent, and the world. Each person became totally infected with the Holy Spirit so that wherever they went they were living instruments of revival. Of course the enemy was at work and always will be, but God prevailed. Just as long as there is complete surrender, God will always prevail.

CHAPTER FIVE

Give Me This Mountain

W hat we all need to understand is that the enemy establishes himself and his kingdom in every area of creation. Like the tentacles of an octopus slithering in everywhere, the devil invades and corrupts all parts of that creation. It is clear for this reason that the Word speaks of the whole creation being redeemed from the sting of death.

"For we know that the whole creation groaneth and travaileth in pain together until now" (Rom. 8:22), and we are to preach the Gospel to every *creature*. In the same fashion as the tentacles of that great octopus must be severed one by one to extricate the foe, so the spiritual tentacles of the enemy have to be extricated from each avenue where he has gained access and the ascendancy. When the power of Pharaoh's magicians was broken, the land of Goshen where Israel resided was freed. While all of Egypt experienced terrifying darkness, Goshen was in the light.

Now, although God had given us great victories over the activities of the witch doctors and their powers and spells, there was another area that the Holy Spirit wanted to address. The witches and warlocks had called up spirits that would change their form, taking on the appearance of hostile animals and reptiles, for the purpose of both terrorizing us and killing us. One witch doctor turned lizards into crocodiles for the purpose of eating another pastor and myself, but in the same way that the Spirit warned Joseph to flee to Egypt with Jesus, He also warned us. The enemy was thwarted. Spirits had been called up and made to appear as serpents, hyenas, and other wild animals, which were launched to attack and devour us. Greater, however, is the Christ who dwells within than the prince of this world. Due to His anointing and authority, one powerful arrow of the declaration of His Word literally melted the enemy before our eyes.

I had one pastor, Chakanza, who had formerly been a witch doctor. He could sit on a small reed mat and fly 200 miles in a night (by the power of the devil) to kill someone and return home that same night. His constant companions were spirits, which manifested as hyenas, lions, and snakes, and his powers worked against all and sundry. Then one day, he met a power that he recognized to be greater—far greater—than the power he was experiencing. He had gone to a Gospel meeting with the intent of disrupting it and making the evangelist look a complete fool. But the evangelist was a vessel who knew how to take hold of God. None of the magic that Chakanza sent against the evangelist worked. He was forced to listen to the Word, which was so forceful and affected him so deeply that he rushed forward and cried out, "What indeed, must I do to be saved?"

The power of God was so much greater that the very next day found Chakanza preaching the Gospel of the resurrected Lord Jesus and directing others to salvation, causing both drought and storm. I was reminded of how Jesus had stilled that demonic storm on the Sea of Galilee, which was an attempt on His life. The disciples had marveled, but Jesus, in essence, had told them that they could do the same.

> *And, behold, there arose a great tempest in the sea, insomuch that the ship was covered with the waves: but He was asleep. And His disciples came to Him, and awoke Him, saying, Lord save us: we perish. And He saith unto them, why are ye fearful, O ye of little faith? Then He arose, and rebuked the winds and the sea; and there was a great calm. But the men marveled, saying, what manner of man is this?* (Matthew 8:24-27)

The devil is the prince of the power of the air and has proved himself over and over to be the force of destruction through hurricanes, tornadoes, and, in Africa, through drought, floods, and cyclones. The first issue with which the Holy Spirit wanted us to deal was a certain mountain in the northeast of the country called Inyangani. It is the highest peak but was a very sinister and foreboding mountain. There is little doubt that certain key witch doctors under that powerful spirit of Mbuya Nehanda had established some sort of a positional stronghold on the place. It sounded much like the prophets of Baal who set up their groves on the various mountains of Israel and Judah. There was always something very strange about Inyangani, and reports of "activity" upon her peak always sent ripples of fear coursing through the local natives.

Of course, the local white farmers made mockery of such things as nonsense, though there were times when their local farm workers reported seeing strange lights upon the peak. Three things could not be denied however. First, a very thick, swirling mist would appear over the mountaintop at different times. There were times, of course, when the cold winds were blowing and would bring in a natural mist, but there were other times when this dark and foreboding mist would appear, often on a calm and sunny day. Second, the very face of the mountain looked evil, and many local farmers did identify with this phenomenon. Third, and most significantly, was the sudden and unexpected disappearance of people whilst out hiking on the mountain. The local natives would merely comment, "Inyangani is hungry again."

It was against all rules for people to hike alone there, and usually experienced trackers would lead groups to the peak. The climb was by no means naturally difficult, and the view at the top was spectacular. I realized that the disappearance of people was supernatural and seemed always to coincide with the appearance of that foreboding mist.

We seemed to be dealing with a horror scene from some novel or movie, but it was all very real. The Holy Spirit spoke clearly, "I want you to take up a position of abiding on that mountain, for it is the key to the whole nation. You may not speak about it until I direct you."

I must confess that I was a little afraid of that place and had never had a desire to ascend the summit. The last disappearance from the mountain had been a young schoolboy. It had been a clear, beautiful day as a group of students in their early teens had begun the assault of Inyangani. They were all excited, and, under the watchful eye of both teacher and game scout, they made their way to the top. Suddenly, about two-thirds of the way up, that frightening mist descended, so thick that the climbers could not even see the person in front of them. As is usual with teenagers, a few of the boys had become stragglers. At first they joked about the mist, but soon they became terrified. All their bravado melted away rapidly. Calling to one another as they heard the game scout doing farther ahead, they managed to bunch together to wait it out. All but one decided to remain where they were until the mist lifted. That one decided he could easily make it to the main body of climbers who sounded as if they were not far off. Leaving the group he groped his way upwards and was never seen again.

By late afternoon the mist lifted and the search began. The following morning saw the helicopters, army, and police with dogs arrive for a thorough search, but there was not a sign of the boy anywhere, not a single indication, no tracks, no scent, nothing. The natives continued shaking their heads and declaring, "That mountain is hungry again."

What was definitely unearthed in that great search were clear signs that sacrifices had been offered upon the mountain! And the remains? Human skeletons!

I soon began to eat, breath, and sleep that wretched mountain. I saw it with the eye of the Spirit, saw the groves, saw the idolatry and the evil. I saw too a nation under the slavery of satan, groaning and sighing in their bondage. The Spirit showed me the efforts of the colonial and subsequent Rhodesian governments to stamp out witchcraft but to no avail.

"This is not a natural war," the Spirit warned one day.

I had become enraged at what had been done: the fear, the violation of people's lives and of families, and above all at how the powers of darkness had perverted the glorious light of Jesus from being revealed. I was a student in the Holy Spirit College and He continued, "You have to die to every natural decision and reaction. Remember, I need obedience and abiding, or you will derail the whole strategy by your emotions."

He continued, *"You are fighting a supernatural war for you 'wrestle not against flesh and blood, but against principalities, against powers, against the rulers of darkness of this world, against spiritual wickedness in high places… Praying always with all prayer and supplication in Me'"* (see Eph. 6:12,18).

I went to the Word and wept my way through Jeremiah:

> *Oh that my head were waters, and mine eyes a fountain of tears, that I might weep day and night for the slain of the daughter of my people…. For the mountains will I take up a weeping and wailing, and for the habitations of the wilderness a lamentation because they are burned up, so that none can pass through them; neither can men hear the voice of the*

cattle; both the fowl of the heavens and the beast are fled; they are gone (Jeremiah 9:1,10).

Then, I was indignant through Isaiah where it says,

The ox knoweth his owner, and the ass his master's crib: but Israel doth not know, my people doth not consider. Ah sinful nation, a people laden with iniquity, a seed of evildoers, children that are corrupters: they have forsaken the Lord, they have provoked the Holy One of Israel unto anger, they are gone away backward (Isaiah 1:3-4).

I found great comfort in the Messianic promises—*"and there shall come forth a rod out of the stem of Jesse, and a Branch shall grow out of his roots: and the spirit of the Lord shall rest upon Him"* (Isa. 11:1-2)—and applied them to the very situation in which I found myself. Finally, I "angered" my way through the Book of First Kings. The difference, however, was that this time it was His anger and not mine.

Now, at the same time that the Spirit had us abiding for the mountain, He had us also taking up the cry regarding the breaking of severe drought, which had hit the nation for six consecutive years. The Spirit showed that the two were interwoven; the prince of the power of the air was able to disrupt the wind patterns and, in actual fact, establish his own. Farmers were going broke, the rural people who existed off the land were in great poverty, and the whole nation was being affected. The Minister of Home Affairs, a medical doctor who had been barred from practice, had become a witch doctor. Using his very considerable office he gathered a great convocation of witch doctors and spirit mediums at the Great Zimbabwe ruins to call on the ancestors to bring forth rain and prove that their gods were greater than the Lord Jesus. It is just such a situation that spells victory for the intercessor—a confrontation with God by the world.

We had been agonizing for some seven or so months over both Mount Inyangani and the drought. I marveled that the situation had become so similar to the account of Elijah and the prophets of Baal in First Kings 18. We had so interceded for the whole Rhodesian situation for years, and it looked, through the natural eye, that all was lost when the communists took over in a rigged election that swept them to power. It was a death of all deaths to any intercessor who had proclaimed any other result—as I had.

But, just when it seemed all had been lost, the hand of God came sweeping down and declared to the new communist government, "Thus far and no farther." Today, God's restraining hand remains upon them, and they have never—even now, 17 years later—been able to institute their wicked design for the land, though they have tried. Christianity is still taught in the schools, but it would appear that the church is losing its position because the leadership is fearful and will not stand against gross sin in the land.

The great battle came during our meetings, which had continued daily. The word of Elijah went forth in the spirit to the whole nation of Zimbabwe, *"How long halt ye between two opinions? If the Lord be God, follow Him: but if Baal, then follow him"* (1 Kings 18:21).

We were greatly exercised by that prophet's bold declaration: *"As the Lord God of Israel liveth, before whom I stand, there shall not be dew nor rain these years but according to my word"* (1 Kings 17:1).

What a mighty position of intercession that prophet had gained concerning the rain. The Holy Spirit spoke, "I want you to gain that same position."

I was tempted to argue, "But who am I, Lord?"

However, when one considers it was not Elijah and nor is it us but the Spirit who both enables and executes, there could be no issue about being in the class of Elijah because it is really the class of the Holy Spirit. Again, there was much victory through the high praises of God. It was not just something we did of our own but we were specifically directed by the Holy Spirit. I well remember the seriousness regarding the issues with which we were contending but we were a joyful people and this expressed itself in our propensity for singing. New songs were always being written and composed because they were expressions of the heart of God for us at that time. We were definitely unconcerned as to whether anyone else enjoyed or even approved of the praise, for we knew it was God's direction in our situation. Many of those same songs would be commercialized if they were written today, but they were His songs and we were not in the business of merchandising nor remotely concerned about such things.

What was most important was that we carried the burden whilst about our daily tasks but were not to display any kind of heaviness. The real victory came through Elijah's mocking the prophets of Baal. It was amazing, for the Holy Spirit said, "Mock the enemy and challenge him, for he is undone."

Oh what victory we experienced as the presence of the Spirit came down and the Glory of the Lord was tangible. We watched the events at the Great Zimbabwe ruins and marveled that we could have been living in Elijah's day and confronting Baal. The witch doctors sacrificed, drank their blood and potions, cut themselves, and cried out to their demon gods whom we had bound in the spirit. They guaranteed that by the next day there would be an abundance of rain—while in actuality it was hotter than ever and the drought continued unabated. Like He did for Elijah, God gave such assurance for rain through our abiding intercession that we knew we had only to ask and it would rain. Oh the victory. Oh the defeat of the enemy. It was complete!

"I want you to go up to that mountain now and redeem it," declared the Holy Spirit. "The victory is complete," He continued, "but even as Abraham was commanded to walk the land, I want you on that mountain."

It was about a six-hour journey followed by a climb of several hours. We left the very next day and collected a couple of local farmers for the assault of the mountain. We carried the communion emblems with us as we ascended the most treacherous face of Inyangani. Somewhere near the summit we sat down for a breather, for it was very steep. The view was magnificent. It was a crystal-clear day with a most breathtaking view. There was not a cloud in the sky. As we sat there, it seemed as if we were on top of the world and the song of the Lord began to fill my heart. Such was the presence of the Holy Spirit that I decided to have communion right away. We prepared the emblems and laid them on a granite rock, and I was reminded that God *"preparest a table before me in the presence of mine enemies"* (Ps. 23:5).

Instantly and without warning, a great wind began to howl around us, and a thick dark mist descended. It was the enemy, and he knew that he was defeated. We could hardly see one another but we partook of the Lord's Supper, literally "in the presence of [our enemy]," the devil. It was his last tactic, but we knew we had the victory; we had paid for it in months of travail. I stood and read the Word of the Lord to the enemy, reminding him that he had been defeated on Mount Carmel and that he was defeated both on that mountain and at the Great Zimbabwe ruins. We cast the emblems upon the mountain slopes and claimed the territory through the shed blood of Jesus Christ. Anointed words poured out as, with Holy Ghost boldness and authority, we reminded the devil that he had been defeated at Calvary nearly 2,000 years ago. Such was the victory in the midst of the darkness that we were rejoicing. I quite felt like that great prophet triumphing over the prophets of Baal as he laughed and mocked them. We indeed mocked the devil, for the victory was all ours. He could not prevail. Oh, the assurance that intercession gives is beyond words.

Just as fast as the wind came up and the mist descended, so it stopped and the mist lifted, not drifting away but disappearing completely in a matter of seconds. Since that day, never has there been such a mist on Inyangani, and of course there has not been another disappearance.

A few weeks later, I was visiting that area again. The mountain *looked* different. A local farmer who was not even saved remarked, "You know, Inyangani has changed. It has a somewhat soft look about it, and I could swear that the thing almost smiles."

Even the local natives declared in triumph that Inyangani was defeated and would never be "hungry" again.

The day after the victory on the mountain back in Chipinge, I immediately went out to Don's farm. By seven in the morning, the temperatures were hot and humid. I had such faith as I knelt on the soil, which was so dry that it was fine red powder. I reminded the devil that his power over the weather pattern was broken and I called upon the Lord to send forth rain, not with pleadings but with the full assurance that the matter was settled. Nothing and nobody would ever persuade me that rain was not on the way. There was not a cloud in the sky, nor the slightest breeze to move the trees. The coffee was in very drab condition, and Don and his wife were trying hard to put on a brave front, but deep down they were dejected.

"Don't worry," I declared, "it will rain today by lunchtime."

"But the weather forecast says that there is not to be any sign of rain…," they started.

"Believe God," I interrupted, "it will rain. In fact, I can smell it on the wind."

"But there is no wind…"

"It's coming; it's here!" I rejoiced.

Like Elijah, I felt like sending Don to the top of the mountain until he returned with the report of clouds, but instead I departed.

It was eleven in the morning when the phone rang and Don was on the line. He was laughing, crying, and talking excitedly all at the same time. The rain was falling—not just a light shower but a good, consistent, soaking rain. The drought was broken in Zimbabwe. Amazingly, for the next year different farmers would call for us to go to their lands and pray for rain. The news went throughout the whole district, and we had the opportunity to preach the power of the Gospel to those who had formerly been closed or who had been outright critics of us, especially as a result of our working with the natives. How God can touch people at their point of need! He knew just where to go to get a hold of the stubborn and resistant.

Several months later, I was in the Middle Sabi Valley where several members of our congregation resided. They were wheat, cotton, and soybean farmers. It was the end of winter and the time to combine the wheat. The particular couple I was visiting had been through major financial difficulties, so bad in fact, that they had been about to lose their farm but for the intervention of the Lord. They had not even had the finances to pay their water bill so as to enable them to irrigate their crop, but God delivers even from our own foolishness. In the natural, the current wheat crop was their salvation or their complete ruin. The hand of God was so upon the crop that it was going to be a record yield.

It was a Saturday afternoon when "all hell" broke loose on their farm. Throughout the morning very sinister rain clouds had been building on the horizon, but it was not anywhere near time for rains to fall. It was months too early. We watched those clouds and instantly recognized the work of the enemy yet again. We did not waiver. How could we? We had gained the position both over and for the rain. At about two in the afternoon, the storm came howling up the valley, so heavy and so low that it seemed we could almost lift our hands and touch those clouds. They were heavy and thick and black with evil. As if the devil was taunting us, the first enormous drops of rain began to fall. If those clouds had released their water on that wheat, the whole crop would have been totally ruined, along with the couple. We marched out onto the lawn in front of the house and began to speak to the devil once again just as we had on Mount Inyangani, reminding him of Elijah's dealing with him. In the mighty name of Jesus and by His blood we declared the enemy defeated, and we commanded the storm to depart. As if a thousand devils were put to flight, the winds shrieked and howled and carried those clouds, at great speed, farther up the valley where there was devastating destruction.

Shortly thereafter, Sheila, the farmer's wife, received a call from her sister who farmed five miles up the valley. She was extremely distressed, believing that Sheila must now be simply ruined. However, not another drop of rain had fallen after the prayers, and the crop was completely saved. Years later I used that gained place of intercession again and again whilst on my long march to prison in Mozambique. Ah, the abiding presence and authority of the Almighty is even over the works of His hands:

> *But the men marveled, saying, What manner of man is this, that even the winds and sea obey Him!* (Matthew 8:27)

CHAPTER SIX

Let Go!

I USED TO THINK I was born to be rich and live in a palace. The Holy Spirit had to remove that ambition from within so that I was utterly dead, dead, dead to such things.

"For," He said, "as long as that area of self is alive, you are flawed for the work and purpose that I have for you."

He continued, "You can never demand of anyone that which you yourself have not given up or that to which you have not died."

The intercessor carries the sentence of death. As Paul says, *"Always bearing about in the body the dying of the Lord Jesus, that the life also of Jesus might be made manifest in our body"* (2 Cor. 4:10).

The work was growing, nay *exploding*, and it was exciting to be a vital part of God's Revival. Naturally there were setbacks, upheavals, and the element of human nature that will always seek to frustrate the program of God.

Several years before, God had dealt with me on the issue of loneliness, and I had broken through with Him on that score. I still, however, enjoyed people and a good social life of both entertaining and being entertained. I enjoy cooking and am a good cook. On many occasions I had used my cooking skills to win people over so that I could begin to minister to them. There's an old saying, "The way to a man's heart is through his stomach," and I had certainly seen that work in the military. I loved to hold dinners and, of course, my ego would get excited when I was highly praised for the wonderful meal.

"That's pride," said the Holy Spirit one afternoon as I was in the kitchen cooking. "That's pride and it has to go!"

The blessed Holy Spirit has a way of getting directly to the root of a matter, but just at that point I did not want to hear Him. He had come in and clearly ruined my dinner for that evening.

"Think of all the time and energy you are wasting on something you enjoy, simply to impress, when you could use that time more profitably."

I suddenly realized that, in terms of an *eternity* of fellowship and enjoyment, this earthly pilgrimage was a time to work. As usual, when the flesh is touched it is going to kick and fight all the way, and I was not giving up without that fight—even though I knew I had already lost the battle. I tried to argue that I never had lavish parties. Those parties I had were not that often, and I did not own a television, satellite, or video for any kind of entertainment.

"No matter," emphasized the Holy Spirit, "it's still *you* and self must go."

He was poking and prodding, and I did not like it because I was already charged, tried, and condemned: GUILTY! We are so very slow to learn. All that the Spirit wants is honesty, and then He is able to quickly deal with an issue.

"Thanks!" I said. "You've just ruined my dinner tonight."

He distinctly chuckled and was gone, leaving me to brood over what He had said. I knew I would never be left in peace over the matter. I guess what was most infuriating at the time was that I already knew that He had won! It was merely time to see how the whole thing was going to be worked out.

Next, He got me on the issue of money and souls. What I enjoyed most about money was the control over it. I like good things and was always very comfortable in the homes of the wealthy, though I also had no problem going into the huts of the natives.

I have always loved that classic picture of the little hut of that great missionary, C.T. Studd, which was built right in the heart of the African jungle. He came from a wealthy, aristocratic background and was left a fortune by his father, yet he gave it all away—all except 2,000 pounds, which he reserved for his bride-to-be. She said, "C.T., what did the Lord tell you to do?"

"Give it all away," he replied.

"Then you'd better do it, for I'll not marry a disobedient man."

C.T. never lost his class, and over his simple mud hut in the heart of Africa hung his estate name, "Buckingham Palace."

"Well, Lord," I said one day, "I don't have to be a pauper to serve You! I get tired of everyone thinking that Christians must look poor, talk poor, and act poor."

"No," He said, "I was not poor—that's why Judas wanted the bag. It was always very full. But…"

"But what?" I interrupted.

"It's your attitude towards money that counts, and you don't need a lot of it to have a bad attitude." He continued, "It's 'the *love* of money that is the root of all evil,' and you love it."

"But I don't have any. I don't have bank accounts, insurances, stocks, or anything else."

"Yes, but you *love* it. You don't have to have any or much to love it. That's the problem with Africa. You love money but don't have much."

Once again the Spirit was getting down to where it hurt, only this time Jesus was in on it with Him.

Since I had been saved I was always a *giver* to the work of the Lord. When I began to earn a salary, I thought very little of giving it all away on a monthly basis because there was a need in the ministry. I loved to give and learned that I could never outgive God. From the day I entered full-time ministry, I had decided never to take a salary but to live by faith. The only persons to know this were the various church secretaries and treasurers. A salary was always entered into the books, but it had regularly been distributed to a needy cause without anyone else knowing. I marveled at how the Spirit had prevailed upon people and stirred them to give to me even though the majority were faithfully tithing and believed that I was well taken care of through my salary.

"That's all well and fine," continued the Spirit one day when I thought things were going well, "but I'm not in the least satisfied because you're still in charge of your life where I should be."

I began to protest but to no avail.

"Your believing in Me and trusting in Me is good and I have counted that to you as righteousness, but I want you to go even further now. I will tell you when you may have a dinner and who to invite. I will tell you how to spend your money, when to spend it, and on whom to spend it. I will tell you who to bless and when and how."

I groaned and protested loudly, "But then I'm not free. I'm just a prisoner!"

"Wherever did you get the idea you were free?" gently chided the Spirit.

"From the Word You inspired," I snapped.

"Read it again, but this time more carefully," He cautioned. "Now are you agreeable?"

I really saw that I had no choice, and just in case I needed a little prompting, I was clearly reminded of the Rusitu experience and did not savor the thought of the Spirit leaving me to my own devices again.

"I surrender," I declared.

In so doing, I did not realize just how heartbreaking and humiliating this "grave" was going to be. The Holy Spirit certainly knows how to give some knockout blows in the ring, but He kept reminding me that there was a specific goal and purpose and that He was moving me in a definite direction—what direction at that point in time I had little knowledge.

"Much of what you do and give is really to impress people, and that will go," warned the Spirit.

All I could hear echoing in my head was, *"They have their reward…they have their reward…they have their reward"* (see Matt. 6:2).

I saw all too clearly that when we play to the human arena we inherit only a temporal reward—the praises of men—while losing a far greater weight of eternal Glory. The first thing that happened was that the Holy Ghost began to have me invite to dinner people who, in the natural, were "a pain in the neck."

And He warned, "You cook for them every bit as perfectly as you have cooked for those you love and want to come."

I died on two counts. All my friends wondered why they were not invited to the parsonage anymore. I was not permitted to tell them, and worse, they could not understand why I had chosen to "favor" those with whom previously I had had little social dealing. God the Holy Spirit was indeed preparing me for the "whosoever," so that the day of victory would come when I could also declare with Paul the Apostle, *"For I have learned, in whatsoever state I am, therewith to be content. I know both how to be abased, and I know how to abound.... I can do all things through Christ which strengtheneth me"* (Phil. 4:11-13).

I soon began to view people, no matter what their social status, as precious vessels in the eyes of the Lord. Once again, as my attitude changed and I began to be an avenue for Christ to reach out through me, other people changed and became willing and eager to be involved in the work. Some became infuriated that I had "lowered my standards"; but if Christ's act of clothing Himself in human form and coming to earth was a lowering of His standards, then I hoped that I had done the same.

At the same time the Spirit was working the "dinner" issue in me, He was also working the "money" issue. I was not permitted to buy anything for anyone unless He directed. That was also very difficult as I had been so accustomed to presenting people with little gifts or rushing to the assistance of those in need. All that was to stop, and once again the Lord was really dealing with the issue of partiality. He was fully building on the foundation He had established by having me not only *accept* but truly *love* the natives. I would see people in need and think that "such" was a worthy cause to which to contribute, but the Spirit would say, "NO!"

I came to realize just how much money is wasted on ridiculous trivialities, such as giving gifts, which are often unwanted, when such finances could better go to the winning of souls. One thing that the Holy Spirit really worked into my life was the principle of absolute, circumspect stewardship. I learned that I am merely a steward in my Father's house, and as such I really have no say over anything. Actually I saw myself as the unjust steward who was giving away and writing off that which did not belong to him. I saw myself before the Lord as having *"wasted my master's goods"* (see Luke 16:1).

I saw that people who gave to the ministry did so because they believed in me and what I was doing. Therefore, I had no right whatsoever to betray that trust. That is not to say that I believe in poverty, but the Spirit revealed just how corrupt and careless we can be and how very important stewardship is in His economy. And indeed, we are *"stewards of the mysteries of God. Moreover, it is required in stewards, that a man be found faithful"* (1 Cor. 4:1-2).

The Spirit took me to the Word and showed me:

> *Verily I say unto you, There is no man that hath left house, or brethren, or sisters, or father, or mother, or wife, or children, or lands, for My sake and the gospel's, but he shall receive an hundredfold now in this time, houses and brethren, and sisters, and mothers, and children, and lands, with persecutions; and in the world to come eternal life* (Mark 10:29-30).

"Not everyone is going to warmly receive you. They may be as a mother or father, but they may also persecute you or simply give you a difficult time even while having you in their home. The only reaction I want is for you to act like Him."

I have stayed in multitudes of Christian homes across the nations and truly have family in many places. But I have also been accommodated by people who did not want me and subsequently made conditions quite unbearable.

I well remember staying with a couple whose children had rabbits and dogs. The kids did all the housework and did it badly. Dishes were not washed properly, the food was smeared over an old tablecloth, layer upon dirty layer, and the rabbit sat on the table during meals and "did his thing." My host and hostess accommodated me in an adjoining cottage where they had a tenant who was moving out. The sink in the cottage was full of dirty dishes that were growing mold. The refrigerator was filled with old rotting food, and the sheets on the bed had not been washed. At eleven at night I had to go to the basement to wash the sheets and slopped through "water" on the stairs only to find out that it was dog urine!

I have also stayed with people who have sat down to eat without offering me a thing. Such is the persecution of which Jesus is speaking: the rude, selfish, angry, and altogether unlovely who sometimes can make life a misery unless total victory has been gained in Christ. Such is the behavior of some of those who are of the "household of faith." But when Jesus is the essence and sweetness of a person's life, no matter the conditions or the circumstances, His fragrance will always flow forth. That is what the Spirit wanted to establish in me. He declared:

For if ye love them which love you what thank have ye?....And if ye do good to them which do good to you, what thank have ye?....And if ye lend to them of whom ye hope to receive, what thank have ye? For sinners also lend to sinners, to receive as much again (Luke 6:32-34).

Another principle that the Spirit was establishing was that of receiving that others might be blessed. So many times we are unable to receive graciously, especially when someone else has *sacrificed* to give, and so rob the giver of their blessing. I have always paid my way, but now the Holy Spirit was telling me, "I'm going to do all that and in such a way that you cannot repay." That was really a tough one and of course led to many deaths. There were accusations of "taking money from widows and old women," of "fleecing the naïve and helpless," and of "not doing an honest day's work and therefore having no right to eat." Such accusations had to be borne in silence. An explanation would not have been understood even if offered. The Holy Spirit would never allow such anyhow.

Each test case, when passed, took me to higher ground in the Lord. The most difficult test came concerning my dear, beloved mother. The devil had tried to snatch my life in my earliest days. When only a few days old, I had to undergo major surgery. From then on, it was one sickness after another; one drama after another; one accident after another. Nobody was saved in our house then, so we knew nothing of the work of the devil or the redeeming work of Christ. From the day of my salvation, God began to heal all my childhood sicknesses and diseases, especially after I began to fast. Needless to say, mother had fought desperately for my life, which resulted in a special bond of love between us. It had been so hard to leave and go to foreign and often dangerous mission fields watching her sob, "You'll never come back; they'll kill you."

Yet, despite the pleas and tears of a loving mother, there was the equally haunting cry of the Lord, *"Whom shall I send, and who will go for us?"* (Isa. 6:8).

The reply of Jesus had long since settled the matter: *"He that loveth father or mother more than Me is not worthy of Me: and he that loveth son or daughter more than Me is not worthy of Me"* (Matt. 10:37).

Despite that choice and decision, the persuasive powers of a mother are exceptionally strong. Mom had not been long saved at this time, and we were a very close family. I knew the reality, the practical reality of Jesus' setting a sword in the family and dividing it, for I had seen the anguish of a loving mother watch as our choice for Jesus indeed divided the family. Mom was to go to the altar like everyone else. Human emotion and ties must not stand in the way of the higher calling of God.

So I began to die a thousand deaths as there were no longer the thoughtful little gifts, the surprise visits, and the many things that deeply please a mother's heart. The worst part was that I could not say anything, and Mom did not say anything, which made it all the more difficult. She quietly braved so many hurts and misunderstandings. For the sake of He who is all and the call of His higher, eternal Kingdom, we had to go through the fire. She was beside herself when I undertook my first 21-day fast and tried to elicit from me an assurance that I would see a doctor daily for an examination. She wanted to have me examined by a shrink because, in her mind, surely I was going to make myself sick, bring back all the old plagues, or simply fade away.

I had to set my face as flint, and no matter the cries, pleas, letters, or even at times the anger, I had to press on with the calling. Today Mom is the greatest moral and spiritual supporter of the ministry, and she and Dad are also faithful financial supporters. She has completely released me and lays no claim whatsoever upon my life—although, naturally, she is still a mother and is always excited to have me around even if I am only "passing through."

The process of "letting go," of having things and people "wrenched away," is very painful but exceptionally necessary for the maturing intercessor. It is the same as the painful growth of the creature struggling from the cocoon or the chick from the egg. Any interference to make the development process easier or less painful will only weaken or even deform the creature so that it never reaches its full potential. God was working in me to bring out His fullness for His Glory and His alone.

CHAPTER SEVEN

The Separated Life

OVER MANY YEARS, I have come to understand that the working of the Holy Spirit in the lives of those He raises up to be intercessors follows definite principles, and that within those principles He has plenty of room to maneuver in dealing with the individual personality. The life of intercession is a continual dying to self so that the life of Christ might be manifested through the vessel by the inner workings of the blessed Holy Spirit.

There is nothing that brings such death as quickly as fasting and prayer. Like so many of the Christian "arts," fasting and prayer have largely been lost to the Body of Christ because they are such a negation of self and are essentially totally anti-social. The biggest problem with most Christians is that they spend much time reading about these "arts" without ever getting down to practicing them.

Many believers tell me that they were never taught to tithe. Well, something is wrong. I am really not interested in whether one is a tither. I want to know if one is a giver, and nobody should have to be taught such a thing. When Jesus comes into a person's life and the Holy Spirit takes control, that person must, by the very residency of the divine nature dwelling within, become a giver because God Himself is a giver. The basis of the problem, if a person is not a giver, is not the excuse always offered that "It's not my calling," but that the Holy Spirit has not taken control.

The same applies to fasting and prayer. When the fullness of the Holy Spirit fills the vessel, He must by His very nature point to those things that Jesus did and that bring the anointing and power of the Lord. Only *after* Jesus had fasted and won the victory was He able to declare, *"The Spirit of the Lord is upon Me..."* (Luke 4:18). It is fasting, like nothing else, which brings the anointing that breaks the yoke of both the flesh and the enemy.

From my earliest days with the Lord, I remember an unsatiated thirst to know Him, really know *HIM*. There was no sacrifice too great if it would help me experience a greater taste of God.

I grew up in a family that loved fishing, and almost every weekend we were off at the earliest possible moment to fish until the last possible hour on Sunday. Weekday afternoons, holidays, and weekends were fishing, fishing, fishing—until Jesus came in and the Holy Spirit took control. Naturally, there were great agonies of heart and wrenchings that were painful especially since we were a very close family. Suddenly, however, a higher priority took precedence and to the family it was as if a foreign body had invaded the sanctity of the unit and threatened to bring division. Mom was ready to do battle, and she is a real fighter, so it was going to be very tough. None of us realized it then, but the battle was really against the Holy Spirit, and of course, the human element will always lose. As for me, I was caught in the middle between Mom and this Holy Invader, and *it was miserable* to say the least.

Finally, after months of agony, I declared that I did not want to go fishing anymore but wanted to be with God. Dad was of the opinion that I should "take my bed to church," and Mom felt that I needed to see a psychiatrist. Religion was "all right, but this was going too far, and fanaticism was out." There was always the hope and stated opinion that it was all part of my "growing phase" and that I would "get over it," but "it" grew worse and worse as the months and years went by. I no longer wanted to play sports—and I was pretty good—socialize, or involve myself in all the other activities of friends. At every opportunity I would steal away to talk with the Lord, and my conversations developed into travail and weeping as the Holy Spirit took control. (Even today, I really do not have time nor stomach for so many of the "activities" that are so prevalent in the Church. They are not wrong in themselves, but there is a higher agenda and calling of the Lord that is understood only by those who are also drawn to Him.)

Prayer became more than mere conversations; it developed into taking on larger issues, many of a national, continental, and international nature. I would wander away from the group or crowd literally craving the company of One unseen yet so real. I would thirst to be alone, simply to commune and adore the majestic God who had fearfully and wonderfully made me to be an instrument of His adoration. It was not religion or theology, dogma or tradition, but real relationship for which I ached. The more I ached for Him, the more real He became.

Whether walking in the African bush or sitting under the canopy of the African sky, I was drawn to casting my whole being upon the Lord. I would seek the solitude of the forests or simply crawl under the thorn bushes to pour out my heart to Him alone who can change eternal destinies. Hour after hour and days many, whether arising at night or drawing aside during the day, I would seek Him. And the more I sought Him, the more my soul longed for Him. The greatest objective of my prayer was that I might do the will of God and, more importantly, that I be conformed to the will of God and that I might pray not simply out of some form of duty, but with a consuming passion.

So, I fell passionately in love with Him and wanted my life to be a passion for Him. There is nothing else in this life worth living for than Him. Ah, how busy we can become over trifling matters when the enormity of eternity presses in. How the human soul and emotion can craftily relegate this most serious and enormous responsibility to the periphery of life by deeming fellowship with God of little significance compared with the high regard we attach to human endeavor.

By its very nature, true prayer can only provoke a spirit of true worship. Amidst the agonizing, the travail, the pleading, and the wrestling there is a confidence only in the One who agonized in Gethsemane to show the way to the Father and in the Holy Spirit who leads us in intercession because He knows the mind and heart of the Father. Since it is the very nature of each of the members of the Godhead to give total Glory to the other two, the fragrance of the incense of worship must ascend from a heart that is being directed by the Spirit with the purpose of bearing witness of Jesus and giving Glory to God. Indeed, *"the eyes of the Lord run to and fro throughout the whole earth, to show Himself strong in the behalf of them whose heart is perfect toward Him"* (2 Chron. 16:9).

When the Lord finds such a one, He settles upon him and the Spirit lifts that one into perfect worship—worship that is in Spirit and Truth. Part of that worship is the sure knowledge that it is all the working of the Holy Spirit and all the victory of the Lord who alone can answer prayer and is worthy of all our adoration. Such would be worthless and hopeless unless inspired by the blessed Holy Spirit who, when He directs the vessel in worship of the Lord, creates a worship that is pure, holy, undefiled, and pleasing unto Him.

The Holy Spirit does not operate through human systems but through humans themselves. People are to be the pure channels through which the holy oil must flow, and the vessels can only produce that which a Holy God has produced in them. It is a life investment that counts and not the performance of a sermon in an hour. Holy preaching and holy living are produced in the closet. It takes separation to know God.

Moses was on the back side of the desert for 40 years; Paul was in the Arabian Desert for nine; David was a shepherd and then a fugitive. Each in their *aloneness* found the source of true life, power, and godliness. They became thirsty for the "fountain of life," followed hard after the God who found them, and had a singleness of eye for the One they grew to love and fear.

When I entered into the true mystery of prayer, I little realized in the beginning that it was preparation for intercession. And, oh my, did it cost. I lost friends and family, was misunderstood and maligned, ridiculed and rejected, and above all, was the subject of whispers, sniggers, and incessant gossip. But what a small price to gain such a Friend! God became my friend and how can I ever complain?

It became a common comment that "Michael has gone off into another world again…." It was very definitely that. In the very midst of a group or even a worthless conversation, I would soar into the presence of Him for who I had a passion. No words needed to be uttered. There was no trying to prove any kind of spirituality by putting on a display. It was communion with the Lord and far exceeded anything terrestrial and temporal. I could be in the midst of great activity and a crowd, yet I was gone, lost in fellowship with Him. Of course, there were times when people were speaking directly to me and I had gone off to be with the Lord. They suddenly presented a question and I did not know whether it was to be a "yes" answer or "no." After several incidents of a "red" face, I learned to apologize, and my congregation learned to accept their "dominee."

The misunderstanding of people and separation from them grew worse when I began to undertake serious fasting. I read in God's Word about fasting and that was good enough for me. I tried so hard to keep it secret at first, but it was very difficult. The first time my precious mother discovered that I was on such a "crazy, life-threatening endeavor," she quickly called the doctor to explain that I was surely going to die and now really did need to see a "shrink." I at least thought that I would have an ally in the Jewish family doctor who, to my way of thinking, should have known about such things. Well, he panicked all the more, sent everyone into a tizzy, and absolutely insisted that I report for a thorough check-up every day of my 21-day fast.

Oh my, how people tried to encourage me to give up such a "foolhardy" notion by saying that I was being "selfish and irresponsible." They claimed that I was assuredly going to end up sick and damaged and that others would pay the price for my "stubborn religion." But nothing against me worked. I set my heart and would not be moved. So began a life of fasting!

Let me quickly say that there are different reasons for fasting just as there are different fasts. A true fast can be initiated by God, by self, or by circumstances. Numerous accounts in both Testaments tell of God calling His leaders and people to fast and pray either to institute something or as a direct result of sin or a specific situation. There are also many examples where a fast was called because an individual wanted to draw nigh unto God for deeper fellowship and relationship as a result of some affliction of the soul.

Many people cop out of fasting because they say that God has not "called" them to a fast. Well, they mostly would not hear God even if He did. I have embarked on many fasts simply because I wanted to draw closer to the Lord and enjoy Him. Such is a very good and valid reason to fast. Fasting should not be something that we "do" but should be a way of life. It is for this very reason that prayer and fasting are linked together.

Oh the *pure joy* of fasting simply to draw closer to Him! Oh the *authority* that comes out of the discipline of fasting for no other reason than to please the Lord in love and not through works or the carnal mind thinking presumptuously before Him! The *delight* of bringing the flesh under subjection so that the spirit might soar into lofty realms of His presence is indescribable. It is at the conclusion of such a time of fasting that one simply does not wish to return to the mundane life again. To live in that higher realm with the Lord is so satisfying to the spirit that I loathe to break such fasts.

Finally, there is the fast that is necessitated through the crises of circumstance. When Israel faced annihilation at the hands of Haman, Esther called all the Jews in Shushan to an urgent fast. If ever there was a statement of wisdom in urgency, it was declared by Esther: *"If I perish, I perish"* (Esther 4:16). Thank God for that small group of watchmen, wherever they may be, who are able through discipline and willing through compassion, to drop whatever they are doing in order to address the urgency of the hour when the enemy seeks to destroy that which is God's or that which He purposes to accomplish.

Many years ago God called me to an Esther fast three days before Christmas! The fast began at four in the morning and was to end the same time, Christmas day. Somewhere during the fast I received a tremendous burden for three of my students who were studying in the United States. I did not know where they were or what was happening. At about nine o'clock Christmas morning, I received a call in Africa to say that the students had been traveling along the interstate toward Little Rock, Arkansas, when a semi overtook them. The semi was weaving badly from side to side and simply gathered their vehicle under its rear axle, pulverized the car, and spat it out into a nearby field. The car was so badly crushed that it was *"impossible* for anyone to have survived,*"* according to the police. Yet, each of the three students came out of the vehicle without so much as a scratch. Often the safety of others depends on how obedient we are to fast and pray.

In another case there was a local farmer in the congregation who had been crippled from his waist down for many years and who wanted healing. Past preachers and evangelists had dragged that poor man out of his wheelchair and "commanded" him to walk! However, that is presumption unless you have the authority of God for such an action.

The man was an excellent farmer despite his handicap. Prior to his salvation, he had been pretty wild, but he had a persistently praying wife who had prayed him into the Kingdom. In the days before he became handicapped, this man's habit was to rise at four in the morning and be about his farming duties, then after lunch he would have an hour's sleep. One particular and fateful day, he could not get off the bed after his afternoon rest. He was crippled.

Well, I decided I was going to really seek the face of the Lord as to what was the major factor hindering his healing, for I knew and believed that God is more than able to deliver to the utmost. Off I went with my tent and drum of water to spend three weeks seeking the man's healing, for I was sure that God would complete a miracle. He was such an influential farmer, a real "man's man." I knew that his healing would have a dramatic impact throughout the country, for he was also well-known as a former national rugby player.

On about the 18th day into my fast, the Holy Spirit spoke clearly, "Go and ask him what he is going to do with his life if I raise him from that wheelchair."

I must confess I was quite shocked. I expected the Lord to give me the authority to lay hands on him or tell me something dramatic. I felt there was no longer any need to remain by the river, so I immediately packed and made my way to the farm. The man was in his workshop and, as usual, was delighted to see his pastor. I chatted about the farm for a short while and then entered in on the subject of my visit. I explained what I had been doing and why and then asked him the Holy Spirit's question.

He looked at me for the longest time and shuffled uneasily in his chair. Then, hanging his head, he softly said, "You know, Michael, if God raises me out of this chair, I will go back to my old life."

His answer was like a knife piercing the deepest part of my being, for I instantly realized the full implication of what he was saying. "You know then, that you have just condemned *yourself* to that wheelchair for life?" was the instant reply of the Spirit that I gave to him. There was nothing more to be said on the issue, and today the man is still farming, still serving the Lord, and still in his wheelchair.

Fasting is not merely the "body under discipline," but it is a total negation of "self" at every level for the higher purpose of God. Of course there are those who fast and pray for strife and the human arena, but dare we degrade the pure and holy because of the profane? Fasting can be perverted and made into a religious tradition and pharisaical practice by anyone, but in the life of one who is truly in love with Him, it is a powerful weapon for the Glory of God. Times without number has the yoke of the enemy been broken and captives set free because of the discipline of fasting. The enemy hates fasting just as he hates prayer. Jesus, speaking of certain demons, said, *"This kind can come forth by nothing, but by prayer and fasting"* (Mark 9:29).

Prayer and fasting are an integral part of intercession. Nobody can claim to be an intercessor without participating in prayer and fasting, for these actions are very much a part of the constraining power of love and self-denial of the true watchman of the Lord. The true intercessor must invade the world as a man among men, bathed in meekness and humility, and being as wise as a serpent yet harmless as the dove; bound with the bonds of servanthood yet regal as a king with royal dignity— the dignity of the King of Kings. The intercessor must be zealous, compassionate, and fearless, being determined to march into the thickest of battles with the banner of the Lord held high and His trumpet loudly heralding the Truth no matter the price nor consequences.

Such is the mettle produced by prayer and fasting. Such is the caliber of the great lover of God, the wise strategist with God's battle plans, and the ardent warrior who is jealous for the reputation of His God and fired with energy for the salvation of men. Above all, the intercessor must carry the warrant and marks of death that the Life of Christ might be manifest. Everything he does and everything he says must bring the flavor of the Creator of Lights so that the Life of God might flow into the mortality of man and infuse him with divine strength, holy direction, and eternal purpose. Without this, those who are meant to be carrying life can just as easily infuse death and be agents who kill.

Necessary, therefore, is the separated life of those who are intercessors or are in training for that high office. Such are separated to bear witness of the residency of Him within and to manifest His Glory to a dying world. Such are separated to take the Gospel to every creature, not by the wisdom of man and his technological methods, but by the *power* of a life resurrected from death. There must be no confidence in the flesh but entire dependence on the indwelling of the Supreme, Divine Being of the Holy Spirit.

Prevailing prayer cannot be offered by any who have not prevailed with God. Such is not accomplished overnight or in short years. It is a way of life that requires discipline and commitment, drawing one away from the crowd and the pursuits of men, making one a stranger in the world and homesick for Heaven. Prayer is a desire for God that breaks the shackles of sleep and all other self-indulgent desires and catapults the warrior into the realms of His supernatural presence. It is surrender to the Lord in the holiest of devotions and is far beyond the attainment of the casual observer or one who dabbles in sublime pursuits. Prayer, linked with fasting, is the powder keg that explodes the individual into the power house of Heaven and equips such a vessel with that holy anointing necessary for godly ministry rather than human entertainment, for ministry that will be life changing and earth shattering.

Nights of watching in prayer and fasting, doing battle with the elements without and the agonies within, are always crowned with victory in the morning hours as the dawn breaks and the sun ushers in a new day. It was at just such a time that the Lord changed Jacob's name to Israel and left him a prince instead of a deceiving supplanter and vagabond.

I well remember spending many a night in prayer wrestling for some wayward soul or situation. I have always found the dawning of the morning crowned with victory. One night I wrestled for the rebel army in Mozambique as the soldiers were reluctant to come to any meetings. I wept and travailed the night hours. It is not for one, then, to make up that lost sleep during the day. Such is part of the sacrifice that brings His divine intervention. I waited all day in excited anticipation of what would transpire in the evening meeting, which had been saturated with the dew of Heaven and the tears from my eyes for the indifference of men to the love of God.

Lo and behold, they came not in their tens or twenties but by the hundreds in response to the unction of His divine yet unseen hand directing them to hear of His love. It broke the chains, and the meetings with those soldiers were forever different. No amount of prayer and fasting crowned by supernatural results can ever satisfy the warrior just so long as there are still souls—other sheep, even the one—who must be gathered into the fold. Many a wayward soul has been turned because of petitions offered to the Lord in sleepless nights. I know many a friend who, in their rebellion and stubbornness, would have cast their inheritance to the wind and despised their birthright had it not been for the mercy of the Lord constraining them through a night of travail washed in tears. Such secrets are His alone.

A vast difference exists between loneliness and aloneness. The warrior with God simply has to be separated and alone to do battle and fulfill the divine mandate that so heavily rests upon Him. In the divine presence, however, he is never *lonely*. So many Christians are often driven to unholy pursuits because they are lonely and seek solace outside of the Lord. If many more of God's people would drop to their knees in fellowship with Him, they would no longer desire the mundane things of this world to fulfill the void within.

The separated life in search of God has driven me to desperately and earnestly seek Him. Times without number, I have taken my tent and departed into a solitary place with only a drum of water, fasting for 21 days, to break the strongholds of the enemy, to gain higher ground, or to know the mind of the Lord. I remember how we were having a crusade in a certain area that was saturated in witchcraft. Off I went for a season of fasting and prayer, sleeping in the open. It was bitterly cold and I was saturated with the dew each night. Certainly, the nocturnal activities of the devil were disturbing, but that was the very reason I was there: to do battle! He was vanquished of course. Such is the assurance that comes only to those who break through to God and know the outcome of an event before it even happens. If the Lord found it necessary to fast 40 days, then how much more should we, His disciples?

There are numerous kinds of fasting, from the "Esther" fast of three days without anything, to the total fast with water only, to the partial fast. Then, there are fasts undertaken from 1-40 days with only water, and beyond that, supernatural fasts that must absolutely be led by the Lord. It would never enter the mind of a true warrior to compare fasts or to compete in fasts with himself or anyone else. How can such carnal issues enter such divine activities? The victory of days and nights of solitude is always *higher ground*, and once gained, there can only flow forth songs and praises of thankfulness and adoration.

During the worst years of the communist domination of Mozambique when the nation had been raped and pillaged, I began our prayer and fasting conventions. They became famous in those days of the 1980s and over 600 pastors and evangelists would gather from all quarters of southern Malawi and Mozambique — some *walking* for up to three weeks through the jungle just to attend. Many of the accounts they shared of how God had delivered them from communist soldiers and brought them in from their various fields safely can only be written in the annals of Heaven because they were so spectacular.

We would gather in a large church where we simply had a "shut-in" for ten days. Each had his own sleeping mat or shared with a friend, and we would spend the entire ten days in that building praying and fasting, praising and worshipping, and sharing the Word. We all slept in the building, and throughout the night there would be prayers or worship or some spiritual activity taking place. Those who wanted to sleep did so while the rest entered into business with His Divine Majesty. They were days of great darkness and hardship over the whole of southern Africa and indeed the continent at large. The Gospel was in great peril in many lands, and crisis situations *demanded* crisis solutions.

Tea was served three times a day and in the evening; otherwise there was no sustenance. People had not come to eat but to do business with the King. Literally, the life of multitudes hung in the balance as we would break through and petition the Lord so that He might deal in the natural. The presence of God so descended in that building that people feared to walk heavily lest they offend Him, so everybody went on tiptoes. There was no careless chatter and idle gossip because everyone came with one purpose: to touch Heaven so that Heaven could impact earth.

The awesomeness of those days and the fruit of the intercession that they brought will be recounted in a later chapter. Nothing short of tarrying like that and such as we read of in the Book of Acts can bring such supernatural results as to be nation changing. That is what this life is all about: changing the history and destiny of nations that the Gospel might continue to go forth as the Lord promised so that every creature might hear the blessed news of salvation.

In a day when the Church has become flippant and casual about the devil, we need always to remember that he is a powerful being and that the archangel of war himself, Michael, did not bring a railing accusation against the devil. Whilst I am fully aware that he was defeated at the cross of Calvary, it behooves us to remember that we are dealing with an enormously powerful supernatural being who often has legitimacy because of the sin of man.

The defeat of the devil takes extraordinary measures and a battle plan that God has structured and revealed for the enemy's demise. This is the reason why God needs warriors, and such warriors are made in the furnace of God's separation.

CHAPTER EIGHT

Trusting God in All

TRUE INTERCESSORS are not born; they are made. And God was making me through trial and tribulation, through fire and aloneness, as He wove His higher purposes into my life for the ministry that He had planned for me. Only the Lord knows the end from the beginning of our lives, but I have often thought that it would surely help to have a little glimpse too.

The ultimate goal of the Holy Spirit in His workings in us is that we should *"know no man after the flesh"* (see 2 Cor. 5:16) and have *"no confidence in the flesh"* (Phil. 3:3), so that it is all of Him and nothing of self. When once I came to realize that "of myself, I can do nothing," only then was real progress in the making. It did not come easily, and there was, as usual, a death process to experience so that I might clearly see that His ways are higher than my ways. Only that which is holy and separate is acceptable unto Him. I quickly realized that all our efforts and all our programs are worthless and futile without the divine stamp of approval, and how would He approve anything that He did not author?

One day, the Spirit spoke clearly, "It is not more anointing or boldness or power that you need, but more *obedience*. All of these other qualities come out of this one. Faith will increase when obedience increases."

I suddenly saw it in a flash. I had spent so much time striving to *have* and to *be* that I had missed the source of it all and that source is obedience. I realized that the more that I entered into *relationship* with the Father, the more I would *know* Him and therefore *trust* Him.

I saw Jesus' words about love and discipleship so clearly in a new light and understood that He was really saying, "*Because* you love Me, you will obey My commandments." Clearly, this differentiates the servant from the friend. I could only be a friend when I did whatsoever He commanded me. It became apparent that this is what distinguishes the true intercessor from all others. A true intercessor who carries the sentence of death and lives in obedience to the voice of the Holy Spirit absolutely must be a friend of Jesus.

As I pondered the enormity of the calling and, above all, the privilege of what was being offered, the Lord spoke challengingly, "Michael, I have very few friends. I have many preachers and teachers, evangelists and workers, in My Kingdom, but very few I am able to call My friend. Would you be one?"

I became fully aware that it was by obedience that Abraham became "the friend of God," and by obedience that David was "a man after God's own heart," and by obedience that Moses forsook Egypt and became one of God's greatest intercessors for Israel. God's invitation was not to be taken lightly or flippantly. I began to deeply ponder the enormity of the responsibility and comprehend that without the working of the Spirit to bring me to that desire and decision, it was impossible to even begin to embark on friendship with God. It was all of Him for all of Him.

So many Christians today want all of the blessings of God, nay, *demand* all of them as their right, without realizing the accompanying responsibilities. Many of the so-called "blessings" and "provisions" of the Lord have come by way of presumption and the manipulation of people's emotions rather than true dependence on and obedience towards a bountiful Father.

When I began to set aside all other religious activity to focus on cultivating a true relationship with God, things really began to change. How could I have been so blind and so foolishly arrogant? How loving and patient the Lord had been. I was undone before Him. Once again, the Spirit of all Truth had stirred me and directed me into the light, and once again, faced with the Truth, it was my responsibility to respond. Yet once again, I really had no choice because I was in the hands of Someone else who was making all my decisions.

The acid test was going to be proved in a short time. I was soon to leave on a trip for India, about which, at that moment, I knew absolutely nothing. The Lord was directing the whole affair, and I was merely to flow with Him and see His supernatural hand take complete control. The Lord clearly spoke to me that He was going to send me to India. The possibility was so remote in the natural that I was very excited to see just how God was going to orchestrate such an event. Besides, there was nobody that I even knew in India or who had any close contacts with India. But, when God speaks, He will surely perform.

At that time, I was in the midst of a mighty move of the Lord, which was the talk of the country. The General Overseer of the denomination had heard "disturbing reports" and embarked on a journey of investigation to my remote outback of the Zimbabwean bush. His wife had recently undergone major surgery and was suffering complications of one kind and another, including the fact that the wound would not heal and knit. She was along on the journey simply to "spy out the land" because, as she later said, the reports of what God was doing were "too fantastic to believe."

That morning as I awoke, the Lord spoke and said, "You will see the spectacular today."

I was totally unaware of the condition of my guests whose arrival was after the communion service had begun. Sometime in the midst of the service and completely out of keeping with the "traditional order" of things, the Holy Spirit prompted me to call for those who needed healing. The general overseer and his wife were very critical and disapproving. It seemed as if they would have plenty of ammunition to take back to the council with them that "this wayward congregation and their pastor really were 'out of order.'"

I was beginning to sweat a little when the Spirit clearly whispered, "Leave them to Me. I'll deal with the situation."

With that came a calm assurance and peace that only He is able to bring. Different ones were praying and being prayed for when suddenly the unction of the Holy Spirit descended and exploded the whole church into a supernatural atmosphere. People were crying, others shouting, "I'm healed, I'm healed!," whilst some were laughing. The wife of the overseer changed her attitude, stood up, and earnestly sought prayer. Suddenly, she too began to be undone, weeping uncontrollably. The Spirit was really moving upon her in His characteristic way revealing the healing and delivering power of Jesus. It was obvious that He was working deep within, setting her free from emotional scars before dealing with the physical. Soon, she too was testifying amidst tears and rejoicing that God was closing her wound. She could feel the mighty hand of God squeezing her whole stomach back into place. A great miracle was taking place in our very midst, but greater still was the change of heart and attitude that accompanied the healing.

The spectacular had, indeed, taken place and had so impressed the overseer that he instantly insisted that I accompany him to India and head up his healing team! Not only was that invitation extended, but also whilst everyone else was to find their own finances, the overseer undertook to find mine for me so that traveling expenses were not my responsibility.

"You see," I could almost hear the Spirit chuckle, "I told you that I would handle the whole situation."

"You're quite an engineer," was all I could proffer in reply and, indeed, He is. We would find Him never failing if we would only believe and obey.

India was a supernatural encounter from day one. It had to be, since the Holy Spirit was in control and His whole objective is always to bring total Glory to Jesus. The trip was, however, not without some major difficulties, but I was under a strict directive not to complain as the Spirit is the conductor of all things. It was very obvious from the outset that I was not *really* welcome on the trip and was made to feel like an intruder. I was not "in" with the "in" crowd of the denomination because I would not play or be "politically," or rather "religiously," correct. However, I was along to do the work of the Lord and please Him, not men.

This meant a clash with the opinions of men. Whilst most of the team were somewhat serious about the ministry they had come to do, there was also very definitely the idea that they were along to have fun too, and lots of it. I was not in the least concerned about that; there the clash came because I would not be party to their program.

God moved spectacularly from the first night with notable miracles. A mother with three children of varying ages from 12 to about 4 testified that they had all been born deaf and mute. Just as soon as I laid my hands upon them and cast out that spirit, each of the children not only heard but also spoke in their native tongue of Hindi. They had never spoken before! Suddenly the wind of the Spirit moved and the healing Jesus was manifested.

Each night there was a very definite focus on different aspects of healing or miracles. One night the Lord concentrated on the opening of blind eyes, the next on cripples, the next on deaf ears, and so on. Every night there were great numbers delivered from demons, and it seemed that the fruit of the revival fires of Africa were being carried to India. A woman came to us twisted and gnarled as a result of the demons ruling her. She could not even lift her head, but my, she had the worst sewer-like breath I had ever smelled. It was so bad that I had to cover my nose with a handkerchief to save myself from retching. I began to cast out the devils—for she had many—in the name of Jesus, and as each successive demon manifested, it was with a differing animal noise. One demon hissed like a serpent, another bellowed like a water buffalo, whilst yet another trumpeted like an elephant. She had received those spirits as she worshipped the demon gods in the temple. When the woman was finally freed, she was totally unraveled physically, and her foul breath had disappeared.

The crowds swelled to vast proportions, not because of a good adver-tising campaign, but because of the notable miracles and the presence of the Lord to set men free from every kind of bondage. In those days I did not simply pray mass prayers but laid my hands on people. Naturally, this was exhausting, and I would arrive back at our hotel in the early hours of the morning, drained. Each day was spent in prayer, meditation, and the reading of His Word in order to be spiritually, men-tally, and physically fit for that evening. There was no time to sightsee or embark on outings to the beaches, and neither was there any desire for such. I was on divine assignment and was "straightened until it was accomplished."

In the midst of such movings of God, the pursuit of vain things was totally out of place, and when the rest of the team prevailed upon me to join them, I politely but emphatically declined. There was no release of the Spirit to join them, and this *naturally* placed me at odds with the rest and placed them under a conviction with which they did not wish to deal. The outcome of such situations is always unpleasant and does not warrant discussion, especially after so many years. Suffice it to say that I was under sentence of death and I was to *trust* Him in all things. He had definitely orchestrated my being along and would take care of all other things if I looked only to Him and not the "arm of flesh."

Each event and series of situations was for the growth, learning, and the molding of myself in the principles of intercession. As I learned, sometimes with kicking and screaming, to simply let go and trust the Lord, I saw His supernatural hand intervene in all my affairs, especially with people. There came a time when those closest would be infuriated as to why I allowed people to take advantage of me and walk "rough shod" over me. It was the sentence of death and trusting in Him not only with circumstances, but also with people. What peace and joy to rest in the assurance that, by abiding, the unseen hand of One so mighty was upon me and in charge of not only my affairs but also my very life!

There is no greater way to live than to simply obey the Lord. This is true faith and trust developed out of intimacy and the unwavering belief that He *is* supreme and able, under every circumstance, to bring to pass what He says He will do. Once again He emphasized, as He had with Abraham so long ago, that the real reward is not gold, silver, or position but Himself and an unswerving devotion to Him. Jesus said the same thing when He declared, *"Seek ye first the kingdom of God, and His righteousness and all these things shall be added unto you"* (Matt. 6:33).

CHAPTER NINE

The Intercessor—Spirit's Indwelling

T HERE IS REALLY no such thing as an "intercession meeting," for intercession is not "intensified prayer" as Norman Grubb so clearly stated concerning the subject. Indeed, intercession is a way of life, and the true intercessor is very much a man who is among men and not one who is locked away in the closet and never seen. Of course, "closet ministry" plays a primary role in the life of the intercessor, but such ministry is done sacrificially when others are asleep. Jesus awoke a "great while before day" to fellowship with His Father and receive His direction, but He was always out amidst people, ministering to them in their daily activities.

The ministry of the Holy Spirit in intercession is to dwell *within* the frail human vessel and work *through* those who are yielded completely to His divine person, so that Jesus might be manifested to the world and glorified in the earth. The ministry of the Spirit to the individual is the ministry of death so that life might reign. Jesus said, *"Except a corn of wheat fall into the ground and die, it abideth alone; but if it die, it bringeth forth much fruit"* (John 12:24).

Until there is the death of the individual, there can never be the manifestation of the heart of God, for self will always clamor for the ascendancy. He is the Spirit who knows the mind and will of God and reveals such to the intercessor. True intercession is praying the heartbeat of God and continuing thus until there is the absolute assurance that God has heard and will answer. There can be neither doubt nor wavering because praying the heartbeat of God is praying His will. It is not man's selfish desires nor man's manipulation but the pure will and purposes of God concerning individuals, situations, nations, and the world.

Once an intercessor has the perspective of God, such a person can never be selfish nor shortsighted again. So then, the "whatsoever" I ask really becomes the burden of God's heart, and His will becomes my will. God will absolutely give me what I ask in His name because my asking goes far beyond petty, greedy, personal issues. It therefore becomes very clear how important the role of the Spirit is in the life of the intercessor. Furthermore, the Holy Spirit will play little or no role at all unless the vessel belongs completely to Him, for He cannot operate nor be victorious except on His terms.

The difference between the true intercessor and the *casual* praying person is therefore quite obvious. The former is assured of an answer and victory whilst the latter can only hope. The person who prays occasionally focuses mostly on selfish issues whereas the true intercessor carries the burden of the heart of God, which is for nations and the lost. The true intercessor is not bound by time, for he sees a timeless, infinite God who will bring His purposes to pass in spite of man, whilst the person who merely prays focuses on the "now" because he is basically selfish.

For the true intercessor who recognizes that it is all the work of the Holy Spirit, there is no driving ambition for human recognition. He is content to await divine approval whenever, or even if ever, it comes. Such a vessel is jealous only for the honor and Glory of the Lord. The vessel who dabbles in prayer, however, seeks the praises of men and recognition of the world because he has not died to self. Any average person may attend a prayer meeting, but intercession is a burden of God carried in the deepest bosom so that it becomes a way of life. Prayer costs only a little time, whilst intercession carries a great price tag in wrestlings, tears, agonies, travails, and identification, which brings death.

Draw aside with me and look in on the holy, awesome sight of John Hyde, who poured himself out night after night and day after day for the vast multitude of lost in the Punjab of India. After 20 years, this same intercessor stood in the doctor's office to hear the verdict that, because he had exerted so much energy, he had shifted his heart from the left side of his chest to the right side.

"If you do not stop what you are doing," warned the doctor, "you are going to die."

"If I *do* stop what I am doing," replied John Hyde, "I will surely die."

Such is the nature of the blessed Holy Spirit who dwells within to lead us into the secret, holy place of the Most High, the place of Gethsemane where no casual observer may lightly tread, the place where real business between man and God is done, the spot where, despite the sweat and agony and tears, eternal issues are decided because God could find a faithful and obedient servant who will bear His burden.

Intercession is very different from even serious prayer. Rees Howells, the great intercessor of Wales, declared concerning the days of travail for Britain during World War II that, "Prayer has failed; only intercession will take us through."

I am well able to say the same about the situation in Mozambique during 15 years of wicked communist oppression. Serious prayer failed, but when we turned to intercession, matters began to change and the enemy was finally routed in much the same way as Hitler had been. Why? I believe that the enemy is totally unoriginal in all of his campaigns and strategies, for he is not omnipotent and omniscient as is my God. He is therefore forced to rely upon old methods, and much of his power lies in the fact that he gambles on the weakness, indifference, and often downright sin of people and the Church.

For reasons only fully known to Himself, God has chosen to use humans in His battle against the devil who often gains initial ascendancy because there are few, if any, intercessors to stand in the gap. It takes great effort to motivate and mobilize an "upper room" company before such are able to embark on any divine combat operation against the enemy. One of the greatest prerequisites of the Spirit in intercession is a separated company, drawn together in a closely bound community— not necessarily living in community—in intimate union and fellowship with the Lord and one another and dedicated to fighting the Lord's battles for the extension of His glorious Kingdom and the salvation of multitudes. Oh that we would have such groups in this hour. Oh that we would have a people ready to fight the *Lord's* battle, who will be dedicated to one another and not seek personal ambition, personal vision, and personal recognition and acclaim.

The believer can never forget that the ministry of the Holy Spirit is to convince of sin, righteousness, and judgment. This conviction occurs as much in the life of the believer as in the non-believer who knows nothing of the mysteries of salvation. When the prophet saw the Lord and His awesome holiness, Isaiah could only melt like wax before the fire and declare, *"Woe is me! For I am undone…for mine eyes have seen the King, the Lord of Hosts"* (Isa. 6:5).

It is not sin with which the Holy Spirit needs to deal, but *self.* Brokenness comes when the Holy Spirit reveals the purity, beauty, and holiness of the Lord—before whom we are defiled, not so much because of what we do or have done, but simply because, as members of the human race, we carry the marks of sin and are therefore born defiled, though in innocence. My fallen, corrupt nature, measured against the awesomely holy, righteous God of all the universe, makes the sinfulness of sin exceedingly sinful and causes me to cry out, *"In me there dwelleth no good thing"* (Rom. 7:18).

Herein lies the great schism with modern theology, religion, and philosophy, which teaches that man is inherently good and worthy and has rights. May we never forget that *"we do nothing of ourselves"* (see John 8:28). Only the indwelling of the blessed Triune God makes me anything at all so that my only boast must be "all of Them."

If the Holy Spirit would find surrendered, yielded vessels like He did on the day of Pentecost, He would pour out Himself again in similar fashion manifesting the same notable miracles as are recorded in the Acts of the Holy Spirit. The real man of God, having surrendered and submitted to the Almighty in the secret place, having known and experienced Him, steps out clothed with the anointing and power of the holy, living God and manifests Jesus through the Holy Spirit dwelling within. With such a man, there is no pretense, no show, no masks. There is only transparency. The Holy Spirit will always lead the believer to Calvary's cross because the crucified life leads to the glorified one.

One of the greatest problems facing the majority of Christians is their lack of knowledge of the Holy Spirit, who is still often referred to as "it." What an insult that is to this mighty Third Person of the Trinity! He has all the attributes of a person and He is gloriously divine. He has a will, intelligence, power, and emotions. It is a serious matter that requires repentance for the way in which He has been treated and relegated to the back waters of the lives of most believers.

On the subject of the Holy Spirit, John Hyde challenged pastors with questions that need to be directed at every generation:

> Is the Holy Spirit first in your pulpits, pastors? Do you consciously put Him in front and keep yourselves behind Him when preaching? Teachers, when you are asked hard questions, do you ask His aid as a witness of all Christ's life? He alone was a witness of all Christ's life. He alone was a witness of the incarnation, the miracles, the death, and the resurrection of Christ.

He is the Spirit of truth and will always speak the whole truth and lead us into the Truth, for His ministry is to manifest and glorify Jesus. Without His operation, no man would ever know Christ and without Him directing, there would be no true intercession. The true intercessor is he who is saturated in every fiber of his being with the prayer he is praying. Such a saturation is the electrifying presence of the Lord, for the prayer has shaken Heaven and opened her doors so that God has not only heard but also has answered. There are no doubts and no wavering but only the quickening assurance of the Spirit that real business with the Lord has been completed.

I have always found the Holy Spirit to be very fair, but tough. He zooms in to the heart of every matter whether dealing with personal emotions and motives or exposing root issues in national and international affairs. There is no sidestepping with Him. He demands absolute honesty and will not budge until He gets it. He has humbled me so many times and silenced my complaining by simply showing me that I was wrong. If I would just quit grumbling about what I *thought* to be unfair and unjust, God would simply do the miraculous. He showed me that I was actually standing in His way because of my attitudes. He is the sifter and examiner of the deepest recesses of my heart, getting to the real root of every matter, for He is that Spirit of Truth who demands nothing less than the absolute from me. I have found that I can never progress to higher ground until I surrender and submit to the Spirit at the level of His current dealings. His aim is always higher ground in the Lord. The reason that so many Christians "plateau out" in their walk and experience is because of their disobedience to the prompting of the Spirit or their outright quenching of Him.

Dr. Kingsley Priddy, who was staff member of the Bible College of Wales, recounts the visitation of the Holy Spirit in 1937:

> He did not come like a rushing mighty wind. But gradually the person of the Holy Ghost filled all our thoughts, His presence filled all the place, and His light seemed to penetrate all the hidden recesses of our hearts... The revelation of His Person was so tremendous that all our previous experiences seemed as nothing... And we had to confess that we knew nothing of the Holy Ghost as an indwelling Person. That our bodies were meant to be temples of the Holy Ghost we knew, but when He pressed the question, "Who is living in your body?" we could not say that He was. We would have done so once, but now we had seen Him.

I have always found that a major key in intercession is the use of the Word as a legal precedence. Who knows the Word better than the divine Spirit who inspired men to write it? He was the Holy Spirit who brooded upon the face of the waters in Genesis and when God spoke the Word, the Spirit and the Word quickened life. Without the operation of these two members of the Godhead, there can never be any intercession. Jesus ever lives to make intercession *for* us whilst the Holy Spirit indwells and makes intercession *through* us. There is absolutely nothing that we can experience that has not already been encountered by man for *"there is nothing new under the sun"* (see Eccles. 1:9).

Every type of experience is recorded in God's Word as well as every answer to that experience. Anyone who trusts that he can be an intercessor without knowing and being heavily dependent upon God's Word is hopelessly deceived. The Spirit works through the Word. It is for this reason that Jesus taught that true worshippers must worship in Spirit and in Truth, or according to the Word. It is the Holy Spirit who quickens Scripture in intercession and sets such as legal precedence upon which to base our battle, for indeed the enemy is a legalist and must be beaten in the law court of Heaven before he is ever defeated in the heavenly and then in the natural.

The Holy Spirit has enlightened people with the Word time and again beyond anything I could ever understand and has zeroed in upon the issue of intercession with such a powerful precedence from His Word that victory is always assured. Men and women today, who make themselves willing tools of the devil, to be used by him against God and His holy ones, can always be defeated on the same grounds as those operating under similar conditions recorded in the divine Scriptures.

An intercessor is a lifetime partner with the Holy Spirit, with the Spirit Himself, needing and wanting Him to be the Supreme Director for the Glory of God. Nothing less is satisfactory or acceptable and He will operate under no other conditions. He cannot be the *major* partner, but must be the absolute Director.

CHAPTER TEN

The Intercessor—Identifying

I DENTIFICATION IS an integral part of intercession. The greatest intercessor of all time, the Lord Jesus Himself, was the greatest identifier. Jesus,

> *Who, being in the form of God, thought it not robbery to be equal with God: but made Himself of no reputation, and took upon Him the form of a servant, and was made in the likeness of men: and being found in fashion as a man, He humbled Himself, and became obedient unto death, even the death of the cross* (Philippians 2:6-7).

If such identification is what Jesus did for me, it absolutely demands that I make a similar sacrifice for Him, to delight His heart, and for those who are in "gross" darkness and need to see His marvelous light. There can be no intercession until there is true identification. Such is part of the lot of real missionaries who are called to give their lives for different nations and is a major reason why the theory of modern missions is a failure. An evangelist, a preacher, or a teacher is not necessarily an intercessor, effective though that person might be. For the most part, they are casual visitors, but the true missionary, weighed down with the burden of the lost and carrying the sentence of death, is an intercessor if such a person really identifies with the people and carries them in his innermost being, no matter the price.

Look in upon Hudson Taylor of China as he cast aside his Western culture and so completely identified with the Chinese that he became as one of them with his shaved head and pigtail, his Chinese dress and slippers, his food and language. In every way, he became Chinese to win the Chinese and he totally alienated himself from his fellow Western missionaries who despised him for his stand. Yet, he also became the great intercessor for his adoptive land and fulfilled the royal law of the Lord. What identity was born out of a heart burning for the salvation of a people who had never heard of Christ! And what success in the explosion of a missionary endeavor through such great passion whilst his contemporaries remained relatively unsuccessful.

How my own heart has burned for Africa, India, and China. Time and again I have been overwhelmed and undone for these great masses of people who are lost in the darkness of the evil one. What God is needing are great intercessors who will stand in the gap for the people, who will pour out their lives in shaking Heaven on behalf of those people until Heaven comes down and impacts them and changes them for His Glory. God needs men and women who will be ready to give up their lives of comfort and ease, their luxuries and Western culture, and be ready to leave their home shores forever to identify with the lost mass of heathen humanity and point them to the beauty of Jesus.

That is not to say that doing so is not difficult and frustrating especially when the purity of heart is misrepresented and maligned. Many times, I have longed for a stimulating conversation as I have been in the African bush for months at a time. Sometimes, I have even thought that my intellect had totally atrophied and that I had ended up "bush happy" or a zombie. But what did it cost Jesus to be separated from the fellowship of the Father to come to earth? How great was His agony to leave the Glory and holiness of Heaven and be contaminated with the slightest taint of the society of sinful man? For one moment, think of the absolute purity and beauty of Jesus as He took upon Himself the lowliest servitude and became the footwashing slave of mankind to save us. What identification, what love, what intercession of which most know very little.

It is for this reason that we have robbed the world of great moves of God: There are few real intercessors who are ready to give up their all and leave their shores to identify with a people with whom they have fallen in love, or whom the Holy Spirit has burned upon their heart. Herein lies the greatest weakness of modern, "short-term missions": There is no calling to identify.

Identification takes time. How well I remember the ridicule of people questioning why there was a necessity to travel to some far-off country to preach the Gospel when there are enough people at home who need to be won? Such a question immediately reveals the total lack of understanding of the heart of God in identification on the part of those who proffer such groundless challenges.

Perhaps one of the most noble acts of identification by men was that of the two Moravian brethren who sold themselves into literal slavery because it was the only way of being able to get to Jamaica in the early days to preach to the slaves. Those two great intercessors died as slaves, but only after setting up a great network of lasting churches amongst the slaves on the island. What eternal rewards awaited them for so great a sacrifice!

This is the essence of greatness: laying aside everything to become a slave of love to those to whom the Lord calls you. As we look in on Paul the Apostle, we see another servant of such love and dedication that he called himself a *"spectacle unto the world"* (1 Cor. 4:9), *"the filth of the world,"* and the *"offscouring of all things"* (1 Cor. 4:13).

He was heavily burdened with the responsibility of all the churches for whom he declared, "[I] *rejoice in my sufferings for you, and fill up that which is behind of the afflictions of Christ in my flesh for His body's sake"* (Col. 1:24).

True identification means really giving up or being ready to give up everything. Mr. and Mrs. Rees Howells of the book *Intercessor* by Norman Grubb were moved upon by the Holy Spirit to give up their only son whilst they went to Africa. What an agonizing and heartrending sacrifice! But, ah, the price could be ultimately measured in the hundredfold return that the Lord gave them at their first station in Rusitu, Rhodesia (now Zimbabwe), where 10,000 souls were saved and filled with the Holy Spirit. Such unselfish commitment to the high calling of the Almighty yielded incredible fruit.

Was there any difference to the call made by the Lord upon Abraham? And, returning to Paul the Apostle, we read of one who left his riches and his home, his education and his position, his friends and his nation, to so completely identify with the Gentile world that it has to be consciously remembered that he was born a Jew. He counted *"all things but loss for the excellency of the knowledge of Christ Jesus my Lord."* (Phil. 3:8), and later declared, *"There is neither Jew nor Greek…"* (Gal. 3:28).

Such unselfish, sacrificing love can be undertaken only by hearts who have fallen so in love with the Lord that nothing else matters but a burning desire for those who are lost and the mandate of the Lord to reach His "other sheep." This is the hallmark of true identification, which looks beyond the cross of circumstance and situation, deprivation and personal loss, to see the fruit of yieldedness by the eye of faith or total obedience to the high calling of the Lord and a passion for souls.

Nobody can truly pray and travail and weep and intercede for that with which he cannot identify. It is not always necessary to go to a place for the purpose of physical identification, since the Holy Spirit Himself is well able to bring upon the intercessor an identification with persons or circumstances where there is need. Only a surrendered life can identify with the pain and suffering, the humiliation and degradation of sin, and lift the sinner up to see not only the cross but the freedom offered by the life of Jesus. It is in this way that old habits and traditions are broken and liberty from bondage and heathen practices established.

There are many times when God has called me to literally go and identify with a people or tribe. This has often necessitated walking great distances through mosquito-infested country, wild jungle, and the most inhospitable conditions so as to share His love. At other times, the Holy Spirit has stirred me to be separated and fast and pray; and through this, He has brought a tremendous burden upon me and an identification without having gone. When He does this, the reality is so intense that it is as if I had actually been amongst the people for whom I was burdened. The greatest factor in identification is love. Any and all intercession that is not motivated by compassion and love is not really intercession.

I want to look at another great character of identification who changed the destiny of an entire nation. That is what intercession is all about—changing eternal destinies by obedience to the prompting of the Holy Spirit and He can never fail. It is said of Moses that by obedience,

> *When he was come to years, refused to be called the son of Pharaoh's daughter; choosing rather to suffer affliction with the people of God, than to enjoy the pleasures of sin for a season; esteeming the reproach of Christ greater riches than the treasures in Egypt...* (Hebrews 11:24-26).

Israel was married unto the Lord when they splashed the blood of the Passover lamb upon the doorposts and lintels of their houses. Just a few weeks later, Israel commits adultery in the matter of the golden calf, and God is ready to cast them aside and to make of Moses himself a new and obedient nation. God declares that He is a jealous God, and Moses commands the children of Israel to grind the gold of the calf into fine powder and sprinkle it on the water. Fine gold sprinkled on water makes it appear red. Then Israel was commanded to drink this type of the blood—as were the disciples by Jesus at the supper when He said, "Drink ye all of it"—because real cleansing is from the inside out.

Thus begins one of the most crucial and dramatic intercessions that has ever taken place, with Moses pleading to God for God to save His people, Israel. Moses' display of total jealousy for the reputation of God is deeply moving as are his great arguments that God cannot possibly divorce His people and cause the heathen to scorn. It is a holy "chess match," a national crisis of extreme proportions, with God denying all identification with Israel whilst Moses pleads their cause with every part of his being. Moses surely enters into "the fellowship of His sufferings" and draws on every promise and covenant that the Lord had made with Israel. Moses recounts a great list stating why God should remember not only Himself but His very people and concludes with reminding God that He had chosen to make a nation out of the loins of Abraham, not Moses, and that it would be Abraham's seed forever. The *coup de grace* for Moses was when he declared, *"Now if Thou wilt forgive their sin; and if not, blot me, I pray Thee, out of Thy book which Thou has written"* (Exod. 32:32).

Moses' intense identification with a nation in sin, and his desire to see them set them free from judgment and eternal damnation, was so strong that the Lord Himself was moved and He repented. It was not a mere question of saving the nation, but of a total restoration of the marriage covenant with the Lord. The man who gave up the throne of Egypt and identified with God and His people during a 40-year sojourn in the wilderness, thus had power with God. Changing from the lofty palaces and the soft clothes to the dust and skins of Midian as a hireling turned Moses into a true identifier with the enslaved nation of Israel.

There is a call of the Spirit for us to identify with the lost that we might lift them out of their deception; lift them out of their lostness; lift them out of their suffering and poverty in order to bring them to Christ. It is not our words that are going to do it, but our lifestyle. When we break through with God in intercession and find favor in His sight, then we have the liberty to be *bold* with Him and to open wide our mouths, knowing that He will assuredly fill them.

Identification is twofold: identifying with the people and identifying with God. We can have no power with God unless we really know

Him—and that takes time. Getting to feel God, to hear God, to understand God, and to have His heartbeat throbbing in my heart is all part of the identification process. Breaking through with God and reaching a place of authority with Him is not the same as offering up a few prayers and hoping that He will answer.

Moses was desperate; the children of Israel were desperate, whether they recognized it or not; and God Himself was desperate. Moses was busy winning back five things for Israel and God:

1. He was winning back God's presence in the midst of Israel, for Moses declared that he would go no farther if God was not in the midst of them.

2. He was winning back God's grace and with it His salvation, blessings, and provision.

3. He was winning back the marriage covenant and true partnership with God.

4. He was winning back the holiness of God in the midst of Israel.

5. And finally, he was winning back the covenant with Abraham, Isaac, and Israel.

When the battle was done, God set His seal by saying, *"This day; behold, I drive out before thee the Amorite, the Canaanite, the Hittite, the Perizzite, the Hivite and Jebusite"* (Exod. 34:11).

Great victory ensued because Moses was not ashamed to identify with Israel even in her trespasses and sins.

After I had spent many years in the Mozambican bush, the Lord impressed upon me the importance of identification, which became the theme of our ministry and has remained so until the present. A statement of identification is found in First Thessalonians 2:8 where Paul declares, *"So being affectionately desirous of you, we were willing to have imparted unto you, not the gospel of God only, but also our own souls, because ye were dear unto us."* In other words, Paul was saying, "We loved you so much that we were ready to come and live another lifestyle amongst you, sacrificing ourselves in the process, and even being ready to die so that you might know—not only in word but also in every deed—that our God lives and loves and wants to enjoy a relationship with you." This truly is the essence of identification.

CHAPTER ELEVEN

The Intercessor—Agonizing

THERE CAN BE no identification without agony if there is true intercession. This is a crucial part of the "suffering Gospel" of which most want to hear nothing in these days. Paul said, *"[I] fill up that which is behind of the afflictions of Christ in my flesh for His body's sake, which is the church"* (Col. 1:24).

In other words, the sufferings of Christ did not end at the cross; they continue up until today through His saints who give themselves unreservedly for the Gospel and the Church, counting it worthy to suffer for Jesus and for the sake of those who have never heard. The suffering that we are called to endure is mental, emotional, physical, and spiritual. The intercessor lives a dying life; and the more he dies, the more real Jesus becomes and the more powerful is the Holy Spirit who can operate through the vessel.

We are in a mighty battle, fighting against principalities and powers, and this battle intensifies when we take on national and international issues. It is time to carry an indignation and anger inside of us at all the works of the evil one. This, in itself, is a heavy burden. Jeremiah's declaration of suffering was summed up, *"But if ye will not hear it, my soul shall weep in secret places for your pride; and mine eyes shall weep sore and run down with tears, because the Lord's flock is carried away captive"* (Jer. 13:17).

Indeed, we are living in the Laodicean age of the Church when she has been carried away, captive by the materialism of the world, and *this* is a great reason to agonize. Jesus said, *"Blessed are they that mourn; for they shall be comforted"* (Matt. 5:4). The mourning is agonizing over the corrupt state of man and the fact that without Jesus the human race is lost. As we go bearing the precious seed of the Word, we will come again rejoicing, *"Bringing our sheaves with us"* (see Ps. 126:6).

We also agonize at our own casual and often lukewarm condition and find that, as we do, we are drawn closer into His presence. Many times the agonizing we experience is from the Holy Spirit's dealing with some seat of self that we will not surrender or His wanting to take us down another avenue of ministry.

I remember well this farmer who resisted the call of the Lord. His whole life was farming and he was a good and rich coffee farmer. But God moved him to another farm where he went bankrupt and ended with over half-a-million dollars of debt. That was a great deal of money, especially 20 years ago. Consequently, the farmer lost his reputation and his position in the society. It was an agonizing process, but God was killing the farmer in him so that He could raise up the missionary.

At the same time, God stripped us in the midst of our community. We were looked upon as the scum of the earth, and it was God taking us from one death into another. The more we praised and worshipped God, the more we were ridiculed and treated as outcasts. Many times the people in the bar would cease their drinking and chatter to listen to "those crazy Christians" as we did battle, often for the very people who were despising us. The village drunkards accused us of having a barrel of beer in the church and partying! The time came that when we walked down the street, villagers would deliberately cross to the other side of the road, afraid, as if we were stricken by some plague. The white village people and local farmers did not want to even see us; they certainly did not want to talk to us, acknowledge us, or have anything to do with us. It was tough, very tough, especially for our children who were treated as lepers because of our stand.

The agony of it all was crushing, and some were not able to bear the strain of the mockery, scorn, and the continual ostracism. But when victory came it was very sweet. After breaking through with God for the community, the district, and the nation at large, the hardened attitudes changed and people came flocking for prayer and help and comfort. Above all, there came a respect and fear of the Lord as the prelude to a mighty outpouring of His Spirit.

Without a doubt there is a clear correlation between the birthing process in the natural and that of the Spirit with the same accompanying agony. Jesus said, *"A woman when she is in travail hath sorrow, because her hour is come: but as soon as she is delivered of the child, she remembereth no more the anguish, for joy that a man is born into the world"* (John 16:21).

The tremendous effort in birthing in the Spirit is the same. For at least two years, I poured out my heart for the salvation of my Dad. It was a very difficult spiritual battle because he was a tough military man and he certainly fought. Finally I enjoyed the breakthrough and victory, which made the fight seem as nothing because there was such triumph. I had assurance, absolute assurance, that Dad would get saved. I never doubted nor wavered for a moment on that issue because the deed had been sealed in Heaven. The price had been high, but once I had gained the victory through the Holy Spirit, I was able to sit back and watch as God reeled in my Dad.

It took 21 years for his final capitulation and not once in that time did I ever pray for his salvation again. There was no need and to have done so would have meant that I was in unbelief. I had not presumed in my assurance but had fought a fight and won a battle. It had been like a woman's giving birth; the joy afterwards was sweeter than the toughness of the battle before.

A great part of the agony of intercession is giving up that which we are holding on to. How many times have we prevented the Lord from achieving something spectacular because we did not want to surrender and thereby reach a place of intercession where victory is assured? We have no excuse except that we are too lazy to expend any energy and agonize concerning a lost and dying world or the sin in the church. The Bible says,

> *The Spirit also helpeth our infirmities: for we know not what we should pray for as we ought: but the Spirit itself maketh intercession for us with groanings which cannot be uttered. And He that searcheth the hearts knoweth what is the mind of the Spirit, because He maketh intercession for the saints according to the will of God* (Romans 8:26).

It is all the workings of the Holy Spirit who knows the heartbeat of God and is more than ready to reveal such to those who are about His business.

There are four expressions in the Word that describe the agonizing that goes with intercession, and God will never fail both to hear and to intervene when His people sincerely travail, groan, cry out, and weep. Each of the terms is directly related to descriptions of what takes place in the process of childbirth. The prophet Jeremiah declares, *"Ask ye now, and see whether a man doth travail with child? Wherefore do I see every man with his hands on his loins, as a woman in travail, and all faces are turned into paleness?"* (Jer. 30:6).

The very term *travail* means to labor in childbirth, to toil and be in pain or great distress. The Church is the womb of God in the earth, but where there is no travail, there will be either no birth or an abortion. If there is no birth then it brings death to the host. It is through great wrestling and anguish that people are born into the Kingdom, and it is time for the Church to get back to travail.

I see several reasons for intercession, and each carries an intense weight of responsibility. Today, intercession is for the salvation of lost souls and the establishment of the Great Commission, *"Go ye into all the world, and preach the Gospel to every creature"* (Mark 16:15).

Because of his great hatred, the devil means to stop people from coming to a saving knowledge of Christ; therefore he works tirelessly to derail God's purpose by raising up an enemy against both those who would hear the message and those who are sent to proclaim it. This is similar to the many times that the enemy of Israel sought to annihilate that nation through aggression from the outside so as to destroy *the* seed and prevent the coming of Jesus.

Intercession is needed because of sin *within* the camp, which gives the enemy legal right to accuse God's people and prevent them from fulfilling the Great Commission. Satan believes that he will also be able to interfere with the coming *again* of Jesus by corruption within and aggression from without. It is totally naive of any to believe that whole nations and the entire world cannot be enslaved by satan. This will literally be fulfilled under the antichrist's rule. Meantime, we are called to fight for souls, to travail until we bring forth that fruit which the Lord has placed in our hearts to be gathered.

Abundant fruit requires abundant travail, sleepless nights of watching and seeking the face of God, who alone is able to prevail upon the hard of heart. There is nobody, absolutely nobody, who can ultimately resist the Lord after an intercessor has pleaded that person's cause and travailed for their soul with heartrending sobs that shake Heaven. It is time for people to learn to pour out their hearts unashamedly, for we are dealing with the enormous issue of eternity.

"When Jesus therefore saw her weeping , and the Jews also weeping which came with her, He groaned in the spirit and was troubled" (John 11:33). The groaning of which the Word speaks is a deep sighing and mourning under the weight of oppression. It was only when Israel began to groan in her slavery in Egypt that God *remembered* His covenant with Abraham, with Isaac, and with Jacob. Something very powerful takes place in intercession when there is true groaning. The soul power of unbelief is broken and the atmosphere is set free. The agony of groaning stirred by the Holy Spirit within—and it is a great agony—quickly reaches Heaven and there is rapid response. When Jesus groaned He broke all the controlling powers of darkness so that the resurrection of Lazarus could take place.

There can be nothing casual and flippant about such groaning when produced by the Holy Spirit who clearly knows the mind and heart of the Father and directs accordingly so that there is maximum authority granted from on high for the work at hand. I well remember going down into the camps of the ex-terrorists at the end of the Rhodesian war. Those camps were hotbeds of hatred, confusion, and every vile thing imaginable. The powers of darkness literally hung over them like a great cloud. As I entered the zone, I began to groan with great stirrings deep within. The camps were islands of total rebellion where the only law was the whim of the local commander. The inhabitants—who could not be called soldiers—literally terrorized the local population, and the Lord wanted an end of such nonsense. He wanted order established, for His agenda was clearly revival for the whole district.

In the natural, it was totally suicidal to even venture into the vicinity of the camps, but there I was entering into the very heart of them. As I groaned and sighed and mourned for people languishing in the prison of the devil's deception and clutches, God brought an incredible release of His power. I felt it in surging waves as He billowed over me. I had the absolute assurance that He was in control and victory was in His hands. Oh what confidence there is when God steps into the scene and takes complete authority! I knew, after no little amount of trepidation initially, that all was fine. I felt as Daniel must have felt in the den of lions—absolute calm in the midst of a raging storm that could in no wise touch me. That is when I came to realize that the antichrist system will never be able to control nor have any hold on those who are totally obedient to the will of the Master. It was all part of His purpose, and later we had the privilege of seeing the Spirit sweep the whole area with revival power.

The prophet commanded, *"Cry out and shout, thou inhabitants of Zion..."* (Isa. 12:6). There are two "crying outs" in the Bible, and both are intricately associated with intercession. There is the crying out of victory and blessing to the Lord for which Isaiah calls, and there is also the crying out so as to be heard on high. The latter is shrieking or great clamoring or persistent entreating.

For example, the two blind beggars in Matthew's account began to cry out with such noise of desperation that God could not fail to hear them. It was a noise, not from their vocal cords, but an attention-grabbing sound emanating from the deepest recesses of their spirits. When the multitude attempted to silence them, they cried out the more and arrested Christ's full attention. This was not because He heard their physical cry above the noise of the crowd but because He heard their desperation of faith. It is that type of crying out which produces miracles because it is a cry of intercession, and God will never ignore such cries.

Oh that His people were not so reserved and traditional! There needs to be such a crying out in these days so as to be heard in the highest Heaven. Only such will offset the filth of the blasphemy and reproaches of men towards God, *"For because of swearing the land mourneth and the pleasant places of the wilderness are dried up..."* (Jer. 23:10).

When Israel was trapped on the banks of the Red Sea with Pharaoh's army descending upon them, they cried out to God. What a cry of desperation that must have been. What a cry to birth their ultimate freedom from over 400 years of slavery by arresting the full attention of the Lord. And what a miracle took place as the waters parted! Their cry was sufficient for that historical act to be consummated. The shout of Israel at Jericho was another crying out, which caused an entire city wall to collapse.

The theme of the Lord in Isaiah 42 is His indignation against sin and ungodliness to the degree that He says He will: *"Cry like a travailing woman"* (Isa. 42:14). When that happens, the supernatural will be unleashed and the Glory and victory of the Lord revealed in the face of Christ Jesus.

Time and again, I have seen people totally released from controlling spirits and soul bondage by crying out to God. Such heart cries that must be given voice are certainly heard and respected by the Lord who says He does the same! Whole territories in Africa have been released from the powers of darkness by a Jericho-type cry. This is a very powerful tool of warfare that the Lord has given and is very much part of intercession.

It is time to get desperate in our desire to see the powers of darkness broken and the Glory of God established. Only then will souls be swept into the Kingdom. I have cried out for nation upon nation to have a visitation of the Lord and know that such is coming in response to the crying out to God of an army of intercessors.

Then there is the agony of weeping. Jesus wept at the tomb of Lazarus because of the unbelief of Israel. Such weeping was a lamentation or moaning from deep within. It is also a sob or even to wail aloud. The natives in Africa wail at their funerals and because of it, they experience release, whereas most Westerners bottle up their emotions and carry agony for years. There have been several times when I have broken into great sobbing and wailing for different persons who were either in sin or rebellion. I am not ashamed to do this in company as it is according to the urgent prompting of the Holy Spirit. Of course people deliberately misread such a situation, but this is the clear ministry of intercession from the Holy Spirit whose business it is to convince of sin, righteousness, and judgment. He was obviously greatly burdened for the individuals and had found an obedient vessel who was not concerned with opening his mouth to sob.

Such cries have powerful impact in the spirit. They are greatly agonizing and the only thing that I wish to do after weeping is sleep. This is true battle. When Jesus wept He turned the death of Lazarus. Similarly, when Hezekiah wept, his own circumstances were turned around, for he was still about weeping when the Lord spoke directly to the prophet Isaiah and told him to tell the king, *"I have heard thy prayer, I have seen thy tears"* (Isa. 38:5). When Joel called Israel's spiritual leadership to repentance, he emphasized, *"Howl, ye ministers of the altar…weep…then will the Lord be jealous for His land"* (Joel 1:13; 2:17-18).

One of the greatest agonies is what I call, "the death of the intercessor." God will assuredly take the intercessor down a path that will lead to "death"—death of a vision, reputation, confidence in anything that is "self"—that the Lord might receive the Glory. The ministry is not the intercessor's but the Holy Spirit's.

Sometimes God creates a vision or gives a direction that He wants you to follow. There is no doubt that it is the Lord, so you go ahead and proclaim publicly what the Lord has said and what He will do. Then suddenly, it becomes a disaster. You insist, "But I know I heard the Spirit!" And, indeed, you did, but He is going to destroy any reputation you might have when that thing does not come to pass. I'm not talking of uttering false prophecies, mind you, and there is a great difference. Neither am I speaking about flaky Christians who *claim* they are always hearing from the Lord but change their mind every other day about what God is supposed to have said.

A clear case was that God instructed us to invest in a wonderful piece of ground for an entire ministry center but particularly a youth camp. It was a perfect place and everybody poured their life into building and getting the place established. The grounds became so intertwined with the ministry that they could not possibly fail. But fail they did. Through it all, God really chose who were His for a mightier work that was in store, a work of a much larger dimension for everybody.

In the meantime, I never wanted to go near that place again in my life. I was so humiliated, overwhelmed that I had broadcast far and wide the vision, and it had come to naught. "The 'man of God' was not tuned in," people would ridicule or laugh, saying, "God's not answering His 'phone,'" or some such other caustic comment. Of course the biggest amongst God's people is, "How come you had no discernment?"

There just is no answer except die! Finally, God clearly showed that there needed to be a death in order for Him to take us into a higher place of abiding.

CHAPTER TWELVE

The Intercessor—Authority

THERE IS NO experience in the world that can equal that of knowing absolutely, conclusively, and unreservedly God has heard and answered the cries of the heart. Such is the sweetest of victories since it carries an assurance that cannot be changed once decreed from the very throne of the Lord. The key to the authority of the intercessor is when his heartbeat aligns with the heartbeat of Almighty God. At that point, God's Word becomes the intercessor's with no addition or subtraction. Only then, can any say that the Word will not return void but will accomplish that purpose to which it is sent (see Isa. 55:11).

It is also at that point that I may ask whatsoever I will in Jesus' name and it will be given because my desires are His desires. When Elijah stood on Mount Carmel and defied the prophets of Baal, the destiny of the whole nation was at stake. The heart of Elijah had become so one with God that he had been able to declare, *"There shall not be dew nor rain these years, but according to my word"* (1 Kings 17:1). God's Word had become Elijah's word but with all the backing of Heaven.

Elijah had gained a place of authority or intercession for Israel with God whose favor the prophet enjoyed. The greatest responsibility of the intercessor is as watchmen of the *nations*, which is precisely where the heart of God rests. By the very residency of the Holy Spirit, a real intercessor can never be parochial. He has learned the key that sacrificing personal needs and situations for the greater call of the nations will mean that God will always undertake for the former.

Jesus said, *"Seek ye first the Kingdom of God…and all these things shall be added unto you"* (Matt. 6:33). It is when we stand on holy ground in the high places with the Lord that we can open wide our mouths with boldness knowing that what we seek is already granted.

The place of victory or gained place of intercession means several things. It is a place of absolute favor and delight where the Lord does not fail to share the secrets or counsels of His heart. It is a place of mutual trust. God longs to be able to absolutely trust a people who are wholly His. Finally, the place of abiding intercession is a place of revelation. The Lord is very desirous to share the deep things of His heart, especially the truths concerning the marriage supper of the Lamb and our heavenly Bridegroom.

John the Baptist lived for only one thing: to do His will who had sent him. Perhaps one of the greatest declarations of all time was issued from the mouth of that holy man when Jesus came for baptism. He recognized Him and declared, *"Behold the Lamb of God which taketh away the sin of the world"* (John 1:29).

The Holy Spirit is prompting the Church to live as if Jesus is coming today, and therefore declare, *"Behold the Bridegroom cometh!"* (Matt. 25:6).

The greatest revelation given to an intercessor was the revelation of Himself given to John the Apostle on the Isle of Patmos. John, who had broken through the suffering and torment, continued to hang on to the promise of the Lord that He would come, and come He did! The greatest revelation to any intercessor is the deeper knowledge and revelation of Himself.

The Holy Spirit deeply desires that believers—all believers—obtain authority or gain a place of intercession over a great number of situations and in a variety of areas. This is the watchman's fruit of labor: to be able to stand on the mountaintop and know that total authority belongs to him because he fought through with the Holy Spirit and, through total obedience to Him, won. The uppermost issues in the heart of the intercessor, once having gained the place, is the Glory of the Lord, the salvation of the lost, and the holiness of God's people. It is at the, "Right hand of the Father," so to speak, that rulership takes place. Having ascended the mountain of battle step by step under the direction of the blessed Spirit, his is a place of ruling and reigning for the purpose of the exaltation of the Kingdom of God. Nothing else matters. And, once having gained that place in that issue, the intercessor abides there forever. He will always have authority in that matter and will not have to fight the same battles again.

Years ago, the Lord gave us authority over the weather, in particular the rain. In Africa, being subject to so many droughts, there was need at different times to really plead for rain. At those times, rain became a battle between the powers of darkness and light. That is when I took up the cause of real intercession, which continued for several years until complete victory came. I veritably felt like Elijah on Mount Carmel and knew that his word had become so strong that it was a matter of declaring the Word in a given situation and it would come to pass.

Recently I went to India for some crusades. There was water across the whole subcontinent, and I said aloud to the Lord, "But why is there so much rain, this is not monsoon season?"

Instantly, the voice of the Holy Spirit replied, "You won a place of abiding over the weather. You do something about it."

I had a couple of days before the rest of the team arrived, so I settled into some serious intercession. Because of that gained place, however, victory quickly was assured and I knew without a shadow of doubt that no rain would disrupt a single meeting for the entirety of the crusades. I made a declaration to that effect and never wavered once, even though the rain was pouring down.

The first night of the first crusade, it rained heavily to within half-a-mile of the crusade grounds and suddenly stopped. The Lord had said we would preach *every* night without the rain disturbing us. The clouds were certainly menacing and heavy and right over the platform and large drops fell. It was almost as if the enemy, himself, was deliberately provoking a confrontation, but the assurance was mine. The preaching was concluded, the sick prayed for, and several testimonies of miracles given when Heaven opened in a seeming deluge. I was soaked and began to grumble secretly and inwardly when the Holy Spirit quickly silenced me by saying, "I told you that you would preach every night...."

For 17 nights, not a drop of rain interrupted the crusades and, in fact, it was quite dry. As I traveled to Hyderabad to catch my outbound flight, the clouds started coming in and the rain began to fall in great sheets. I smiled quietly, victoriously and knowingly thanking God for all the years of battle and final victory over the elements. Oh how somebody on the continent of North America needs to gain the victory in intercession over tornadoes and hurricanes thereby saving multitudes of lives and untold billions in damage and destruction! The Lord does hold the whole earth in His hands as well as all the affairs of men. It is a little thing for Him to turn the weather.

Amy Carmichael, who spent 57 years in India, gained a place of intercession for orphans and temple children whom she would rescue from the degraded role of being sexual objects for the temple priests. In the same way, George Meuller gained a place of authority for the orphans and strays of Bristol. Such love poured out by these two giants in their respective spheres can only be recorded and rewarded in eternity. Both had gained such authority with God that whatsoever they asked in the name of Jesus was granted. Their whole lives were dedicated to His purposes and they won respect and favor from the One who holds the affairs of men in His hands.

Moses certainly gained a position of power and authority for the nation of Israel, and I believe that the nations are the real issue of the heart of the Lord. I gained a position of intercession concerning the powers of witchcraft so that today I can walk into any area controlled by witch doctors and almost immediately have the ascendancy over them.

David Brainerd poured out his heart in travail and war for the Indians of Pennsylvania. He was unable to speak their language, but years of preaching to them and crying out to God for revival finally brought the fruit for which he had so long sought.

This brings me to the issue of true Holy Ghost revival. A true revivalist is an intercessor. Such is what marks the revivalist out from great evangelists or other generals of the faith. The true revivalists are assured success because they carry the stamp of approval from Heaven as a result of their identification with the lost, their agonizing for them, and their ultimate victory.

Finney was undergirded day and night by the intercessory prayer of Fathers Nash and Young who preceded Finney wherever the great revivalist went. These intercessors prayed down Heaven before Finney ever arrived so that the town or community was already saturated in conviction when Finney began to preach. What teamwork and selfless sacrifice for the Kingdom they displayed.

But above all, there is the unseen Author and Director who is the One giving the real orders, the very Holy Spirit of God. When He takes complete charge, victory is assured and indeed, the birthing process is complete. The joy of seeing many children brought into the Kingdom makes the agony of birthing them pale into nothingness. It was because of "the joy set before Him" that Jesus endured the cross and despised the shame. Oh, the joy of multitudes redeemed because of so great a sacrifice can never be recorded by man. And, like we who follow in the footsteps of the Master, there can only be joy following the whole birthing process, which is the very law of nature instituted by God that touches every part of creation.

I speak of the price of gaining a place of intercession and many today think it ridiculous. C.T. Studd who spent 9 years with Hudson Taylor in China and 12 years in India, returned to England broken in health and with asthma so bad that he could not even walk. As he lay on his couch, he decided that he was not going to end for Jesus in that way. With determination and, above all, faith in his heart, he arose and traveled to the very heart of Africa to establish a mission the likes of which have not been seen since. The price was that in 23 years, he saw his wife only twice. It was not that they did not love each other or care about each other, but the demands of the work were so great as to necessitate their being apart. And who dares point a finger when Jesus left His Father for the same purpose?

The fruit of such sacrifice cannot be measured in earthly terms. From the "Heart of Africa" mission came one of the greatest mission organizations ever: "Worldwide Evangelization Crusade." All of C.T.'s children grew up to love and serve the Lord, and in the wake of his death, the Congo saw one of the greatest of revivals, as recorded in the classic book, *This Is That*.

If we look upon the agonies, heartaches, and trials, the tribulations, sufferings, and rejections, then too, we must look upon the victories, such incredible victories that cannot be measured by mortal man through the eye of the flesh in the realm of the temporal and the carnal. Those victories can only be spiritually discerned and eternally rewarded. What a place of authority C.T. gained for the peoples in the heart of Africa, and his legacy lives on despite terrorism and revolutions, civil wars and strife, destruction and dictatorships.

I cannot complete this chapter without a look at one of the most powerful intercession declarations in the Word. Psalm 149 really emphasizes that when the high praises of God are in my mouth then I have a "two-edged sword" in my hand. What exactly are the high praises? Miriam and Moses sang them on the banks of the Red Sea. David sang high praises, and Jehoshaphat won a great victory with them. The high praises are a "new song," which comes directly from the Holy Spirit who inspires us according to the will and battle plan of the Lord. Because it is always the nature of the Spirit to glorify Jesus, that new song most certainly is the song of the Lamb, which, of course, acknowledges the power of the blood.

Just as the Lord did for Israel in Egypt when He instituted the Passover, as soon as there is the application of the blood, the Lord overshadows those who are His. Times without number, I have been inspired to sing the new song in the midst of the darkest turmoil only to find that such a song breaks through the heavens to touch the very throne of God and bring release and victory in the natural realm because of the overshadowing of the Almighty. The new song is a real song, but it has a power, an unction, and a victory theme that no other song has at that needed time. I have sung such a song for days and the more I have sung it, the more victory I have obtained. Such a song has carried me into a dimension whereby I have felt transported into the heavenlies as if I were looking down from above just as the eagle does. This gives unprecedented advantage in all spheres.

Jesus declared, *"Blessed are the meek; for they shall inherit the earth"* (Matt. 5:5). Actually, the meek, according to God's Word, are those who delight in the Lord, are hilariously excited in Him, and enjoy the abundance of His peace. As I get excited about God and delight in Him, I am lifted above every earthly care. In the midst of the greatest adversity in the natural, I delight in Him and His peace and joy floods my whole being. Men, the devil, and circumstances cannot get the better of me so that no matter where I am, I am ruling. I am in control and I possess whatever territory I find myself inhabiting.

It is for this reason, that whilst in a bamboo prison cage in the midst of the African jungle, I could rejoice, enjoy the victory despite the natural hardships and deprivation, and inherit the earth. Such victory caused my enemies to fear for they reasoned that I should be defeated and depressed. Instead of being intimidated, I became the intimidator. This is what the new song does; it establishes the standard of God in the midst of turmoil and confusion and puts control of every situation firmly in my hands as His child.

This, too, is a place of intercession—victory over shackles and chains and prison bars—so that the world might see that I have a greater purpose and reason for which to live. When I was finally released from that bamboo prison, I found hundreds of soldiers coming to question me as to why I could sing and shout and praise under my circumstances. What victory for the Lord, but it is nothing of myself. Simple obedience to His Word and allowing the Holy Spirit the rightful place of control will always win the day.

This powerful tool of authority, which can really only be recognized and sung by those who already have authority, has always brought me into the very presence of the throne—that electrifying, terrifying, and awesomely Holy place of Light and Life. It is no wonder that David overcame Goliath after descending from the hillside where he had sung unto the Lord. And, by the truth and revelation declared in the Psalms of the sweet singer of Israel, David by faith knew all about the power of the blood. Only when I attain those high praises through total obedience to the prompting of the Holy Spirit do I have the authority of the sword in hand. The purpose of this sword of the Lord is *"to bind their kings with chains, and their nobles with fetters of iron"* (Ps. 149:8).

Such powers I have seen in operation when all else seemed to fail. When the ruling powers and principalities in heavenly places are overcome and dislodged, the evil and corrupt natural powers and principalities are dealt a major blow and are overcome according to God's established principle: first the spiritual, then the natural. While we are not in the cursing and killing business, it must be clearly understood that the judgment of God will often bring death to those who align themselves with the enemy and stand in the way of that which the Holy Spirit wants to achieve.

Many in this Age of Grace, in which we live, find it hard to marry this to their idea of a loving God, but there is absolutely no contradiction. We are dealing with the same God who killed Ananias and Sapphira. When revival begins, the Holy Spirit becomes very jealous for the reputation of the Godhead. I have preached in absolute fear when the Spirit has moved, and I have watched men openly flaunt His grace and ridicule the Holy One of God. If the ministry of the Holy Spirit is to convict of sin, righteousness, and judgment, then there is no hope left to a man who insults Him—the only Person who can draw lost men to Christ and salvation or a backslider to repentance.

I do believe that God is highly indignant and angered when His Holy Spirit is ridiculed. Any mistreatment of the Holy Spirit by men automatically places them under the hand of God's judgment, for it borders on blasphemy. The execution upon the kings and nobles and punishment upon the peoples includes the judgment written and declared on sin from its inception. Such judgment, which is clearly in the hands of God, can be very swift and, in a practical form, even deadly.

Intercession is a lifestyle. It is the principles of God intricately worked into the life of the believer who sets his faith and target by the standard of the Almighty and goes through to victory no matter what hindrances and enemies might stand in the way. I believe in believing, praying, and living dangerously for God. Because of that, I have gained a place of intercession and authority for many nations especially on the continent of Africa.

Because of Christ's obedience and total willingness to go to the cross, He commanded absolute authority as He hung there gaining the only place of intercession ever for total sin. There was no defeat but only absolute victory in the midst of such pain and suffering, and He carried such authority and victory that He could have come down off the cross in the same way that He could have ascended from the Mount of Transfiguration had He so wished. He was in absolute control because He had suffered and agonized to reach the place of authority and therefore victory. No man took the life from Jesus. *He* laid it down and *He* took it up again. Because of that complete authority and intercession, He seated *Himself* at the right hand of the throne of majesty in the heavens—the place of supreme authority—where He ever lives to make intercession for the saints.

CHAPTER THIRTEEN

The Healing of Rod

S OMETIME BEFORE my first trip to India, the Holy Spirit had begun preparing me through the sudden illness of a dear friend at the time. Rod was one of those gems that every pastor desires. There was nothing he was unwilling to do, and in his quiet, humble way he achieved a lot. He shunned the limelight, was a man's man, and was also exceedingly popular amongst the ladies as a real gentleman. I had grown to know Rod and his family intimately during the terrible terrorist war in Rhodesia when I would travel the land-mined roads to visit them on their remote farm. I had become a spiritual mentor to them despite the great distances, the petrol (gasoline) rationing, and the dangers that I encountered in getting to them. Finally, when the war ended, I was transferred to their district as the resident pastor of that entire rural community.

Life there was tremendously exciting, active, and above all, spiritual. Most in the church were young believers both in faith and age and were ready to be taught and to believe for the impossible. I was their natural commander, and they were excited to follow. The church became known as a fellowship of love throughout the land, and people would visit just to experience the presence of the Lord and the real love of His people. The exciting moves of the Holy Spirit that directed the activities of the church were preparing people for a revival that the Lord intended to use to bring peace in the very turbulent days at the end of the war. Of course, there were the community skeptics and critics who sought every opportunity to point a finger, and such an opportunity was not long in coming.

I taught a very practical Christianity, simply believing that what Christ said He would do, He did, and what He commanded us to do, we should also do without debate or question. I was not at all theological and had been trained, not in a seminary, but in the very school of the Holy Spirit Himself. Consequently, when the Holy Spirit was honored, He manifested Jesus, whose presence we were very accustomed to enjoy as He became tangibly real in service after service. His supernatural fragrance would often fill the church with the most delicate of perfumes and many were healed as they simply sat and worshipped Him.

Then suddenly, into this idyllic equation, disaster struck—a disaster that challenged all I had taught and my congregation had believed, rocked the faith of the fellowship, and brought down upon us the scorn and wrath of the entire community. Rod was enormously popular in the whole district and both he and his wife descended from original settler stock. Consequently, almost every influential farmer was either a close or distant relative; and all of them agreed that religion had its place but that Rod had taken things "too far" and become fanatical. Of course, it was all his "young pastor's fault" with his new and, to them, "weird" teachings. Nevertheless, they were prepared to "tolerate" that side of Rod because of his integrity and because, after all, he was "familie" and they stuck together like glue.

Then of course, Rod's mother-in-law had "become saved" as well, and she was *the* most influential lady in the entire community. She commanded enormous respect, and all decided that her new religion was better left "untouched" as a subject of any kind of discussion. "After all," people reasoned, "her husband had been murdered by terrorists, she had played a model role in the community thereafter, and she was 'now' entitled to a little comfort and enjoyment. If she was satisfied with her newfound religion, well then, they were happy for her, just so long as...."

So the gossip went without ceasing because nobody was *really* happy that she should be happy! After all, she was a widow, and everyone thought that widows should spend the rest of their lives in mourning or should get married again. She had certainly had enough of those men who *thought* they might be suitors.

On a pastoral visit during the week, Rod's wife mentioned that he had been having some pain in his back. I took the matter seriously and prayed for Rod with clear instructions that he should take care and watch the situation. By Saturday Rod was in bed and by Monday he was flown to the capital in a state of near paralysis. The incredible verdict of the specialists was that his spinal fluid had become infected and that Rod would never again walk. He would be paralyzed for life.

The news shocked the whole community, and quite naturally, the tongues began to wag. It was a very tough time to say the least. Apart from the anxiety of a friend in real trouble, a myriad of questions needed answering: "Why Rod?" "What kind of God...?" "Look how Rod served his Lord and this is his reward?" Within the fellowship, people were putting on a brave front but were being sorely tested and buffeted, some even allowing the enemy to get the better of them.

However, the Holy Spirit was in absolute control and spoke very clearly to me, "I want you to take up a place of abiding for Rod so that he is completely released from this affliction."

Who was I going to believe: the evidence of the "specialists" reports or the Word of Almighty God? I had no problem believing in the total authority of the Lord, but the issue was getting that belief from my head to my heart and to really trust the Lord for Rod in that particular situation when all evidence was stacked against there ever being any kind of healing.

I instantly went into intercession—an intercession that consumed every day for the next several weeks. The church was placed on a chain fast and early morning, noontime, and evening prayers were instituted until there was a clear answer from Heaven. The tongues of the critics wagged non-stop, but we set our faces as flint to the task of intercession. Almost every other day, I would drive the three-and-a-half hours to the capital, lay hands on Rod, anoint him with oil, and then return to take up the fight with the support of the congregation. They were stalwart, and it was very necessary to keep them focused in on the battle, lest fear, doubt, and unbelief took hold of them.

So much was at stake, and the battle was tough. Practical answers simply had to be provided, but I could say nothing until I had heard from on high. I rejoiced that I did not have to go through the battle of "*my* reputation" being on the line. That was the least thing that concerned me, so the enemy was not able to use it against me. Nor was I much concerned about what the community thought, so the devil was not able to have a footing in that area either. The root issues were simply a real compassion for Rod and his family and that God would be supremely glorified through a total healing.

The toughest part was watching Rod's deterioration into a quadriplegic day by day while refusing to accept the status quo, for the eye of faith was declaring something totally different. There was no presumption, false declarations, or statements about Rod's healing. I would make no declaration without a clear mandate from the Lord, and because I had not gained a place of authority regarding Rod's healing, I was not prepared to speculate in any kind of emotional way. Yes, I believed what the Word had to say with regard to healing, but to transfer that into practical reality was the issue. Anything I said had to be based solidly on victory with the Lord, and we certainly enjoyed our share of victorious prayer sessions.

I was in the hospital and about to anoint Rod again when the Spirit questioned distinctly and deliberately, "Michael, are you willing to take his place?"

"What do you mean?" I countered, though I knew and did not want to really face the full impact of the blow I had just received. It is very easy to want to take another's place in the emotion of a situation, but when the Spirit of Truth Himself was proffering the question, there could be no casualness or flippancy because He was searching the inward parts.

"Unless you are willing to get up into that bed and become what Rod has become, you have no right to pray for him nor cry to Me for any kind of healing."

Suddenly, I felt as if someone had emptied a 44 gallon drum of iced water all over me. I felt sick to the depths of my stomach, and my face must have instantly turned ghostly pale. The blood drained from my face, and I was left shaking with fear. This was no game. There were no lofty and noble sentiments. I was actually face to face with the reality of becoming a quadriplegic so that Rod might go free. Was I really willing? At that moment, I had to say, "No," as I tried to bid a quick farewell and leave without stumbling from the room, thereby facing a barrage of questions about my own condition. All I wanted to do was vomit. Gone were all my lofty, noble ideals. Crippled for life! All the work, all the ministry, all the promise, and me, a vegetable? Impossible!

I instantly resorted to the typical reply, "Surely, God, You would not want this, would You?"

"Oh, but I do," interrupted the Holy Spirit before I reasoned my way out. "Unless you are willing to take his place, I cannot heal Rod. It is up to you. You wanted to take on this assignment."

"You mean I'm the only link between this condition and his healing?"

"Precisely," replied the Spirit in an ever-so-gentle tone.

"Well, that's just not fair," I grumbled, but He was gone and left me to continue being sick, mad, and whatever else. It was not a pleasant drive back, for all I wanted to do was run away and hide. How could I possibly direct a meeting that night? I was upset, and there was no unction upon me. The Spirit had left me to my devices, and I felt like a hollow sham. This was not a light request, and at that point, I really was not even prepared to *consider* the possibility, let alone seriously agree to do it.

I felt like a hypocrite. All my religion was vain. The Holy Spirit has a wonderful way of having such an effect on a person when He really touches on truth issues.

I fled to my trysting place beside the river hoping to find some solace in nature, but there was none. I cried, shouted, pleaded, but no relief came. I guess that I secretly hoped the Spirit would change His mind. He did not, of course. I do not remember how long I was there, but the Spirit came again and simply said, "Die."

That was the issue. Was I really ready to die so that another might live.

"Michael, it is not Rod asking you to die, but Me!" He demanded. "Are you willing to do this for Me?" He continued questioning. "Supposing this is all that I wanted you to do your entire life, wouldn't that be good enough for you?"

It was at that point that the Holy Spirit really had me. There was no satisfactory answer that would ever justify any response in the negative, so I decided that it was better to yield my will to Him and go for broke. Anyway, I knew only too well that I was under sentence of death and that without the Holy Spirit, I might as well be dead. He was not going to stay around a disobedient vessel. I pondered the enormity of the decision. I thought about being a total vegetable and concluded that it was infinitely better being such in the hands of the Holy Spirit than having all my faculties and being without Him.

"Either way," I finally chuckled, "I'm a vegetable. So, Lord, I might as well be a vegetable because You want me to be so. That makes You responsible for me."

I surrendered there and then and began to laugh and laugh and laugh. I imagined my new role, but more, I felt how disappointed the enemy must have been that victory was all the Lord's yet again. I enjoyed a praise session as the windows of Heaven opened, and I danced and leapt and shouted in victory. I made the most of it, wondering when the paralysis would hit me and cripple me for life, but it was really no longer an issue. The unction of Heaven was upon me and I felt the hand of God's approval. It was glorious.

"You may now declare that Rod will be healed," spoke the Holy Spirit, "for I will utterly deliver Him and raise Him up."

My victory shouts then knew no bounds as I rejoiced with such triumph and felt Heaven was in with me on the celebration.

I returned in a couple of days and announced far and wide that the Lord was going to heal Rod. Such confidence and assurance comes not from any lofty assumptions, but from the knowledge that the Lord has spoken and it shall be performed. Naturally, there were doubts amongst many who wondered what right I had to make such statements and build everybody's hopes when the specialists had declared their verdict.

I could not wait for the next trip to the hospital, not only to tell Rod that he was to be healed and raised up whole, but also, that there was nothing in the world that could stop me from taking his place. Rod smiled and quietly said, "Thanks."

Still I knew what I was saying and the import of it. The tide had turned, and I also knew beyond any doubt that Rod would soon be walking. God was going to perform a miracle, and I was not presuming. I had gained a place of intercession for not only Rod, but many similar situations. Once having been made willing by the Holy Spirit to pay the ultimate price, victory was His. I did not give a date or time for Rod's healing, but it was to be soon.

From then on out, it was one series of triumphs after another for me as I stood back and smiled while the community gossiped and actually became quite nasty. Rod's mother-in-law stood firmly with her pastor in the face of the onslaught, much of which she quietly bore, shielding me from the worst. But such things make the real giants in the Kingdom and prepare people for their own victories.

From the instant of my willingness to take Rod's place, the affliction ceased and he began to noticeably mend. Within a couple of weeks, to the amazement of the doctors and specialists, Rod was walking and released to return home but with a severe warning that he would never be completely normal again. We all knew better, and what a time of celebration we enjoyed! The critics were silenced and the Lord vindicated. Rod's recovery was a mighty testimony; though the community would not bow but rather accepted that Rod was purely "lucky." From that point, however, despite the ongoing cynicism, there was a secret respect as we proclaimed the Lord with great power, for indeed, a notable miracle had taken place.

I must confess it was quite a little while before I felt the assurance that I was not going to end up a cripple. That was my fault and not the Holy Spirit's, who assured me that it had been only the willingness and obedience for which He had sought. Once that had been given, the place of intercession had been gained and the victory complete. Rod never looked back, and there was not a single aftereffect. He walked and lived normally and became a very active missionary, which he continues to be some 15 years later. What God does, He does well.

CHAPTER FOURTEEN

The Argentine War

INTERCESSION IS not taking on situations and events purely out of needs or necessities, for of such, there shall be no end. Rather, when the Holy Spirit directs that intercession be made, He is fulfilling the dictates of the strategies that the Lord has upon His heart in doing battle with the enemy. It was one night whilst in our regular prayer meeting that the Lord clearly revealed, "There is going to be a war between Britain and Argentina and I want you to intercede for a British victory. I am holding you responsible and will brook no failure. Multitudes are depending upon this."

With that, the Lord was gone, leaving me to ponder the enormity of the situation. At that time, hardly anyone had ever heard of the Falkland Islands, and they certainly were not an issue in international relationships. What I had been told by the Lord seemed ludicrous, but I had learned to know His voice and, better still, to know that the more outrageous the assignment, the more that it was, indeed, the Lord.

The Holy Spirit clearly revealed that no matter how sophisticated a nation's arsenal was, victory was not necessarily guaranteed by man's might nor by man's power. I was immediately cast upon the Scripture that "some trust in chariots and some in horses but victory is assured only in the name of the Lord."

Britain was by no means ready for a war at that time, *"But sin is a reproach to any people"* (Prov. 14:34), and many were the sins of the land. God does not look at systems of government and decide, "good democracy, bad dictatorship," because He does not judge according to the standard of man. If anything, democracy is the people's choice, which has always been an anathema to God, for *"every man will do that which is right in his own eyes"* (see Judg. 17:6).

I came to realize after a while that it was not so much that the Lord wanted Britain to win that war, but He wanted Argentina to lose. In retrospect then, it was not a great victory for Britain at the time but rather but a resounding defeat for Argentina.

The Holy Spirit will never give up territory that He has won. He showed me that any place where He had moved in mighty revival was His territory. The real failure of any move of God is ultimately that the next generation is rarely trained and equipped to continue the work. On the contrary, children are often forgotten in the excitement and fervor of a revival or move of the Spirit and so become alienated and disillusioned with the things of God. The Spirit distinctly said one day, "I always brood over a place, territory, or nation, awaiting a person who will truly pay the price for another of My visitations, no matter how deep in sin that place, territory, or nation might have sunk."

What an incredible call to the Church to stop playing religious games in the nations and to seriously get down to winning territory for the Lord through intercession. Argentina was the territory of the Holy Spirit, and any other power was a usurper. It was a time of great travail during which the Spirit revealed one of the major keys of the situation to a lady intercessor. She was one who had little general knowledge and was ignorant about Church history. She stood up and declared, "I see a man seated upon a throne, and he has three crowns upon his head. He is looking south and is very much involved with Argentina. It sounds strange because I have never heard of a king wearing three crowns!"

She had been very reluctant to reveal that key piece of information for that very reason, but the unction of the Spirit had come upon her so strongly that she had been compelled to speak out.

The great Argentine revival of 1951 had been the mighty triumph of intercession by a single missionary, R.E. Miller, and later, a small Bible school in City Bell, not far from Buenos Aires, which had also given itself to intercession for a mighty outpouring of God. The Holy Spirit Himself had orchestrated the whole affair, seeing the end from the beginning and intervening in the history of Argentina to bring very necessary change. There were three very powerful factors at work in that land in 1951, and all three had to be broken before God could achieve His purposes: the powers of Rome, the military, and Eva Peron.

In the words of Miller:

> As the war in the heavenlies progressed, intercession reached out for lost souls; for the cities mentioned, for this great country so utterly bound in paganism, idolatry and Catholic tenets of religious pretense which satisfy by ritual but leave the inner life a pitiful vacuum…

Miller continues in his account of the events of intercession:

> Then one Friday morning in September the Word of the Lord came forth directly and in mighty power, "Weep no more. The Lion of the tribe of Judah hath prevailed." Instructions and promises over Argentina followed, telling of the wonderful things He was going to do. With this word came a mighty release… Coming down from the glorious heights in the presence of God into the stormy atmosphere of the outside world, we heard strange news. A revolution had broken out in government circles. It was abortive…but a great Hand had reached down to shake the very seat of the Argentine Government.

Later on, the intercessors received a direct word concerning Eva Peron:

> Eva Peron shall tremble…. She will see the thunder of My Presence fall upon her heart. She will tremble for she shall see Me just as I am.

Then the news leaked out throughout the country that Eva Peron was seriously ill:

> That beautiful but wicked, powerful but evil, adulterous and unrepentant one who ruled with her husband in a strong dictatorship and had made men tremble, was stricken by the Lord; now she would tremble…. Eva Peron, the one who had become an ardent spiritist and was taking the country into open spiritism was inexorably taken down into a terrible, rebellious death, screaming for life, tearing out her beautiful

hair in rage. Nevertheless, death took her into the presence of her Divine Judge.

Concerning the revival, Miller concludes:

God did not sovereignly choose Argentina to bring forth such tremendous things for naught. Here in a country steeped in idolatry and paganism, filth and degradation, God brought forth one of the greatest single mass operations of Divine Grace ever recorded in Christian history. Nearly a decade later, we are still reaping the positive effects from that outpouring of His Spirit…. The last chapter has not yet been written, for as yet, it has not been enacted. The story is still not ended, nor has it all been told.

Some 20 or so years later the Lord was consummating the incredible Argentine revival through a small, unknown group of intercessors in a remote African village. The last chapter was, indeed, being written as the Holy Spirit planned the final severing of the tentacles of the two forces that had continued to keep Argentina enslaved.

The Spirit spoke distinctly, "I want the defeat of Argentina because when she is defeated, the military junta will be overthrown, ending dictatorship forever in that land. And, with the overthrow of the junta, the power of Rome will also be forever broken. No force will ever be able to prevent Me from freely presenting the Gospel in Argentina again."

Wherever the Roman church has established herself on the face of the earth, there has always been instituted the most repressive systems of civil government. Similarly, every nation that has been under the yoke of Rome has been technologically backward and has developed slowly, if at all. This is an amazing contradiction, but nevertheless true, considering the importance that Rome has always placed upon education.

There is only one man who sits upon a throne and wears three crowns: the Pope—who commanded absolute authority over the whole of the South American continent, including her most ruthless dictators. It was time for the whole system to be forever swept into the sea, and God was about to do it.

We began to earnestly intercede only to find that the heavens were like brass. It was going to be a tough assignment, and I knew that before any headway could be made, the "strongman" over Argentina had to be bound. It was at this time that the Spirit revealed why revivals do not continue, but He explained, "My work in that land was never completed and now is the hour."

There was no earthly reason why there should have been a war between the two countries, so there was need for a reason of provocation. I was exercised in the Word through Daniel's 21-day fast. In a mysterious way, that fast assisted the archangel, Michael, to overcome the prince of Persia. I realized the importance of an extended fast to bind the powerful princes who ruled over Argentina. Consequently, I called the intercessors to a 21-day fast. I knew that we were dealing with some mighty religious spirits and they are often the strongest. The realization dawned upon me that we were not only fighting for Argentina but the whole of South America, which languished under the same ruling powers.

I was burdened greatly for those under the severe bondage of tradition as I recalled the words of Jesus, *"You make the Word of no effect because of your tradition"* (see Mark 7:13).

We were given to prayer every night and often through the day when people could come. The burden was heavy as we began to carry Argentina like a baby, travailing and crying out to the Lord to birth a mighty deliverance for her tens of millions. The intercessors were so serious about their assignment from the Holy Spirit that many began to research the history and geography of the land and any other information that might be useful to the task ahead.

Everything we had was thrown into the fray as we waited patiently for the breakthrough. Twenty-one days came and went with no visible victory nor even the slightest inkling of a crack in the heavens. We prayed on and on, firing volley after volley at the enemy. It seemed as if we were systematically chipping away at the powerful walls of some mighty fortress. And indeed, we were! What stirred us to continue was the experience that our own neighbor, Mozambique, was enduring after 500 years of ruthless control under Rome, and more recently, a totalitarian communist regime that had enslaved the nation and treated men worse than dogs. The condition was no better in Argentina where the military dictators were a legacy both of the same religious system and the autocracy instituted by the Perons. Our hearts ached for the freedom of the Gospel to go forth, and we were neither going to give up nor let up in our bombardment of the enemy until the break came. Our confidence and trust was in the Holy Spirit who knew exactly what was required and had assigned us the task probably because He knew that we just would not stop.

The breakthrough came as in Ezekiel with the Lord putting His hooks into the jaws of Gog to bring them against Israel. I knew we had him at that point! He was defeated and we were on the victory roll after months of war. Oh, the victory and praise that we enjoyed knew no bounds! For weeks thereafter, all we could pray was for the Lord to put His hooks into Argentina and draw her against Britain. And that was not all. We were very impressed that they should come, in the words of the great prophet, *"to take a spoil, and to take a prey; to turn thine hand upon the desolate places that are now inhabited…"* (Ezek. 38:12).

Just how prophetic that was, we had very little idea at the time, but were soon to discover. We felt as if the enemy was perpetrating a war *against* his own desires—which is out of character for him—knowing that it was going to be his demise, but he was helpless to stop the sequence of events that was to follow as they were orchestrated by a higher power than he.

There were whole nights when we danced the victory dance, shouted the triumphs of Heaven, and laid bare the workings of the enemy. How we rejoiced over words like "humiliation" and realized that we were about to see Him "[make] *a show of them openly, triumphing over them in it"* (Col. 2:15)—and a military one in the natural at that! The intricate web of strongholds that had enshrouded Argentina were being broken, and this time for good. We saw, in the Spirit, a vast bush fire raging up the entire continent beginning from Argentina and devouring everything in its wake that was not of God. Nation after nation was going to be touched by the blessed Holy Spirit, and multitudes were going to be swept into the Kingdom. Nothing, absolutely nothing on earth or in the heavens, was going to be able to stop this impending move of God.

I must emphasize that at that time, none of us knew anything about a previous revival in Argentina or the intercession that had preceded it. Such knowledge came only years later, yet again confirming that our arrow was "bulls eye" with the Spirit.

I was absolutely confident that our prayers had reached the throne and that God had answered. We saw, as it were, the Pope fall from *his* throne, symbolizing that his authority had waned. Spread out across the entire Atlantic was an enormous cross depicting the absolute victory of God. The powers and principalities were dislodged, and freedom was coming to a land that had languished under total slavery. Indeed, the sigh and cry of Argentina had been heard and respected by God, and He was intervening. Our excitement knew no bounds after the long protracted war that we had fought. Whole nights were taken in praising the Lord and literally enjoying the triumphs that are recorded in Heaven. Then, quite suddenly, it was all over and we returned to our "normal" spiritual activities, if I might call them by that. Soon, Argentina was forgotten as the Holy Spirit laid other nations and issues upon us.

It was a very excited telephone call in the early hours of the morning that brought the news months later that war had been declared. The Falklands were, indeed, both the "hook" and "spoil" of Ezekiel's prophecy. Of course, the British would never believe that they were a mere pawn in the hand of the Almighty. It was not really British honor nor the ownership of a few windswept islands in the South Atlantic that had stirred up the spirit of good old British gunboat diplomacy once again, but the unseen hand of Almighty God. His agenda is far more serious than anything man can comprehend, for He always deals with eternal issues, and the eternity of an entire nation lay at stake.

History adequately records the rest of the saga in the natural. It was a major and embarrassing defeat for a military nation that was thoroughly humiliated in the eyes of the world. An open show of the enemy assuredly took place. It was the Exocet missile that won the day for Britain who retained ownership, and more importantly, her pride, over those windswept sheep islands of the Falklands. The military junta in Argentina was overthrown, ending once and for all the ruthless dictatorship. A seeming great wall of water began to burst upon the land in waves of new revival. Just as the prophet Isaiah describes: *"When the enemy shall come in like a flood, the Spirit of the Lord shall raise up a standard against him"* (Isa. 59:19).

It is time that the Church realized that the flood is the Lord's standard and not the enemy's wicked plans. The flood of the Lord was to sweep the whole of South America and bathe the entire continent in a mighty move of revival, which continues to the very time of this writing. The power and monopoly that Rome had enjoyed for over 150 years was broken, and multitudes were set free from the bondage of religious tradition and ritual to become true worshippers of the living God and His only Son, Jesus Christ. What a triumph that has been fully recorded in the libraries of Heaven!

Our intercessory battle for Argentina was excellent preparation for an even greater war against the enemy that we were to fight—a war that continued for many years and, in a similar way, was to release the whole of Southern Africa. Often the greatest tragedy of victories gained in intercession is the failure of the Church to go on the offensive with aggressive evangelism once all the walls of the enemy have been shattered. It is of tremendous encouragement that such was not the case in Argentina where the Church was poised to take the whole nation and has done so. What eternal victory!

CHAPTER FIFTEEN

The Vietnamese Boat People

Ignored, shunned, cursed, and beaten off as a mighty cancer and leprous blight upon the face of the earth were the Vietnamese refugees. Given a rare and "magnanimous" opportunity by their communist dictators to leave, multitudes had seized the opportunity in the belief that the nations would give them sanctity and refuge. In some of the most callous and disgustingly brutal decisions made by modern governments, multitudes upon multitudes of Vietnamese perished in the most gruesome of deaths, mostly on the open seas, because nobody would open their doors. Whilst men's hearts were constantly hardened against their plight, nevertheless, there is a God in Heaven who sees all and is deeply moved as the devil inspires man's inhumanity towards his fellow tenants of this planet.

The international holocaust, for it can be termed nothing less, continued for some years. Boatload upon boatload of Vietnamese were returned to sea if they ever reached the shores of any nation. For the most part, vast numbers perished from the elements and deprivation as they sailed on or in anything that floated. The whole crisis became totally intolerable and enough was enough. God was going to move and directly intervene in that total blight on the history of mankind.

It was a beautiful African winter's day, and I was in my kitchen cooking. Everything was going so very well. Vietnam was far away and though we had all heard and read about the "Boat People," as they came to be known, there was little I could do in landlocked Zimbabwe. As I stood at the stove stirring some exotic sauce I had concocted for a dinner—a rare event by then, I might add—the Holy Spirit came into the room. Certainly, I have found that He does not trifle and He went straight to business.

"Do you remember fasting for all those who were in solitary confinement in communist prisons?" He questioned.

"How could I possibly forget? After that, we ate for them, and You told us that every mouthful we ate *on their behalf* You would multiply for them when they partook of their bread and slop."

"Correct," He replied.

"Well, I never did hear the outcome of that," I interrupted.

"You will read about it in Heaven. Now I have another assignment!" He retorted. "The Boat People."

"Ugh," I groaned as I looked at my delectable sauce.

The Spirit totally ignored me and continued, "I want you to take up a position of abiding for those people until international doors open for their refuge. I have a great work for them in the future and, like the Japanese, they will be lost unless something is done. Those that they perceive as Christian nations are slamming the doors in their faces. Change that."

"But where do I begin?" I tried to reason.

"Live as they live and see how you like it." With that, He was gone.

I pondered the issue for a few days and wondered whether I should find a lake and a boat and spend the next few weeks simply floating around on the water. That being a little impractical, I settled for my tent routine, except that this time it was not by the river nor in pleasant surroundings. I planted the tent in the open veldt. An African sun, even in winter, can be strong, especially when it blazes down on a tent all day and heats it up to oven temperatures. I cooked inside by day and froze by night. I rationed myself to a cup of water a day. By the end of the third day, I was not a happy person and tried to justify myself by convincing myself that I was achieving nothing by "this ridiculous escapade."

"Unpleasant, isn't it?" chided the Spirit on the fourth day. "And you've only completed three days. What about those 'Boat People' who are weeks on the open sea. How do you think they feel? They are dirty, hungry, wounded, and without shelter. Here, you are simply hot and cold in this tent."

I understood clearly that unless I overcame my physical discomfort—which was not even a matter of life and death to me as it was to the boat people—I would never be able to intercede for them and open doors of refuge that they so badly needed. It was not pleasant, and I gained little comfort as I read from the prophet Ezekiel whom God called to lay on his left side for 390 days for Israel and a further 40 days on his right side for Judah.

Actually, I became quite terrified that the Lord might require me to live in that tent for a whole year. I could think of nothing worse. Why was it that I felt like a caged animal this time when I had undertaken numerous fasts and been subjected to the confinement of that tent many times in the past? I started to think that I was an utter failure as the process of identification and accompanying agony began to take shape. I knew it was the sentence of death that was upon me, and until and unless I died, I would never be of any value whatsoever to the suffering boat people. There was no reason why I should have been perturbed. After all, I reasoned, I was the Lord's vessel. Should He desire to keep me in that tent for a whole year or more, then it was His business and I had absolutely no right to complain.

I was greatly challenged by the life of the famous Welsh Revivalist, Evan Roberts. After a very active role in leading the revival of 1904, he went into a life of seclusion at the home of the Penn-Lewis. In a letter that Evan Roberts wrote, he declares:

> These last seven years of seclusion are exactly of the same pattern. But then my work was public and people could see the results. Now it is chiefly hidden, with its results in the unseen and waiting God's own time for their revelation…. God is my Master. What He bids, I do. Where He commands, there I shall stay. Should I deviate or abandon my course of life and work because man fails to understand me? I will not do so. I am responsible to God. He is my Director. It is His work I am doing; and knowing that my work is in line with His expressed will I will follow it gladly, and will do so.

I was utterly humbled by the life of intercession and testimony of Evan Roberts and decided that God had absolute and first claim on my life. So what if I died in a tent just so long as I was about His business and will? The words of Jesus burned into my heart, *"I delight to do Thy will, O my God"* (Ps. 40:8).

After I had run the gamut of emotions, the Holy Spirit said, "You are not obliged to do this. I will relieve you of any responsibility for those refugees, but..."

I never allowed Him to finish because I knew that I really was *obliged* if I was going to remain on target with the Lord. "It's fine," I hurriedly replied, "I'll just continue."

It was no good trying to tell Him that everything was wonderful or for that matter trying to explain anything. I did not want to end up in the same shoes as Ananias and Sapphira so it was best to say as little as necessary and rather keep quiet. He is, after all, the Spirit of Truth! Nothing can be hid from Him, even our thoughts.

And so, I settled down to the monotony and routine of a boat person stuck in a tent in the middle of Africa. One of the first things I experienced through the Holy Spirit was the bitter disappointment of being rejected. It became so real that I felt that I was with those Vietnamese as they were insulted and sent back to sea. Humiliation upon humiliation was heaped upon them just as it had been upon the Jews of Europe who had been denied access into country after country. Initially nobody wanted them, including the "land of the free and the home of the brave." The same then, applied to the Vietnamese. And yet, those were the very people who had stood by America during that terrible war. Such treachery, such humiliation, such contempt was poured out upon a people who sought only for freedom and the right to live without being oppressed.

"I know all about it," said the Lord one day. "I was a man of sorrows and acquainted with grief, the grief of the sin of mankind. I was despised and rejected so I feel it very keenly when My creation continues to behave in this fashion. They still have not learned."

The Great Intercessor had spoken, the One who lives to make intercession according to the will of the Father.

"I want these people freed," He continued, " because I am going to use them in evangelism and they will be an asset wherever they go."

Then, with ever-so-encouraging words, He declared, "Continue with your intercessions for your cries are being heard on high."

I began to see that this was not so much a battle against the powers of darkness as a battle to make men aware of the situation and compassionate towards the suffering. I thought of my own position *before* the Lord had instructed me to intercede. I had heard about the "Boat People" and felt sympathy for them, but there was little I could do. After all, they were far away in Indochina and very remote from me. I was about *my* business. Therein lies the issue with mankind—selfishness in the face of great deprivation—but God is not at all like that so He quickly made His business, *my* business, and there I was, then, about *His* business.

At the same time I was in my tent, the team of intercessors was at home bombarding Heaven on behalf of the boat people. Daily meetings were in operation, and they were weeping and travailing, touched by the plight of the suffering. I have often found that women are more easily touched than men and I believe that it has to do with their bearing children and nourishing them. When a man, however, begins to weep and travail in intercession, something very powerful takes place in spiritual realms and strong powers are broken.

The Vietnamese Boat People were no longer remote, and none of us could be careless and casual about them anymore. They were fast becoming a part of our lives as we carried them in our bosom. The strategy of intercession was powerfully at work to set them free from their plight and achieve the purposes of the Lord. Meanwhile, we were all learning that the Lord had promoted us into a realm of responsibility for international affairs.

The time came, when I was so married to that tent and its conditions, that I knew if the Lord did, indeed, want me to stay there forever, it would be quite fine to do so. I do not know exactly how or when, but the presence of the Lord came down and filled that little tabernacle in the African wilderness. Such a love pervaded us—me in my tent and the team back at home base—for those Vietnamese that it was going to be strange to live without them. Intercession had been going on for some three months, and through the fasting and prayer, the sacrifice and tears, and His divine love and burden, our hearts and lives had become inextricably interwoven with the boat people. Newspapers and magazines and reports of all descriptions had been avidly devoured to see if there had been any change towards them. Whilst I did not spend the three months in that tent—for as soon as I embraced it, the Holy Spirit released me from it—not once thereafter did I not feel very much a part of the sufferings of those Vietnamese. It was all part of the workings of the Holy Spirit who, Himself, was deeply moved and burdened with their terrible conditions and was a partaker of their sufferings. There was no great victory celebration but the gentle assurance that victory had come. As sure as I was of that victory, was as sure as the burden for the Vietnamese boat people simply drifted out of our lives.

One day they had been so real, and then suddenly, the Vietnamese were no longer a part of us. We had gained the place of intercession. A month or so later, the United States, in a decision that seemed to contradict former policy, announced that they were prepared to take a quota of Vietnamese refugees, and thereafter, a literal tide of conferences, help, and open doors for the boat people became the order of the day. Indeed, yet again, the Holy Spirit had won a tremendous victory for a suffering people who were to be future instruments in His Hands.

I was in Jerusalem in 1987. My dear friend, Bara, is a Japanese tour guide in Israel, and I was spending some time visiting him and his family and experiencing Israel, once again.

"I have a treat for you tonight," announced Bara one morning. "We are going to a Vietnamese restaurant in Rehavia. My friend Quan owns it. He has an amazing story to tell…"

"A Vietnamese restaurant in *Jerusalem*?" I questioned in amazement. "That's hardly believable."

"Yeah," agreed Bara, "But it's true. You'll hear the story for yourself tonight."

Quan loved the Lord and was full of life and vitality. We had arrived early at his restaurant so that I might enjoy quality time with him before other clients came. He began by describing the terrible conditions that had led to his decision to leave Vietnam and how he had miraculously escaped death by hiding under an overturned and derelict fishing boat where he had remained for four days whilst the government soldiers had camped out on the beach a mere stone's throw from where he was. As if that were not bad enough, he and his family and friends used everything they had to purchase an old boat with the intention of making their way to Hong Kong, for they had heard that there were many refugees there. About 13 family members and some friends were aboard when they set sail with great dreams that freedom awaited them and they would be made welcome wherever they went. They found this to be nothing but a myth, and whilst they never reached Hong Kong, they were shunned and literally chased from every place they attempted to land.

"Our cries to God seemed to be in vain," said Quan. "We were discouraged, without many supplies, and all the money we had was used up. We had already buried a couple of our children at sea, and others were suffering greatly from exposure and malnutrition after we had been weeks on the water.

"Finally," declared Quan, "We gave up and gave ourselves to the elements after we were finally rejected yet another time. There seemed no point in trying to survive. Nobody wanted us. It was almost three months that we had been on the seas, and we had been treated as lepers wherever we went. We were adrift somewhere in the South China Sea headed towards the Philippines but really drifting aimlessly, being carried by wind and tide. There was no more fight in us. I was sick. My family was sick, and our friends were sick. We were emaciated, covered with salt sores, and some were delirious. All I could hope was that the end should come quickly. Many ships had passed us, but none would stop and help. We resigned ourselves to the fact that our end had truly come.

"Then suddenly, God intervened. It was late morning one day when a ship suddenly appeared and actually circled us. I do not remember too many details because I was only semi-conscious. Actually, I thought I was hallucinating when I saw the ship. But sure enough, we were drawn alongside, and a miracle took place! Helping hands began to lift our emaciated bodies on board where we were fed and our wounds attended by men speaking a strange language. I soon found out that it was Hebrew and that we had been picked up by an Israeli merchant ship. It was too much to believe and only something God could have engineered.

"The following afternoon, the captain sent for me. We both could speak English. He was so kind and we had spent such a pleasant night after having eaten our first real meal in months.

"'Yesterday after picking you up,' he began, 'I radioed the relevant authorities in Israel as to what I should do with you all. Well, this morning I received a communiqué from the Prime Minister of Israel himself. Let me read to you the exact text of what Mr. Begin has said,' he concluded."

The message from the Prime Minister said: "I received your report regarding the Vietnamese boat people whom you rescued today. My heartiest congratulations. As you well understand, Captain, we ourselves were a landless people for centuries and know what it is like to be wanderers and pilgrims on the face of the earth. We therefore, cannot ignore the plight of these who are suffering so. Bring them *home* to Israel with you and we will give them refuge."

The tears were pouring down our faces as Quan concluded, "So, I am a full Israeli citizen now and will give my life for this land, which rescued us and gave us hope again."

And the exact time of their rescue? The end of the three months of travail undertaken by a small insignificant group of intercessors in an African village. As we traveled home that night too overawed to talk, though Bara had heard the account before, the Holy Spirit began to softly speak to me in the silence. "Do you see, Michael, what I am able to do with a vessel yielded unto Me?" He questioned. "I wanted you to hear the outcome and see the fruit of your labors, which were not in vain."

CHAPTER SIXTEEN

The Vision

T HE LONGER THAT I walk with the Lord, the more I know that
He is a God who has definite strategies and who works according to a fixed set of plans. Nothing, absolutely nothing, is a happen-
stance with the Lord for He is a God of order. Consequently, He has a
plan concerning the nations, and it is for this reason, too, that there is a
judgment of the nations. In the Word, clear evidence is given that God
concerns Himself with nations as much as individuals. It is also very
clear that the Lord is visiting the nations to take out of them a nation for
Himself: *"A peculiar people, a royal priesthood, a holy nation of worshippers who
will show forth the praise of the One who has called men out of darkness into His
marvelous light"* (see 1 Pet. 2:9).

This was God's purpose in His calling of Abraham and making
that great patriarch "His friend" and creating a nation out of him.
God wanted all the world to see, in living reality, the testimony that He
is not a God who is far away in the heavens, but He desires a *relationship* with men, and He will pour out His favor upon those who obey
Him. The Lord was launching us into a worldwide ministry of intercession for nations.

In intercession one night, the Lord began to burden us with certain
key nations in God's order and plan for world evangelism. It was of
great concern to us, then, that communism was expanding across the
world and that those to whom God had given unlimited resources for
the purpose of the Gospel were doing nothing with those same
resources except to squander them on their own lusts. We realized that

if the commitment and zeal in the Christian West were the same as the communists and revolutionaries had for their causes, then the whole world should already be converted. But those whom God had raised for the purpose had lost the vision in their desire for personal ambition and wealth.

Jesus commanded, *"Go ye into **all** the world and preach the gospel to **every** creature…"* (Mark 16:15). The reason we were not fulfilling that command was because the Church had really lost God's purpose and become too temporal in both outlook and activity. The Spirit was sweeping over the meeting, and we were in great travail as only He is able to bring upon the intercessor. Different ones began to see different nations and specific places, and some even began to speak those languages under the unction of the Spirit who was arresting our attention and focusing us on His agenda—which is, after all, the very heartbeat of God.

Suddenly, one person and then another began to receive clear pictures of dismembered parts of a human body that were in the strangest fashion. The decayed members of that dismembered body were brought together into a whole body again. That body began to take on the appearance of specific nations. It was as if we were watching a slow-motion movie picture as the scene unfolded.

The "head" of that decayed and failing body was the nation of Great Britain. The Spirit spoke clearly that Britain had lost her God-given direction and calling because she was a nation that had become "pleasure-loving" and desired only comfort and ease. The disease from which the head was suffering was cancer that had caused great and sordid growths within, thereby blinding the eyes. The brain was no longer able to function, as the roots of the cancer had invaded the control center of the body. Confusion had been established and wrong signals were going forth based on whatever opiate the brain was receiving.

The Holy Spirit explained, "I made Britain the nerve center from which My Word was to go forth to all the world. I raised up a strong and principled people who were ready to pay any price for the cause of Truth. They stood against that evil of Rome and sent forth missionaries to the ends of the earth. It was for this purpose that I made Britain the greatest colonial power ever, so that through her, I would be known in the nations. It was I who made Britain rich and gave her the knowledge wherewith to build and create and become industrial."

My mind was immediately cast upon the exploits of a people who had known God or, at least, greatly feared Him, and I thought, *What incredible inroads the British had made, especially during the Victorian era.* Indeed, there were always traders and industrialists who were selfish for their personal visions and ambitions but even their work the Lord had exploited as they had opened the vast interiors of the continents. Then there was Victoria, that "born again" queen, who had worked tirelessly for the total abolition of the slave trade worldwide. She had annexed Nyasaland to the British crown on the word of David Livingstone for the sole purpose of stamping out Moslem Arab slavery in Central and East Africa. The Word of God was translated and carried far and wide by an army of persevering missionaries who were ready to pay any price to fulfill the specific command of the Captain of their faith. Deprivation, disease, and every opposition of the powers of darkness were not sufficient to prevent the greatest Christian endeavor since the first century.

God had raised Britain twice to stand against the onslaught of the devil against Christendom in both World Wars. In particular, it was the power of intercession that had won the day time and again during the darkest hours of Hitler's attacks on the tiny island nation. Once again, God's purpose in the British victory was that nothing should disturb the preaching of the Gospel to the ends of the earth, that all men might hear and multitudes be saved. If Germany had won, the whole world would undoubtedly have been plunged into a darkness far worse than communism.

Following the "Winds of Change," which engulfed the world after the Second World War, Britain opted out of her God-given responsibilities and, in so doing, degenerated into an insignificant player in the world scene. Sadly, the post-war generations settled down to a life of comfort, resting on the laurels of the past. The gods of Britain became the soccer ball and the beer bottle, creating a pleasure-loving society that does not want to have any responsibilities, especially in world affairs. Esthetic pleasures have taken precedence over eternal destinies and every Britain demands the right to do what is in his own best interests.

As of this writing, the British Royal Family with all their sordid escapades is merely an indicator of the moral and religious decadence of an entire nation that is in gross sin, the consequence of having largely rejected God. The fact that an entire nation could idolize an adulterous, Jesus-rejecting princess in preference to God shows how far the nation has slipped.

In the vision He gave us, God distinctly revealed that He had called Britain to evangelize the world and that such a God-given mandate had not yet been consummated. The choice was Britain's: either repent and turn back to the God so that there would be times of refreshing and a renewed vision for the world, or stagnate into division and decadence and become inconsequential.

In the vision, the upper chest area of that corrupted body was portrayed as Australia. Externally, the chest appeared bronzed and muscular, as of a strong athlete, but inside it was filled with parasites and putrefaction. The lungs were collapsing and a horrifying sickness was taking control of the entire chest. Today, we know that disease to be AIDS.

"Australia I called," said the Lord, "to preach the Gospel to Asia and the islands of the Pacific. Alas, My people have become corrupted with immorality and the false worship of the philosophies and teachings of the New Age, which is the vain deceit of the enemy to develop the mind at the expense of the spirit. Blessed with My high calling, Australians and New Zealanders have substituted this and rather filled their lives with the fun of sun, surf, and sand."

The greatest of honors is that God places such incredible responsibilities upon some nations with the reward of supreme blessings as they fulfill their mandates. Conversely, failure brings the judgment of the Lord and generations of bondage. There is no doubt that part of the reason why the Protestant lands developed and became world powers was because of their belief in the Bible and the "Protestant work ethic," which enjoins a man to freely work and enjoy the fruits of his labors. Industrial development and modernization took place in the Protestant nations while their Catholic counterparts lagged far behind because of the autocratic systems of religious and civil government.

Though originally founded as a penal colony, Australia soon became an important settler nation with abundant reserves of natural resources to be exploited for the purpose of the gospel. To a large extent, this has not been done. The call of the Holy Spirit, through Queen Esther, echoing down through the centuries is: *"Thou art come to the Kingdom for such a time as this"* (Esther 4:14).

Equally, the consequences are also just as real that "Enlargement and deliverance shall arise from another place but thou and thy father's house shall be destroyed" (Esther 4:14).

Smith Wigglesworth prophesied of a great revival that would come to Australia in the last days and such is desperately needed now. Australia has not yet fulfilled the call of the Lord. The result will be that God will raise up a people who *will* fulfill His call, but the consequences for Australia will be terrible.

The Lord went on to reveal the lower torso as the continent of North America, which was founded, in particular, for the purpose of spiritual freedom and also for the financing of a worldwide Gospel outreach. When statistics declare that Americans spend more on pet food every year than the gross total given for all missionary endeavors by all organizations, it certainly speaks loudly about the condition of the nation. That lower torso was bulging and debauched through gluttony and riotous living. Peritonitis was eating away at the inner organs and sapping the strength and vigor of the nations of North America, which had been planted by God for the purpose of taking the Gospel to South America and the East in particular. In actual fact, the lower torso was identified with the face of Elvis Presley, who had once enjoyed a relationship with God but sold it for fame and fortune. Major spirits of deception have seduced the continent and created conflicting signals about truth and what to believe.

Perhaps the greatest tragedy of all, with particularly the U.S.A., is that of "exported religion." Because of the wealth of the nation and the increasing desire for U.S. dollars, American religion has been exported worldwide and accepted as an international role model. After all, "It has to be right; it's from the U.S.A." People no longer scrutinize whether teachings really line up with both what the Word actually says and with the entire sentiment of the whole canon of Scripture. It "sounds good and pleasant; it must be right."

"America has, like Esau, whom I hated because of it, sold her birthright for compromise and has rejected Me," said the Holy Spirit. "Religion has replaced relationship in a nation that no longer knows the difference between right and wrong; where anything and everything is acceptable. My standard is no longer upheld, and sin has become a reproach. I founded the nations for My purposes and enriched them for the Glory of the Gospel. Alas, as Israel of old, they have committed whoredoms and turned to every vile thing replacing Me with their false idols and worshipping of the creature." He continued, "I strategically placed nations on the face of the earth and enriched them so that the wealth that I gave them power to obtain should be used to present My Truth to the ends of the earth."

On one trip to the United States, the Spirit spoke clearly:

America, America, I will visit thee one more time. I will flow from the east even unto the west. I will blow with My Spirit: I will visit thy sons and thy daughters; I will visit the fathers and the mothers. I will restore the family. I will bring unity and a bond of peace. I will visit the Church with new revival. Restoration and enlargement shall follow. Shall not I use you again? Shall I not remember Mine own who have given themselves in battle to keep the lamp a-burning, at home, on the mission field, and in the tears and fasting? Your former Glory shall return. I shall make thee the mother of many peoples.

Even as I have prospered you for a purpose, thou shall charter the oceans and seas and isles, carrying not the weapons of carnal war, but the mighty sword of the Spirit. With rubies and sapphires, diamonds, beryl, and sardius shall you bedeck the southernmost isles. Thou shalt sacrifice thy priests and prophets to Africa, Asia, and the great enemy lands of Islam, as well as the southernmost isles. Thou shalt scatter, but thou shalt surely increase. My hand shall move upon thee. I shall bring new prosperity as I begin to visit. Thou shalt find the mountains of gold, even as thou considerest that which I have given. This prosperity shall be, yea, for a new planting of My Word to the nations. Thou shalt not again forget that it is I that prospers thee and it is for a purpose: Thou shalt not again squander it as the prodigal, but thou shalt one last time cast thy bread upon the waters and I shall fill thine own storehouse with abundance.

Take the sword again, thou Levi; move thou among they brethren and use it. Life is surely within thine hands. Purge the priesthood, purify the temple that My light may again shine.

For a brief moment, the nation seemed to rally, but I fear that such a word will be fulfilled only in coming tribulation.

Those parts of the body representing South Africa, the fourth nation, were the loins and legs. They were portrayed as the members of a marathon runner who had dropped from the race because of muscle cramp and fatigue. There was a real cry from the Holy Spirit to the nation of South Africa, "Whom shall I send and who will go for us?"

There was no South African to say, "Here am I, Lord, send me!"

"Indeed," said the Spirit, "I planted South Africa to be a light and testimony to this great continent of Africa, known as 'The Dark Continent.' I ordained South Africa to take My Word, My precepts, and My name to all of Africa. I planted in their forefathers that pioneering spirit so that they would move ever onwards bearing the Gospel with them. But alas, the people were seduced and deceived. I gave them the riches of gold and diamonds and much more to empower them and provision them for the great task of the mission fields of Africa, but they settled down to enjoying the fruits of the land selfishly for themselves. Indeed, because I had planted that adventurous spirit in them and they did not use it for My Glory and honor, they therefore corrupted it. The 'Isaac' that I promised and purposed became an 'Ishmael' in their midst, and their energies and efforts were established in building personal kingdoms. Their hands turned against the very peoples I had sent them to win while they sat and enjoyed and squandered upon their own lusts, the riches I had given them."

The full extent of our intercessions for South Africa and the resultant victorious peace that accompanied her transitions are told in my book, *What Is Your Destiny?* As an intercessor who had touched the throne for South Africa, I was able to declare six weeks before the elections and transition, "There *will not be civil war* in South Africa." Indeed, such assurance can come only from the throne itself. I could take such a stand because I was not indulging in wishful thinking and hopes but in the absolute word of God as spoken in the throne room.

The price of 15 years of travail and tears, of agonies and cries to Heaven, gives the intercessor the right to make bold statements of fact, having paid the price to move the heart of the Almighty and change the destiny of what might have been in any nation. Hearts were changed, lives redirected, and a nation turned. Again, the failure of the Church to take up the gauntlet, as also was the case in Zimbabwe after independence, is not the failure of intercession, but of God's people to take advantage of the victory afforded by the intercessor. The South African church has not taken the gracious second opportunity of the Lord, seized the initiative, gone on the offensive, and preached the Gospel to Africa. South African businessmen may be found everywhere in Africa for their cause of financial enrichment, but the Church remains myopic and tragically paralyzed by religious bigotry.

The feet of the decayed body represented the nation of Kenya, and it seemed quite prophetic that the Lord should have chosen two nations from Africa. The feet were stilted and the toes broken. The prophet declared, *"How lovely on the mountain are the feet of him who brings good news"* (see Isa. 52:7), and Paul writes that our feet are to be shod with the "Gospel of peace." Ah, what a contrast that is to those feet which run to mischief and create strife. Kenya, a jewel in Africa, rich and majestic but divided by tribalism and overtaken with corruption and great sexual immorality, has lost her vision and direction. Not only was Kenya ordained for the winning of North Africa, but also of sending forth evangelists to the whole world.

The vision and accompanying burden was going to be a huge ministry, which has actually continued up to the present. I never wished to visit nor minister in the U.S.A., but the Lord has taken me there time and again not only to preach but also to intercede. Abraham walked in the land, but still God did not give the nation into his hands. Before that time of full possession, all the Canaanites had to be judged and removed and many wars of cleansing had to be fought. God wants a separated people who will not be contaminated by the perversions of the inhabitants of the lands. Some of those wars were against invaders, but many were against the corrupting influence of sin and its accompanying spiritual adultery and idolatry. Through the travail and tears for peoples who had been chosen but rejected their mandate, the Spirit said emphatically, "I will take you to those lands and there you will minister for Me and help to stir up a remnant for Me, a jealous people who will love Me with their whole being."

At the time, it seemed impossible, but it is not by man's might not by man's power but by His Spirit that all things are achieved. All the Lord wants is a believing, trusting, and obedient people, and He will work miracles. We were a group of simple Africans in a rather remote village in Africa, and how would God possibly take us to the world? The ways, wherefores, and whys belong to Him, but He has done exactly what He has said because many have been faithful to the burden and calling of the Lord as He presented it so many years ago. And again, it is proof of intercession that the burden is the Lord's and will also remain mine for just as long as He designs or until the task is fully accomplished.

My dear friend, Mr. Howells, of the Bible College of Wales, interceded and carried the burden of communist Eastern Europe and the Soviet Union for over 40 years. What an intercessor! I remember visiting him at the college and asking, "Mr. Howells, what has the Spirit been saying to you?"

When he walked into the room, it was as if Jesus had walked in, and then, with a face shining as an angel, he declared with such simplicity yet absolute assurance and triumph, "The Lord has said I may stop interceding for Europe and the Soviet Union. The wall is coming down and they will all be free." That, I might add, was perhaps two years before the Berlin Wall came down. Ah, what victory, but only after a lifetime of travail and agony of which most know nothing. But then again, to know the secrets of the inner chamber and the intimacy of the Lord is worth all the suffering. He had knowledge that the Wall was coming down long before the event, for the Lord had given the triumph to a general who had fought the devil for over a generation for the liberation of enslaved millions to bring them not only freedom in the natural but also the glorious Light of eternal Life through the one and only Gospel.

I have carried these nations in my bosom for almost two decades. No matter what happens in the natural, and sometimes the directions these lands are taking is very discouraging, yet I must always look through the eye of faith and the sure knowledge that the Lord never gives up on any person or nation unless He clearly says so. Great things are still to come forth from these lands, even if by a remnant. Jeremiah gave his life in travail for Israel only to see the nation taken into captivity, the king have his eyes put out, and His beloved Jerusalem razed to the ground with the magnificent Temple of Solomon destroyed. What intercession he made for a wayward land that never repented. But, ah, looking down the tunnel of time as the Lord does, what fruit of revival was sown into the remnant seed by those same intercessions of that great prophet, so that another prophet of a later generation was able to declare, *"The Glory of this latter house shall be greater than of the former..."* (Hag. 2:9).

The victory lies in *that* it happens, the results being the Lord's, and not "when" or "if" it happens. I have walked, ministered, and wept in all these nations except Australia, to where I shall yet be going. I have sighed and cried out to God time without number for a mighty outpouring of His Spirit, that He would indeed rend His heavens and come down upon these lands and give a little reviving in order for that sick body to be completely healed so that the nations might hear of the love of One who died for all mankind. Naturally, it is always wonderful to see mighty and fruitful outcomes of intercession, but ultimately it is all His Glory. In terms of eternity, time does not matter as long as there is a final victory. This there will always be, experienced or not by the intercessor's generation, if only he fulfills his high calling.

Things are happening rapidly as this Age is being closed, and the Lord has said that they who know Him shall be mighty and do exploits. Whilst I am very excited about what is happening, yet as an intercessor, I can never forget that over half of the world's population has never heard of Jesus. The task ahead is still enormous. As darkness covers the earth in the last days and darkens the people, the Glory of the Lord will shine brighter and brighter, brighter and brighter in the face of a people who love Him absolutely and uncompromisingly. In this way, the whole world will know that there is a God who reigns in the heavens, and man will be left totally without excuse on the day of Christ's appearing. The Spirit is still heralding a call for watchman to join the great choir of intercessors.

CHAPTER SEVENTEEN

The Jungles of Zaire

I T IS ONE THING to fight in intercession and see the results as the Holy Spirit leads but altogether a different matter when the intercessor is very distant and the outcome can in no way be determined by individual personality, involvement, or influence. So it was one night that the Holy Spirit burdened the team for a situation in the heart of Africa. We knew beyond any doubt that we were up against some of the strongest powers of darkness and also had no doubt that we were dealing with matters in the deepest jungles of Zaire. It was there, in those jungles, that the Holy Spirit had moved in 1954, bringing an amazing revival and outpouring upon unprecedented numbers of jungle natives. That outpouring had been in response to the intercession of mighty warriors such as C.T. Studd, Mr. Rees Howells, and others who had travailed even decades before. Such men never saw the fruit of their travail in those dark areas of Africa, but as sure as they had broken through with God in victory, so victory came.

As the unction of the Spirit was upon us, He began to burden us that we needed to prevail over a situation of tremendous bondage. We were quite used to dealing with the enemy through the witchcraft of eastern and southern Africa and were now called into battle in central Africa. Unlike for the boat people, I was directed not to take up any particular position of identification in the matter. The burden, however, was heavy indeed.

The only word that we received from the Holy Spirit was when He revealed one night, "I am greatly exercised for this people who are enslaved by the wicked wonders of a mightily powerful witch doctor. There is much sacrifice of people, and I have heard the cry of many for freedom. Your intercessions must reach the throne and set free this tribe."

The anger began to rise within my spirit as I thought of the terror and tyranny inflicted upon whole tribes because of the selfish choices of a few who wanted absolute control. The rule of the enemy is by fear. The rule of the Holy Spirit is by "love, peace, and a sound mind." I marveled at how the devil is going to rule with gripping fear through the antichrist himself. But, in the midst of his reign of terror, the likes of which the world has never seen, there will be a place of total authority and peace in the eye of the tornado where there will also be complete security.

This witch doctor in the jungles of Zaire was "found out," and we were going after him like a pack of hound dogs going for the kill. The stranglehold of darkness was about to be broken and people set free. Night after night we came against the enemy as we cried out to the Lord. It was not in the defeat of the magicians of Pharaoh that we found our break as we had done at other times. It was not in the conquest of the antichrist that we met victory. We came at the enemy from every seeming angle, but his walls appeared impenetrable. It was on that point that I had him. We had been traveling with Israel in the wilderness, had crossed the Jordan, and suddenly come face to face with that great and foreboding city. The Word of the Lord came distinctly through Joshua, *"Now Jericho was straitly shut up because of the children of Israel...See, I have given into thine hand Jericho"* (Josh. 6:1-2).

We needed to penetrate our "Jericho," and God who is the same yesterday, today, and forever had given us the Holy Spirit blueprint for total victory in the capture of such a formidable city.

The strongman had to be bound before we could conquer that situation in the jungles of Zaire. We already had our spy on the inside of the tribe, namely, the blessed Holy Spirit. The key to Jericho was a role reversal—the fear that Jericho had inflicted on all had come upon them. Instead of Israel being intimidated by that great and formidable city, Jericho became intimidated by Israel. The fear generated by an army marching daily in absolute silence would have been electrically terrifying. Furthermore, silence speaks of judgment and not only Jericho but all of Canaan was about to be judged through the people of the Lord.

The cup of sin and iniquity of the Amorites was then full, and God was therefore able to deal with them. In the same way, the wickedness of this tribe was full, and God wanted a people set free and a heritage for Himself in the jungles. After all, *"The earth is the Lord's and the fullness thereof"* (1 Cor. 10:26). Enough is enough where the Lord is concerned.

Daily, weekly, for some two months we continued to war against the strongman of Zaire. There were days when we were in absolute silence; there were others when we would shout and blow our trumpets and sing the victory song whether in the natural or in the spirit. Each time we were attacking "our" formidable city, and though at first it seemed as if we were making little or no headway, we were actually causing a breach in that which had been so tightly bound for so long. There was no fasting on that one—we simply warred. We were utterly cast upon the Holy Spirit as our Planner and the Lord as our great Captain, for we were not physically seeing any results or obtaining any kind of report. Yet, there was never a doubt that this was a bona fide assignment and that God was wanting to accomplish something mighty that only He knew.

We had to go forth, "knowing not where we were going" but trusting Him implicitly for direction. He never fails. The battle became stronger and the burden heavier. We knew by the Spirit that this people, whoever they were, suffered great hardship and slavery to the prince of darkness and that their freedom depended on our performance. Failure would not be entertained, no matter how things appeared in the natural. The last week was an exhausting one as we threw everything into the fray. True intercession is incredibly exhausting, and there have been many times when I have felt as if I have been beaten and bruised. This was one of those situations where I felt daily, as if I had been through a wringer. Great stamina was required so healthy eating was essential.

One of the most exciting moments of intercession is the breakthrough. How can I ever forget such times, for they are so powerful that they become indelibly marked upon the mind of the intercessor. It was a Wednesday night, and from the outset I could discern that this was to be a night of a "Jericho shout." There was tremendous excitement in the air and such liberty as we had not known for weeks. We began to shout at the enemy and, like Gideon's band, it seemed as if 1 voice was magnified into 10,000 voices. We shouted, danced, and praised for several hours, the excitement knowing no bounds. I can understand how people who have no discipline can become extreme and allow themselves to be carried away in times of such spiritual excitement because the intensity becomes almost physically unbearable. We are dealing with power, the most real power in the universe. It is the *dunamis* of the Holy Spirit, and it is supernatural power coming down to infuse mortal man for a divine purpose. Such power is so strong that it is difficult for the frail human frame to contain such. But we must never forget that the spirit of the prophet is subject to the prophet, and there must always be order. Suddenly, just as instantly as the excitement had begun, it finished. We departed that night knowing that something significant had been achieved. We knew for sure the next morning!

Overnight, Zaire was taken cleanly out of our lives. We had gained the victory, that place of intercession where the intercessor can, *"ask in* [Jesus'] *name and that will* [He] *do that the Father may be glorified in the Son"* (see John 14:13).

We had asked the heartbeat of Almighty God under the direction of the Spirit. Now victory was His, and because it was His, it was ours too.

Flight SN 146 was en route to Brussels via Kinshasa, the capital of Zaire. This was some two years following our great intercession for the jungle stronghold of that country. The battle had long been forgotten in light of other responsibilities. One of my missionaries was on board that flight and by Providential intervention another missionary boarded the flight in Kinshasa and was assigned a seat next to this fellow. They took a little time in sharing testimonies whereupon the man from Zaire began to recount an amazing story. He came from the edge of the jungle where they had established a mission station with a school. For years they had been trying to penetrate the interior of the jungle and had "tamed" a very powerful tribal chief whose son began attending their school. Every year the missionaries would visit the chief and seek permission to begin working in the interior. Every year the chief refused their request. The main problem for the chief was that he was under total control of a very wicked witch doctor who terrorized the entire jungle. The real power of the witch doctor came because of the incredible fear generated by diabolic rituals, which included regular human sacrifices.

"Without warning or any prior sickness, the witch doctor suddenly dropped dead one day," recounted the missionary. "And, within a couple of days of the death of the witch doctor, the chief also died unexplainably. It was almost as if the hand of God came down and took away their lives."

"When was that?" asked my missionary as he calculated dates. It was the exact time we had broken through with the Lord in intercession.

"The greatest miracle, however, is that for 20 years those jungles were closed to us. Now the son has become chief, and God had prepared him in our school. He was born again with us, and since becoming chief, he has opened the whole interior and we are experiencing a mighty move of the Holy Spirit amongst the tribal peoples of the jungles."

What an intercession-answering God!

CHAPTER EIGHTEEN

Egypt, Uganda, Ethiopia

THERE ARE THREE nations in central, north, and the Horn of Africa that are significant in God's plan of events. Two, at least, are featured in the Word. Egypt, that illustrious nation that enslaved Israel, is also the nation that gave sanctuary to Jesus. A classical ancient civilization, Egypt is neither Arab nor essentially Moslem. I do not see any strong evidence of her aligning against Israel in the end days. A land of perversion and always used as a metaphor to describe the carnal world, Egypt may be redeemed and used for God's purposes as she has already been in the past.

Uganda, called the "Pearl of Africa," is beautiful with a rich kingdom heritage. Almost in the center of the continent, Uganda is the source of the great Nile River flowing out of Lake Victoria. Uganda was chosen by the British in the 1940s to be the homeland for the Jews. With that, many Jews began to settle in the country and to establish businesses. Jewish architects designed and built the National Bank of Uganda Headquarters and the Entebbe Airport. Consequently, when it came to wanting to know about the design and layout of the latter in preparation for the Israeli raid, the blueprints of that airport were housed in Jerusalem. At one time, tyrant Idi Amin prepared to blow up the National Bank Headquarters in Kampala only to find that it was so strongly constructed he was unable to do so. As a Moslem, Amin wanted nothing at all to do with Israel or Jews and to destroy everything Jewish.

Ethiopia, like Egypt, is an ancient civilization with a deep Hebrew and Christian heritage. It was from Ethiopia that Sheba came to see the magnificence of Solomon's Temple and palaces and declared "the half has not been told." The last Emperor of Ethiopia, Haile Selassie I, claimed direct descent from Solomon and Sheba. He was called the "Lion of Judah." A friend of mine worked for the Emperor in the 1950s and complained to him one day that the remote rural peoples of Ethiopia would not cooperate with him. He was sinking boreholes throughout the country. The Emperor took off his signet ring and gave it to my friend telling him to stamp any clay tablet with it and he would never have trouble again. I handled that same ring, which was a solid nugget of pure gold. It was emblazoned with the winged lion of Judah. Every time the chiefs were shown that symbol thereafter, they would literally prostrate themselves and do whatever they were commanded.

The Holy Spirit said, "I want you to take up a position for these nations. Part of your abiding will be to visit them."

At that time, Amin was still the tyrant dictator of Uganda, and communism was strongly entrenched in Ethiopia under the evil totalitarian regime of Mengistu. In Egypt, President Anwar Sadat had been assassinated and an effort made to turn Egypt into a fundamentalist Moslem nation. The main key to each of the nations was the ruthless annihilation of Christians and the protracted and systematic persecution of any who attempted to preach the Gospel. Because the Great Commission is so paramount to God, the interference in or prevention of the Gospel freely going forth is of the utmost concern to the Holy Spirit.

In Egypt, the intercessions of one servant had brought tremendous international repercussions. That person had been on an international flight passing through Cairo. Whilst waiting for the flight change, the Holy Spirit spoke and instructed, "Go to the Hilton, book the *presidential suite*, and fast and pray for 40 days and nights."

After an argument with the Lord, the intercessor finally obeyed. On arrival at the Hilton, the next issue was paying for the thousand-dollar-a-night suite. Again, the Spirit rebuked, "You do what I tell you and I will take care of the rest."

The intercessor moved into the suite and, much to the consternation of the staff, was never seen, did not eat, and hardly used the bed. For 40 days, the intercessor battled with the princes of Egypt until victory was assured. At the end of those days, the Spirit ordered early on the following morning, "Climb to the top of the great pyramid of Cheops."

Having taken a taxi out to the pyramid, the intercessor climbed to the top of the pyramid and stood looking out over Egypt. Suddenly, the anointing of the Spirit came upon that watchman. He ordered, "Prophesy! Prophesy to Pharaoh of Egypt and declare unto him, 'You make peace with My Land, O Pharaoh. No more war with Israel...'"

Unknown to the intercessor was the fact that at that very moment, Anwar Sadat, Pharaoh of Egypt, was flying into Cairo in his jet. Having declared the word of the Lord to Pharaoh of Egypt, the mission was over. The intercessor received an anonymous check for the exact amount of the entire bill at the presidential suite and continued with other business.

Later, the entire negotiations for peace between Egypt and Israel were conducted in the presidential suite of the Cairo Hilton, which had been saturated in prayer for 40 days and nights. Then, when President Anwar Sadat landed at Ben Gurion Airport, Tel Aviv, on that great historic occasion of peace, he was asked by the press why he had come to Israel to make peace.

"Because," he replied, "when I was flying into Cairo in my presidential jet, God spoke to me and told me to make peace with Israel. I have obeyed."

It was not only peace with Israel that was required, but peace with God; and peace with God can come only through the blood of Jesus. We were wrestling with an ancient spirit of manipulation and control. That same spirit had manipulated Pharaoh in the day of Moses and was still very active. Egypt is the northern gateway to Africa and was powerfully evangelized by the early disciples. The initiative was lost, however, when the Church became ensnared by traditions, esthetics, and gnosis. They lost their power, and with the advent of Islam, were swept up by yet another deception. The gods of Egypt are as strong today as in the day of Moses. But, when Moses threw down his staff it became not just any, but the powerful, most poisonous of all snakes, the Egyptian cobra. The significance of that was not lost on either Pharaoh, the god of Egypt, or his magicians. Both knew they were getting a thorough beating by a greater power.

In similar fashion, Egypt received another thorough beating in the June War of 1967 (also known as the Six-Day War) and again in the Yom Kippur War of 1973, which prompted Egypt to make peace with

Israel. God never forgets, and His books will always tally, and that, very accurately. He is a God of restoration and always gives another chance to those who will cry out to Him.

To the team that went down into Egypt, the Lord spoke, "I would have compassion upon you and forgive your iniquities and deeds of the past for you succored My people, Israel, and allowed them to grow into a mighty nation. I would have compassion on you as you sheltered Me as a babe… Say to the sons of Ishmael 'I AM' hath sent Me unto you to bring forth a people of power called by My name."

Our cries for Egypt were for a nation that would change from being an aggressor to one that would be a supporter of Israel and, indeed, a stumbling block to those who opposed Israel. It was a cry too, for a powerful remnant to arise who would stand against the persecution of Islam and shine as a mighty light in the darkness of a worldly land steeped in ancient bondage of false gods and false worship. We cried out for a land that would turn and acknowledge the God of Heaven, cease to fight against Him, and open the door for the preaching of the Gospel.

The team that went down into Egypt walked the streets of Cairo, sailed the ancient Nile, and prayed and travailed for a nation steeped in sin and every perversion. They shook the city and every false idol and god. Three months after their trip, Cairo experienced an enormous earthquake, which shook the mosques and destroyed many of the domes of those places of false worship. Being a poor nation, there were no finances for repair, and every damaged mosque was forced to close its doors because of the dangers of collapse.

According to Ezekiel, God has put fear in the land of Egypt and diminished her so that she no longer rules over the nations. She has, indeed, taken a back seat in policies toward Israel and even within Africa. It is almost as if God has pulled the teeth of Egypt and she does not even roar anymore. The power of intercession is able to turn the aggressor who will assuredly be judged if they oppose the Lord and His ways. The Holy Spirit is very jealous and will blow with a strong force against those who oppose God's very own.

Because of Britain's move to establish Uganda as a Jewish homeland—though it failed because it was not God's will—there is no doubt that the wrath of the enemy came against the land. Idi Amin released an avalanche of persecution and terror upon Uganda that clearly expressed the anger of the devil. He opened the door to powerful Islamic forces, which would operate from Uganda to the rest of the continent. We visited a devastated land and saw the "forest of death" filled with the skulls of those who had been butchered by the tyrant. We lifted up a cry for Uganda that God would restore her as "The Pearl of Africa" and that she would stand against the onslaught of Islam; furthermore, we prayed that out of great revival would come a mighty army who would "shine with a luster that came from God" and march against the devil to take the Gospel to all of Africa. We cried out for a people who were beaten down and robbed, a people who had lost the will to survive, a people who had no self-worth.

As we traveled to Uganda to identify with the land and pour out our hearts in abiding, we taught the principles of intercession, believing the Holy Spirit's command to raise up a band of His warriors in the land who would take up the burden and stand in the gap. The Spirit had spoken, "I am calling forth from your midst an interceding people who will do battle in the spiritual."

We travailed for national revival, which would be the only answer to the calamity of a nation that had suffered one destructive government after another. Little did we realize how much the Lord would prepare the land for the future, but as ever, the power of intercession prevailed to change natural conditions and, therefore, the course of history.

There was absolutely nothing operating in Uganda. Hotels were closed; the cities were filthy; the roads so pot-holed that they were impassable. At every turn there were roadblocks with gun-toting thugs in tatters of uniform, if any uniform at all, throwing around their weight because of a rifle. Dirt, squalor, and disease were rampant at every turn. Perhaps the best illustration of the condition of the land was the hospitals with multitudes lying sick and dying and no medicines, doctors, or services. Electricity had failed, water was not running, and there was a general breakdown of services.

"Pray for order and authority and sound government. Do not look on the natural," said the Spirit, "but look through My eyes and turn this situation."

We preached, prayed, and wept through the land and stirred up the people to take hold of the Holy Spirit. I knew that Lord had a mandate for Uganda, but it needed to be realized by the people to be fulfilled. We carried the nation for some time after leaving her before the burden lifted. We had surely identified with the people by being in their land and experiencing their lack, their poverty, their suffering. Gunshots rocked the city of Kampala every night and put fear into most. There was no guarantee that you would see another day, but as ever, the Lord was faithful to His servants as we were on divine assignment, thereby, meriting His protection.

Soon, the Church where we had ministered began to explode as they began, themselves, to intercede. They were compelled to keep knocking down their walls and building larger. More importantly, their influence increased in the land as God visited them and manifested His mighty hand. A new government came into power, bringing peace and prosperity that has continued for over a decade and changed the face of the nation. Most importantly, they have taken their stand against Islam and its onslaught down the continent, leading to a wave of awakening across the nation. Yet again, God honored our travail and had mercy on a people who were lost. It is marvelous to see how the nation has changed. Perhaps the best example of that change is mirrored in the capital. Once a dirty, broken-down town, Kampala has become a sparkling city and shows Uganda as the "Pearl" once again. It is Jesus, however, who is shining forth from Uganda as the people have embraced Him. And, in embracing Him, they have embraced all that He brings: peace, joy, prosperity, and hope.

Ethiopia, that proud nation which always took her cue from Egypt, was brought low and "great pain shall be in her." The nation failed to rise up to the call to be a real light and preach the Gospel to North Africa. Instead, traditionalism and feudalism kept the land in darkness despite having the Gospel and a strong Jewish heritage. The emperor had been assassinated, the church destroyed, and communism ruled ruthlessly raping the nation. Ethiopians had become worshippers of idols of communism, which adorned the streets and cities of the land. Great deception issued forth from the Coptic Church, which promised only ritual and the worthless worship of the creation of men's hands in the form of idols that festooned every church building. Religion was dead and true Christianity was systematically stamped out by the communists.

The Spirit declared, "Ethiopia is a nation that is cut off, for she is salt having lost her savor. Her abominations have risen to Me, and judgment has come. I hate the idols and deception that have cast a veil over the people and robbed Me of their worship. I have given her into the hands of the enemy, but I would have compassion upon her so that restoration might come and Ethiopia might be the light I have desired her to be."

The Spirit directed us to take up a position for change, but change would come only after things became worse and there was a real cry in the land for a visitation of God. Ethiopia was to be a nation with purpose—the purpose of the Gospel. For ten years, famine wreaked havoc upon the land, and the little that Ethiopia had was pillaged by her Russian overlords who took every conceivable supply in return for worthless weapons. Relief aid that poured in from the West was literally transshipped immediately to Russia. Supplies never reached the people who died by their hundreds of thousands from famine and war.

"There must be a cleansing of the people and the land," declared the Spirit. "Until the people really decide that they desire the Lord, there can be no improvement. The tyrant rules by the will of the people. Only when that will changes will the enemy be dislodged from his seat. Pray for a people to rise up from the people who will honor Me and rule with justice and righteousness."

Civil war was going to be the only cleansing for Ethiopia, contrary though it might seem to most people's understanding. We began to deal with the ruling principalities and to bind the strongmen who held the nation enslaved. As we did, there was the emergence of a new force from within Ethiopia that offered independence to Eritrea in the north. Such a tactic sandwiched the communist government and her forces.

Civil war had been raging against Eritrea for more than a decade in Africa's Afghanistan, where Russia, just as in the latter, had embarked on a "scorched earth" policy and literally burned the nation with napalm and other chemicals. But God is a restorer, and in His hands, the desert will blossom again. That is precisely what happened in Eritrea. The country is a mixture of Christian and Moslem, but the leadership is Christian. Combining with Christian forces from Ethiopia who rose up against their communist masters, their united strength dealt crippling blow after blow to both Russian and Communist Ethiopian forces. The Russians were utterly routed and humiliated in another colonial war that they lost. The hand of God was against them, confusing them and bringing their global plan to nothing. The inspirer of their designs, the devil himself, was being defeated by the intercession of an army of warriors who were destroying him in the heavenlies with the resultant defeat of his natural armies inspired by his design.

In an astounding series of victories, Mengistu's forces were overwhelmed and the tyrant fled to seek asylum at the mercy of Mugabe in Zimbabwe with whom the Lord is still to deal. In amazing answers to intercession, the nation was instantly freed and Eritrea was granted independence from Ethiopia. A hunger for the Lord swept the nation as peace descended upon Ethiopia. Yet again, God heard the travail of His people, who took upon themselves the burden of the enslaved so as to set them free. An awakening has swept the land, and Ethiopia has become a popular place for preaching. Prosperity has returned, and famines have disappeared. The nation has become a standard against the onslaught of Islam, and the Spirit is going to use Ethiopia to bring down Sudan and set multitudes in *that* land free.

The Lord saw the travail of His people and was pleased. He heard our cries and our sighs for a nation in bondage and answered. It is so tragic that men have to pass through such circumstances, which might have been avoided, before they are willing to change.

What victory in intercession! What joy to see the fruit of travail change a nation from war to peace, from destruction to prosperity, from hatred to joy! I believe that the Lord is satisfied.

CHAPTER NINETEEN

The Killing Fields

THE ONLY SIDE that an intercessor may take is the side of right-eousness. While facing the city of Jericho, Jesus appeared unto Joshua who asked Him, *"Art Thou for us, or for our adversaries?"* (Josh. 5:13).

With sword in hand, Jesus replied, *"Nay; but as captain of the host of the Lord am I now come"* (Josh. 5:14).

The greatest need amongst all Christians today is to live by the standard that Paul declares in the Word: *"There is neither Jew nor Greek..."* (Col. 3:11).

I was born a Rhodesian—a very small but unique tribe of less than 200,000 people of all the peoples of the earth. Practically the whole world stood against her either by boycotting or sanctioning her or by attacking her borders or aiding her attackers with all forms of arms or ammunition and she survived for 15 years. Defeat finally came because of betrayal by friends and treachery from some within. Before the final demise of Rhodesia however, I had, like Paul the Apostle, *"Counted all things but loss for the excellency of the knowledge of Christ Jesus my Lord"* (Phil. 3:8).

Since the making of that decision, I have no nation nor national identity, outside of a necessary passport, nor allegiance to any earthly system of men. I simply look for a Kingdom whose *"builder and maker is God"* (Heb. 11:10), and pledge full allegiance to the standard of Heaven. Such a position affords great freedom and liberty to be and do what the Lord alone desires.

The communist manifesto of Robert Mugabe and his communist/terrorist alliance had screamed out in headlines that Christianity was to be abolished, churches closed, religious holidays banned, and the future of Zimbabwe purged of white Rhodesians through a reign of terror and extermination. Sufficient was the available evidence through both the Elim missionaries who had been so brutally massacred and in the reign of terror that had purged Mozambique of all white settlers after the communist takeover there; it was a crisis and such situations demand drastic measures. Pol Phot's slaughter of two million in the "Killing Fields" of Cambodia and Machel's own "killing fields" closer to home in Mozambique spelled out exactly what was to be expected and toward what the nation was headed.

"Unless there is serious prayer and intercession," declared the Holy Spirit one day, "there will be a terrible outcome for the future of the land. Disaster may be averted though. The enemy must be thwarted in his designs," continued the Spirit, "and only then will I be able to move."

"That's a huge assignment…" I pleaded.

"Yes, but begin with My people. If they will humble themselves and pray and seek My face and turn from their wicked ways, then will I hear from Heaven and forgive their sins and will heal their land," interrupted the Spirit.

"Yes," I agreed. "As ever, the barometer for measuring the condition of the land are the people of the Lord."

"There is invasion from without and sin from within. Both need to be addressed and time is short," He concluded.

Despite a spiritual awakening that had swept the land for most of the 1970s, as it had many nations, there was a slothfulness amongst God's people in Rhodesia to fulfill the "Great Commission." A certain pride had invaded the nation, which had become hardened and somewhat cynical. The black church was marginalized and had become very politicized. Many black Christians had turned to the ancestral spirits and had compromised through intimidation by terrorists. Others were filled with anger and hatred for nothing and nobody in particular, but mainly because they were confused and knew that they were in sin.

Witchcraft across the land had increased alarmingly, and it was necessary that people's attention should be focused on the real enemy of mankind—the devil. One thing is abundantly clear. No matter how tyrannically a people think they are being treated, there is a God in Heaven who sees and hears all the travails of men. The moment any peoples turn to terrorism and justify the slaughter of multitudes of innocents in the cause of so-called freedom, they are terrorists and tools of the devil whose very nature is to kill, steal, and destroy.

Israel, even under the slavery and bondage of Egypt, never took up arms and resorted to terrorism for freedom. Rather, their sigh and cry was heard by God, and He had respect for that intercession and intervened. They who live by the sword shall die by the sword. It is for this reason that Africa has been so plagued with one revolution after another, one massacre after another, and one genocide after another. Any people get the government they choose. When Israel cried for a king like the kings of the nations around them, God allowed them their rebellious choice. Thereafter, they suffered tyranny for 40 years. Similarly, when Africans took up arms and chose, by violent revolution, to overthrow the existing colonial governments, they sealed their choices and fate. The history of the continent since 1960 is testimony to those choices, and the confusion, fear, and hatred brought by the devil through the rebellious will of man emphasize the facts.

God will tolerate no side-taking and justification in intercession. There is one standard, an absolute standard, and it is His Word. Everything and everyone must be measured against this absolute and, on the basis of the Word, stand or fall. Our emotions and false human loyalties cannot in any way sway us in intercession. And so, I began to travail and sigh and cry for a land so beaten and bruised. It is important always to remember that men who perpetrate wicked deeds are really the tools of the devil even if willingly. Deal with the devil and wicked men no longer have their motivating force to give them legitimacy. The enemy had to be dealt a crippling blow, and I poured my whole life into the task of interceding for the land and holding back the dark clouds that gathered on the eastern borders.

The Spirit quickly took me into Jeremiah where I learned to weep through the great testimony of that mighty prophet. Ah, what a love he had for the land and the people. As I read through his testimony and prophecy, I began to weep for Rhodesia and all of her peoples. It was no longer an issue of who was right and who was wrong, but of sin being a total reproach to an entire nation, of the enemy of mankind merchandising every opportunity brought by divisions and differences, and of his manipulating people's decisions through fear. All fears had to be broken, and fear hung over the nation like a giant octopus, enslaving both blacks and whites. Fear was driving men to make ridiculous choices. The Word, however, positively declares that, *"They who wait upon the Lord shall renew their strength…"* (Isa. 40:31).

Days of separation and fasting followed as I wrestled with the Lord to break that bondage, and there could, of course, be no fear in my own life. I followed Jeremiah from one crisis to another as he pleaded for the preservation of Judah until that, too, was no more important. What was of utmost importance was that God be exalted and His Light be manifest to a dark world. It was the devil and sin that had robbed men of their dignity and honor. It was idolatry and witchcraft that had turned the same men into animals, and it was ultimate rejection of God Himself that had brought trouble to the land. As I interceded—and there were many in the land who were travailing—I realized that God was presenting Himself at every juncture and forcing all men of all colors and persuasions to make a choice: either for self or for Him.

I so identified with Jeremiah that I wept and wept for sin and for the rape of the nation. I agonized with families, both black and white, who had lost loved ones. I cried out for the cessation of blood-letting that was terrorizing the land. I travailed for those who were enslaved by witchcraft and was angry at the enemy for destroying multitudes of lives. There were many false "pillow prophets" who prophesied good things and peace when the holocaust was coming, and a whole nation was going into real slavery for they were deceived into believing that they were being offered freedom.

I fought alongside Esther, fasting her fast on numerous occasions, for the salvation of multitudes of blacks and the white population from annihilation by a man so filled with hatred and indoctrinated by wicked communism that he could not see any reason. It was in Esther that the decree of death was finally broken and the nation saved from wholesale slaughter. As Esther won favor with Ahasuerus, so I broke through to the

Throne and pleaded for God to deal with the ragings and threatenings of a demon-possessed instrument of death.

The days of wrestling seemed to simply flow one into another, and time became inconsequential in terms of what was threatened. There were days when I just did not eat, not because I was fasting but because the battle was so tough. The weeks rolled into months and the months became a year and then two. It was assuredly an assignment of death, and I was glad that I spent most of my life separated and alone on an isolated farm. It was there that I could devote much time and concentration to the battle. The responsibility was enormous and the burden very heavy, but the fight simply had to continue. Little did I realize at the time, but the Holy Spirit was preparing me for many more such battles for the freedom of nations.

There were three main areas that needed addressing: the threatened massacre of multitudes, the captivity of the land and imposition of totalitarian oppression, and the future of the Gospel within the nation. I realized my hands were tied to a great extent because the will of the people demanded that which was coming, and God Himself would not circumvent their will. Within that framework though, I could pray that vengeance be not exploited, that wickedness be restrained, and that the honor and Glory of the Lord be magnified.

The great victory in Esther, where the extermination of Israel was prevented, spoke prophetically that there would be no wave of annihilating massacres in the land. This victory was offset by Jeremiah's bonds and yokes, which the Lord commanded him to place upon his neck as a sign of the bondage coming upon Israel. Such bonds and yokes were coming upon Rhodesia, soon to be "Zimbabwe," and nothing was going to prevent it from happening. Such was the will of the people.

Captivity was again confirmed in Jeremiah 32 where God declares, *"I will give this city into the hand of the Chaldeans, and into the hand of Nebuchadnezzar, king of Babylon, and he shall take it…and they have turned unto me the back, and not the face…. But they set their abominations in the house…. And they built the high places of Baal…"* (Jer. 32:28,33-35).

The plea of the prophet to throw open the gates of Jerusalem and save the city and nation seemed very applicable. The battle was no longer man's but the Lord's, and God was fighting for the salvation of multitudes. A nation under bonds and yokes was far better than a nation obliterated.

History records the outcome. The Holy Spirit spoke very clearly, "I have said, 'Thus far and no farther.'" He declared, "You may have the land, but the people are Mine, and you shall not wipe out My name nor My posterity."

Whilst the terrorist hordes took the nation and sought to unleash their reign of terror, the unseen hand of Almighty God restrained them at every turn. Today, after 18 years, I marvel that those same men, still frothing and fuming in anger, have not exhausted themselves fighting a relenting battle against the Lord Himself. They still have not recognized this fact. But, he who wars against the Lord and His declared Word shall never prosper.

In the confusion brought by the Lord spiritually and naturally, the enemy turned upon himself, as Midian had done, and began to slaughter his own. In a diabolic ethnic cleansing of Ndebele by Shona, tens of thousands were massacred as a tribute of the devil's hatred and a picture of what had been prepared for the entire nation. A 900-page report spells out the extent of those massacres that broke the will, power, and size of the Matabele nation.

God is not mocked and His Word should never be defied. He had put His hooks into Robert Mugabe and said, "Thus far and no farther...." And though breathing war, hatred, and destruction, man has always had to submit to the higher purpose of Heaven. The Ndebele leader, Joshua Nkomo would not submit to that same Authority. He continued to breathe fire upon every white, and as a result, brought the whirlwind down upon his own nation.

What a testimony of the power of intercession and the fact that God's Word is "yea and amen" and should never be taken lightly even by the mockers and scorners who dismiss the relevance of Heaven! They will find out just how real Heaven and the judgment throne are when they stand before Him. To my knowledge, not one of these leaders has ever acknowledged the Lord and bowed their knee to Him, to their own folly. They "have their reward" now, the praises and accolades of men and the financial rape of the land for their personal gain. Eternity with its separation from the Father of Light and Life is too grim to comprehend unless there is repentance. Every wickedness that they have perpetrated upon this planet, no matter the extent, can never come close to how terrible eternal separation from God will be.

And as far as the Gospel is concerned? Not long after the takeover in Zimbabwe, the first president, Rev. Canaan Banana, himself a Methodist minister, set the plans in motion for a single, state-wide church with himself as head. He wrote a most blasphemous book, the title of which was, *Jesus, the Revolutionary*, wherein he portrayed some major biblical themes—such as the Ten Commandments and the Sermon on the Mount—through the eyes of a terrorist, with relevance to a terrorist. The work was heralded by liberal theologians as a great work, but is too wicked to even quote. Jesus said that not "one jot" nor "one tittle" will pass from His Word (see Matt. 5:18), and that deceived man will find out, to his demise, that God's Word is absolute.

The victory of intercession was that, to date, Christianity is still taught as a subject in the schools. They could not silence the Church, wipe it out, nor even drive it underground. Gospel crusades have been liberally held by many and Jesus exalted time and again. If there be any fault in Zimbabwe, it lies with the spiritual leaders of the land who remain fragmented and have failed to build a strong voice, take the initiative, and go on a dynamic offensive with a united front. Instead, most have cowered in the background, afraid to speak out against any and all evil in the nation. This is cowardice and compromise.

CHAPTER TWENTY

Shire Revival

HAMAD SOUL Chakanza was a short dumpling of a Malawian who looked exactly as I imagined Paul, the Apostle to have looked. At an early age, Chakanza had been inducted into the most powerful rites of wizardry, becoming one of the most powerful and feared satanists in Malawi. He could sit on a small reed mat and fly 200 miles to kill someone and return home all in one evening. Terrible laughing hyenas were his charioteers—when he was not flying on his mat—and he was protected by lions, snakes, and other wild animals that he could command at will, using his magical powers. The man ruled by fear and terrorized far and wide. He knew the devil and his power much better than most Christians know Jesus and His omnipotent power.

One day, Hamad Soul Chakanza went to an evangelistic meeting with the intention of disrupting it and mocking the preacher. He encountered a power at that meeting that was greater than anything he had ever experienced. The power of the blessed Holy Spirit descended upon him and touched him with holy fire and the terror of God. Chakanza was soundly converted and instantly delivered of all his demons. Victory was so complete that the next day found him preaching the Christ whom he hitherto had mocked. From that moment, he devoted his life to the Gospel and winning many whom he had previously terrorized.

I received a letter one day from that wily preacher who was hundreds of miles away and whom I had never met. It was a plea to "come over to this 'Macedonia' of Malawi and help...." I was in deep intercession for India at the time, so I sent some representatives. They returned with reports of the great need for the preaching of the Gospel and the training of workers.

I have learned that need must not necessarily be the cause of motivation in the Gospel. What is required is a clear mandate from the Lord, and such was not long in coming.

"I desire to visit and pour out Myself upon those people," emphasized the Holy Spirit. "I want to prepare them for that which is coming."

"Only You can see the end from the beginning. I guess, at this point, I just do not wish to know," I replied.

"Precisely. Now, in case you think that you are just going to go on a simple trip, let Me warn you, it is going to be semi-permanent."

"But what about this place?" I questioned. "Everything is going so well. I committed to…"

"You have no right to make any promises or commitments to anything or anyone that has not been cleared with Me," He interrupted. "You are mine and take orders from Me alone. Is that clear?" He questioned.

"Very clear," I quickly answered.

There is another side to the gentle nature of the Holy Spirit and that is His military, authoritarian character, which is absolutely precise.

"But what about this work?" I continued to press.

"It's mine, and I will take care of it," He replied, leaving me in no doubt that, without Him, I could do nothing.

"You have not been My instrument to equip these people for nothing. Just as the bird forces her chick from the nest to make it fly, I am going to use the same principle. I am going to scatter this people each to their own work…."

"But they are not ready!" I protested.

"Why is it that My people always want to hold on to that which I have given?" asked the Holy Spirit. "They will soon stagnate unless they exercise the ministry that I have given them. I am closing this work and sending most to work in My vineyards. This place, in case you did not realize, has been a Holy Ghost training center."

In years to come, I realized that this was actually a success. A work having to close because most were being promoted into the higher service of ministry was precisely what the Lord had emphasized when He said, *"Except a corn of wheat fall into the ground and die..."* (John 12:24).

I learned then, and very emphatically, that we are mere stewards and that the work is the Lord's. Without Him I can do nothing and have no right to claim any victories as my own. It is all Him for all of His Glory.

It was New Year's Day 1984, when I departed for the new shores (a mosquito-infested place of 120-degree days with 80 percent humidity) of the lower Shire of Malawi, the area that had been the death of multitudes of missionaries since the days of David Livingstone. I was transported in an old, broken Peugeot pickup——a real workhorse. The chassis had snapped cleanly in half at one stage and had to be welded together with a piece of rail; every time it had to be started, a spanner was required, and there were seldom any brakes. The result was that the jalopy rolled down a hill one day and landed in a river. We launched a rescue attempt to retrieve the only wheels that could take us into the bush. Little did we realize that soon we would be resorting to the mode of transportation with which the Lord created us: our legs!

I always accuse the Holy Spirit of "tricking" me into that mission. He simply laughs. If I had known what I was getting myself into beforehand, I am sure that I would not have agreed to the venture— though I really had no choice. There is absolutely no choice when He dictates the policy.

My supplies were meager, and the only camping equipment that I possessed was a small mattress, sheets, blankets, and a mosquito net, completed by my best china and tablecloths. I owned no tent and was to spend most of the next few years sleeping under the stars, getting soaked during the rains and baked by the sun. Yet, true to His word, the Holy Spirit swept through village after village manifesting the Glory of Jesus. I was so poor at one stage that all I could afford to eat was sugar cane and mangoes, washed down, of course, with tea. There were not even sufficient funds to purchase diesel, so I walked...and walked...and walked. Wherever I went with Hamad Soul Chakanza, we found the people open and very receptive. The Holy Spirit descended, and as only He can do, He convicted multitudes and brought them into a relationship with Jesus.

We literally stormed into strongholds of the enemy and smashed his gates, tearing down the veils that he had established over the people of the lower Shire. There was such a hunger for God that no matter the conditions and the discomfort to the flesh, I was always ready to minister. I lived in the clouds and reveled in the heavy anointing that continued for almost two years. God was preparing the people for the influx of over a million refugees from Mozambique who were going to need to see the power and Glory of the Lord.

There was no desire nor even request for the things of the world—village after village simply wanted the Gospel—and the only need was for Bibles. It was the day of their visitation, and no distance was too far to walk to feed the hungry with the precious Bread of His Word. In the heat and humidity, I lost pounds and began to look like a scarecrow, but none of that mattered. The witch doctors feared our arrival in their areas. Time and again, I saw all His gifts in operation as the Holy Spirit moved to glorify the Lord and defeat the enemy. The word of knowledge exposed hidden strongholds of darkness as the gifts of healings and miracles manifested the power of a God who proved Himself greater than all the strength of the devil. Because of that power, multitudes were convinced and turned to the Lord.

God was raising up an army who would preach far and wide, and as we went from village to village, we gathered a train of people who would follow us everywhere, desiring nothing but to be fed with the powerful Word. Without even trying, I had established a mobile Bible school that was equipping men and women for the future. In five years, Chakanza's work increased from 6 branches to over 300 churches and 10,000 members of which I knew for certain.

Once again, I was seeing the principle of the hundredfold increase to those who gave up homes and families and whatever else for the cause of the Gospel. The Lord was answering the travail of many years, and I, though undeserving, was being blessed with fruit, abundant fruit. What a faithful God He is, who honors the labors of His children! All of the riches of America and Europe could never be attractive compared to all the hardships and lack of Africa coupled with the outpouring of His Spirit. One is death, the other life.

The Holy Spirit sent out, two by two, teams of men and women who wanted nothing but to be used of Him. They were simple people, many never having been in school, but they went forth everywhere preaching the Word and confirming with signs and wonders. I was living and seeing the Book of Acts in operation and marveled that He is indeed, *"The same yesterday, and today, and forever"* (Heb. 13:8).

Night after night, I would tie my mosquito net in some overhanging branch, usually of a mango tree, roll out my simple mattress and make up my bed. With hundreds of mosquitoes whining in frenzied efforts to get at me and suck my blood, and the native believers singing and worshipping often until early morning, I would fall asleep in the greatest peace and contentment, for *"He giveth His beloved sleep"* (Ps. 127:2).

I found this to be absolutely true and very welcome in the tough conditions. There were trying times, of course, especially when it rained and I was soaked or I had to cram into a native hut shared with 12 other people plus chickens, lice, cockroaches, and rats. The latter had the infuriating habit of nibbling at toes and fingers whilst I slept.

The enemy, of course, was not going to stand idly by and watch his territory plundered. He attacked me through sickness and often laid me up with dysentery, fever, or some other problem. Just as often though, I saw the miraculous healing hand of the Lord deliver me from all the works of the enemy and raise me strong to continue with His work. I took up a place of abiding for all of that sickness and disease. It would be a few years of real battle, but the day finally came when I had complete victory over the enemy in those areas. Witch doctors using their spells and potions often sought to kill me or at least disable me, but as He promised, He has given us power over all the works of the enemy.

Naturally too, the enemy raised up one and another to hinder the work, and some who were with us in the camp turned and tried to devour us. The most frightening thing that I saw was men dropping dead whilst trying to interfere with the move of the Spirit. It is particularly dangerous to stand in the way of the Spirit when a person knows the truth of what is happening. There is, however, more mercy for those who are totally ignorant.

Selfish personal ambition and greed often motivated men to stand against the Holy Spirit, who becomes very jealous and can therefore be dangerous when He is moving in revival. The Holy Spirit vehemently protected me because I was His chosen vessel for that place and time. Sadly, Chakanza himself, even after having seen the great moves of the

Holy Spirit, turned and opposed Him and stood strongly against me only a couple of years later. Like Balaam had done so long before, pride caused him to run after the riches of a modern Balak. Then suddenly, despite only being in his late 30s, Chakanza dropped dead of heart failure one night. It was the hand of God's judgment, I have absolutely no doubt. I always tell people, "Just go with the flow of what the Spirit is doing even if you do not understand. But, whatever you choose, don't stand in His way. If you cannot agree with Him, move out of the way because when He is flowing in revival, He will steamroll you if you oppose Him."

As I walked through the land, I realized that this, too, was intercession in itself as well as preparation for the intercession that I was going to lead for Mozambique. I was so thrilled to be alongside the Holy Spirit as He worked. He certainly is a worker and very particular about His *modus operandi*. When we do the work His way, we will have His approval and, therefore, His results—which far outweigh anything man is able to achieve, even with all the modern equipment of a technological age.

I saw the full reality that it is, *"Not by man's might, nor by man's power but by the Holy Spirit"* (see Zech. 4:6)—who certainly glorified the Lord throughout the lower Shire of Malawi. I knew, too, that I was reaping the fruit of the intercessions of many who had labored there before and the martyrs who had lost their lives in various ways: malaria, sickness, and disease, and being killed by hostile natives of earlier times. God's bookkeeping is absolutely accurate. The heavenly accounts were being balanced by the Lord who forgets nothing, especially those who have given their all in His service. No move of God or mighty revival is His sovereign act; God works and moves according to the cry of His people or is prevented by the distinct lack of their cry.

CHAPTER TWENTY-ONE

Crying Out for a Plundered Land

DICTATORSHIP IN temporal government is bred by the totalitarian rule of the devil and his demon powers in the spiritual realm. In the same fashion as the military junta in Argentina had been supported and legitimized by the Roman Catholic system, so the pattern was repeated in Mozambique. The Papal system is totalitarian and Babylonian after its founder, Nimrod, and does not believe in any kind of personal freedom. Where Rome is weak in a nation, she makes great issue of demanding human rights and freedoms and takes advantage of the confusion created by political turmoil. When once Rome gains the upper hand, however, she—like the Islamic system—becomes totalitarian.

Mozambique stretches for some 1,300 miles along the southeastern coast of Africa. It was a Portuguese colony for almost 500 years until given independence in 1975. Vasco da Gama had annexed Portuguese East Africa to the Portuguese crown as a supply base for their spice ships en route to and from the East Indies. Though an exceptionally rich land both minerally and agriculturally, official policy had been to limit expansion into the interior, leaving such development to the church for the most part.

The result was that the Roman Catholic church became the greatest controlling force in the colony. With absolute and autocratic powers, the Roman bishops and priests ruled over the interior from their strategically situated mission stations. They held great sway over the officials and governors whose policies were influenced by them, always to their own advantage. Much of the power was through fear and intimidation, which they wielded over the people because of the threat of excommunication. The Roman church brooked no rivals in Mozambique. Any and all evangelism by other organizations and churches was strictly forbidden and only the Jesuits were permitted to do any real missionary work.

When the great intercessor, Mr. Rees Howells, established a mission in the neighboring Southern Rhodesia in 1905, he was the Holy Spirit's instrument for unprecedented revival on the eastern border with Mozambique. Fired with a passion for the souls of Mozambique, an army of evangelists invaded the land purposing to preach the Gospel. They were met with the most incredible opposition and an onslaught from the powers of darkness that had kept the nation enslaved. The evangelists were imprisoned, tortured, beaten, and many killed. The remainder was driven from the land by military force, for Rome would brook no rivals in her absolute monopoly and manipulation of the population whom she held in shackles of spiritual darkness. It would be another 70 years before Rome's monopoly would be broken and that by the equally wicked system of totalitarian communism.

Into the Mozambique equation came the terrorist independence war, which began in the 1960s. FRELIMO, the acronym for the Portuguese FRente de LIbertacao MOcambique (Mozambique), became a Marxist organization under its second president, Samora Machel, who was trained in Russia and Algeria. Machel had taken over as supreme leader of FRELIMO after planning and executing the assassination of Eduardo Mondlane in Tanzania in 1969. Mondlane, who was the founder of FRELIMO, was too moderate for the bloodthirsty Machel.

Independence was suddenly granted to Mozambique in 1975 by the new socialist government that had seized power in Portugal. The Marxist forces of FRELIMO, backed by their Russian and East German overlords, embarked on a systematic raping and pillaging of the whole nation. All property was instantly seized and nationalized. People were massacred by the thousands while homes and factories were looted. Churches and missions were closed and their properties seized for military purposes. Prisons were filled and slave labor camps established. Everyone was a suspect for everything and anything. SNASP, the brutal secret police that was trained and patterned on the wicked East German Stasi, began to interrogate the entire nation—or at least what was left after the blood-letting.

Machel was every bit as wicked as Stalin or Hitler. His excesses became so great that some of his own leadership rose up against him and established the freedom fighting force of RENAMO, REsistencia NAcional MOcambicana or the National Resistance of Mozambique. Meanwhile, the extermination that Machel had begun continued unabated. He slaughtered hundreds of thousands of Mozambicans. In particular, he moved against the Church, imprisoning, torturing, and killing any and all pastors and their members with a rage and hatred that came directly from the devil himself.

I witnessed the holocaust there, myself, and saw the wrath of the enemy unleashed. I knew pastors who suffered untold deprivation at the hands of the communists. Enoch, the pastor of a bush church near the famous Cabora Bassa Hydro electric scheme, had been so badly beaten after being imprisoned that he completely lost the sight in one eye whilst the other was permanently impaired. No matter the danger, Enoch had been so blessed by my visiting him and his church that he wept unashamedly.

"You have blessed us so much, so much," he cried. "I know that you love us because you have bothered to come and see us. We really thought that nobody cared, but God has answered our prayers. You are indeed an angel...."

Whilst I was preaching in Enoch's church and preparing to flee at any given signal because of SNASP, there arose from my innermost being the groaning of the Holy Spirit. Indeed, there was the true, glorious, and triumphant Church suffering under such persecution. I was humbled and overwhelmed and provoked to give my all and, if necessary, truly lay down my life as these men were doing. They were nothing in the eyes of the world, but to the Lord, their intercessions were a sweet-smelling savor.

I established a network of underground churches in the nation, smuggled in Bibles, and did whatever possible to encourage those who were under persecution. I saw the devastation wrought by FRELIMO each time I traveled in Mozambique. Every town and village expounded the praises of communism with slogans, paintings, and graffiti splashed on every vacant wall. In actuality the country was bankrupt and shops and supermarkets devoid of goods. Fear ruled and the atmosphere was heavy with demonic oppression. Tanks were scattered far and wide across the country in a "banana republic" where everyone had gone either berserk or paranoid. A person could be arrested simply for not averting their eyes when passing a military installation or tank. A knock at the door at midnight often meant that the hated SNASP had come to haul a suspect off to interrogation and torture; most were never again seen. There were no trials, nor was there a legal system. All crime was "military" and therefore judged by tribunal, which invariably meant the firing squad or life in a slave labor camp.

It was near the completion of a "mercy trip" to the underground churches of Beira, the second largest city in the nation, that I was emotionally overwhelmed by the situation and conditions. There was no food in the land, no freedom, and certainly no friendliness. The oppression seemed worse than ever, and I began to pour out my heart to the Lord in a great complaint against His creation and the gross inhumanity that I witnessed everywhere. If I felt that way, I thought how much more the Lord was pained for those for whom He died. I was agonized and sick as waves of the Holy Spirit's anointing descended upon me. He overwhelmed me with a great agony and burden. I felt so helpless at the enormity of the task and wondered just how whole nations could so quickly and easily spiral out of control and into anarchy. Deep down, I knew the answer was rejection of God and His order in preference to the devil and his order. I was absolutely broken when I thought of the 500 years of tyranny that Mozambique had suffered and endured. I began to remonstrate with the Lord, "Israel was only 430 years in bondage, and You set them free."

"I heard their sigh and cry and then their groaning. That is the moment when Israel became desperate, and I had respect for their desperation," declared the Lord. "Until then, there was not much I could accomplish."

"You mean that only when Mozambique is thoroughly tired of its situation will You intervene?" I questioned the Holy Spirit.

"No, not when I *will* intervene, but when I am *able* to do so. The attitude of the people keeps Me from working as I desire. I long to visit the land and relieve the distress but am prevented from doing so. There is a way, however. Where are those who will truly stand in the gap?" He challenged. "When will you take up a place of abiding for the nation?"

"But You haven't given me a mandate for that as yet," I complained.

"Well, you now have it. You have seen the condition of the land, and I want it presented to the Throne. I want you to stand in the gap for this nation and take their burdens upon you to the degree that you will be weighed down. Remember, this people is ignorant. They have had 500 years of total blindness and have no knowledge of how to cry to Me. Their freedom will depend upon your performance...."

"That is frighteningly awesome," I interjected.

"It is their only way out of the situation. Besides, I will be with you to direct you," He encouraged. "Unless you intercede to break the cycle, it will continue from one dictatorship to another, robbing the nation of a relationship with Me. This has gone on for 500 years. I have had enough, and there has been none to plead their case."

I began to think of a system that had been so entrenched for that period of time and wondered what kind of spirits were in control. No sooner had I even thought it when the Holy Spirit answered, "Similar spirits to those bound in the River Euphrates of the Book of Revelation."

I immediately knew that the battle was going to be long and hard— just *how* hard I was about to discover! It was going to take five years of hard, concentrated intercession before the breakthrough came. During that time, I walked in the land, drove through the nation, and flew over it. I carried Mozambique in my heart, and my whole life became so wrapped up in it that there was no place else that I wanted to be. Despite the hardships and sufferings, the Holy Spirit had so filled me with the Lord's love and compassion for Mozambique that I was, indeed, ready to die there if necessary.

As I walked from village to village, I acted out various roles to meet the needs of the people. I became doctor, counselor, advocate, prosecutor, judge, and whatever else I was required to be. I realized in another way just what Paul had meant when he said that he was all things to all men. I helped in medical work—certainly not my favorite to say the least, but then, what an introduction—using only a hacksaw blade and knife. There was no anesthetic, and the wound had to be cauterized. Another time, I found a little boy whose entire toe had been eaten away by gangrene. What a mess and how hard it was to administer medication!

Injuries from snakes, leeches, mosquitoes, crocodiles, and invading hippos I easily handled, but to see people in real pain as a result of man's evil to man was too much. Thank God, too, that He answers prayer and heals and sets men free from all sickness and disease if we would only truly cry out to Him. I cried out to Him many times!

Wherever I went, I preached the Gospel, whether to soldiers, villagers, or government officials. I was very much in the thick of their civil war, and though hating the deeds of the communist FRELIMO, I fully understood that the real enemy was the devil who hates all mankind. I could not take sides, and though I worked with RENAMO, I had compassion on all. What was needed was not more war and fighting and hatred but truth and the light of His Word to set men free.

It was very evident that the enemy was desperately attempting to hold on to Mozambique through confusion and hatred, but he had already lost his stranglehold and would soon altogether lose his grip. Ignorance had kept a whole nation enslaved, and the interior of the country still lived in the Dark Ages where tradition, ancestral worship, and witchcraft held multitudes bound. The war, however, was opening up the land and introducing all people to things never before seen or experienced.

Often I would arrive at villages where children would scream upon seeing a white man. Older teenagers would stare in amazement. Most had never heard of Jesus and His saving love, and where people *had* heard of His name, they were enslaved by the traditional and cultural rites and requirements of the system of Rome, which was a robber of any freedom to worship the Living God. Where a people has never seen the demonstrated power and reality of the Holy Spirit, the Lord becomes to them a myth, and religion degenerates into form and rite. This was a picture of the Mozambique where there had never been any evangelistic endeavor.

Darkness enveloped all of those villages where age-old traditions and superstitions were law, but all this was about to change. The many war stories and mighty triumphs—for they are triumphs—are recounted in *Love Constrained* and *Recklessly Abandoned*. However, that which must be revealed is the greatest victory of all: the victory of intercession touching Heaven and making those very triumphs possible.

There was no sacrifice too great for the cause of Christ in Mozambique. His passion filled my life, as did a great Holy Spirit compassion for the multitudes under such terrible suffering in the land. Days of walking through swamps, weeks of being soaked by the rains with nothing dry to wear, thousands of miles on foot, often without food and sometimes in the depths was not enough to deter me. I pressed on and on, always conscious of the urgency of the hour. There were times of such thirst that I was forced to drink water that was alive with all kinds of swimming microbes and worms. Often, I was lifted and carried by the unseen hand of my supernatural companions who strengthened and encouraged me when I was ready to faint by the way.

Then the war itself was terrible. Bullets, bombs, land mines, fighter jets, helicopter gunships, all crossed my path time and again, and yet, the Lord sustained me in all of my ways. I was a special agent in divine service, and He was always my shield and defense. He deflected bullets, exposed mines, blinded pilots, and supernaturally surrounded me with an impenetrable barrier so that no harm would come to me by any means. Many marveled at just how protected I was, and all knew that the Lord's hand was indeed directing me.

Besides those forces against me from without, there was the great burden of carrying Mozambique in the depths of my being. The agony, travail, and groaning that became part of daily life were heavy and exhausting. As a young man, I exerted tremendous energy in my intercessions. Awake often through the night, I cried copious tears for years for the land and learned to sigh a great deal. This became so rooted in me that I would walk around simply sighing for Mozambique. I did not even have to consciously think of the suffering or the war to sigh. Such was the burden of the Holy Spirit as He interceded through me to touch Heaven.

I was carrying a plundered, pillaged nation in my bosom, and there was coming a day when freedom would be birthed and Mozambique forever liberated from tyranny. Just as sure as the intercessor sets his face to the task, victory is certain. There can be no failure just as long as there is obedience and perseverance. As I walked the length and breadth of the land, like Abraham of old, I was possessing it for the purposes of God. Of course there were giants in the nation, but the eye of faith is greater than any of them.

The Lord also possessed His "Melchizedeks" who were planted strategically for my blessing and encouragement as well as theirs. Sometimes, in the most unlikely places, I would find a saint who was prepared to do anything just to bless me in my journey. Such were the markers of a loving, caring, and very personal God who is vitally interested in me in the midst of His whole creation. The Lord had singled out Mozambique for blessing and had chosen me to initiate a move that would bring His purposes to pass no matter the hindrances or the opposition of the enemy.

CHAPTER TWENTY-TWO

The Lord Heard My Cry

THE PRESENCE OF the Lord was very heavy and felt as if He were swirling around the hall in thick clouds. I understood what it must have been like for Israel as they watched Him descend upon Mount Sinai. He was so real as to be tangible. His holiness was invading, yes, *invading* every part of my being. He was too terrible yet too attractive. I wanted more, but I was deeply conscious that I could not contain Him in the slightest. The divine was touching the mortal, and my frail frame was unable to accommodate Him. I felt compelled on the one hand to cry out, "Enough, Lord, or I die," whilst at the same time was too afraid to offend Him lest He depart.

Eternity had violated time and made it meaningless. The infinite had touched the finite and exploded it. Holiness had descended and banished the profane. He was awesome. He was power. He was total purity. This was not a visitation to deal with sin or self as at other times but a demonstration of His mightiness. God was showing Himself, exalting Himself, and proving Himself. There was no place for doubt and unbelief. His Glory banished such negativity. There could be no frivolous behavior in that thick atmosphere, which pulsated with life. I wanted to fall prostrate before Him and hide but felt also constrained to gaze. God was revealing Himself for a purpose. He was allowing us the rare privilege of experiencing His Glory. I knew it was part of our intercessions. There was no noise. How could there be? Silence filled the hall, and if anything could be heard, it was the pounding of my own heart.

This was real; life was electrified. I wished I could be there forever, riveted to that spot with only God to adore. I longed for more but felt my whole being turning to jelly and then water. Like the prophet, I was undone, totally undone. I could not have moved even if I had wanted to. I did not want to. I did not want to offend God in the slightest. This visitation was not something I could say I enjoyed. He was too great for that. He was frighteningly real. There began to ascend from the deepest recesses of my being—so deep that I did not know that such a place existed in me—an unspoken exaltation and adoration of Him. It flowed forth in a fluency never before experienced. Such was the richest and deepest of the blessed Holy Spirit worshipping the Lord. I totally agreed with Wesley's desire for a thousand tongues to praise Him and again determined that I would make the most of the one that I possessed.

I felt compelled to dedicate everything to Him and then more besides. I was conscious that I was horribly unworthy. His grace, however, was so tangibly vast that it accounted for all that I was and left me totally free. I understood at that moment the power of God's ability to forgive and cleanse. Everything was God, everything was Christ, and everything was the Holy Spirit. I comprehended the depths of the Scripture, *"In Him was life; and the life was the light of men"* (John 1:4).

God was simply everywhere and infused everything, and without Him nothing was made nor is anything able to exist. I wanted to embrace the Lord and hold on to Him for all I was worth, never letting Him go. There is nothing to be desired outside of Him, for He is everything.

The Kingdom of God was fully existent in that crude hall in the midst of the blazing African sun in a simple African village. In that moment of enlargement that was to impact me forever, He increased my comprehension of seeking first the Kingdom and all the other things that are needed would be added unto me. Such was the more abundant life that was promised to every believer. I also understood more deeply that He alone is my shield and my exceeding great reward. It is not the wealth and possessions but the Lord Himself who is my prize, and I love Him, love Him, love Him.

Over 650 pastors and leaders had gathered for a ten-day prayer and fasting convention in a small village at the southern tip of Malawi. Many of those same pastors had walked three weeks through the

Mozambican jungles to attend the convention. Some of their accounts of deliverance through which God brought them read as the Book of Acts. One group shared how they had walked for many days and were very tired. They had decided to rest in a dry riverbed under the shade of a large sprawling tree. Soon, they were sound asleep. Suddenly, the pastors were rudely awakened to find themselves surrounded by a platoon of communist soldiers all pointing their AK-47s at them.

The leading pastor leapt to his feet, and the platoon commander began shouting questions at him, "Who are you and what are you doing?"

"We are pastors going to a conference in Malawi," he innocently replied.

"You know very well it is forbidden to pray in Mozambique. We don't want religion here! Today you are going to die," he yelled as he drew his pistol and advanced on the leader.

At that instant the commander was literally picked up by an unseen power and thrown to the ground with great force where he lay unconscious. His platoon, thinking that their commander had been assaulted, rushed at the pastors with their bayonets. Suddenly, they too were picked up and thrown on the ground. The entire platoon lay unconscious. The pastors were terrified and began racing off down the riverbed when the commander arose and shouted, "Wait! Wait! I've seen Jesus. I've seen Jesus. I've seen Jesus. What must I do to be saved?"

At that point the rest of the platoon awoke. All had the same testimony, "We've seen Jesus. We've seen Jesus. What must *we* do to be saved?"

With tremendous excitement, the pastors shared the Gospel with the soldiers, led them to the Lord, and went on their way rejoicing. The platoon melted into the bush again, changed forever.

For ten days, we enjoyed a "shut-in" with the Lord. We all lived in that simple hall, spending day and night with Him. When one was tired, he slept. Variously through the night there was praise and worship and throughout the day there were also teaching sessions. The only sustenance was tea three times a day and water. At the end of such conferences, a couple of cattle were slaughtered and a great feast enjoyed before the pastors embarked on their return journeys. Such grand convocations were held three times a year and became landmark events in the history of Mozambique.

The need for freedom in that land became so acute and the burden so great that we would automatically slip into intercession. Such was the work of the Holy Spirit who was directing us according to the heartbeat of the Lord. Each time we gathered for such convocations, the intercession became more intense. The enemy was not prepared to let go of a nation that he had kept closed for 500 years, but the Spirit had expressly declared that Mozambique was His and He wanted her free. There were days on end when we would be weighed down with the burden of their persecution and tears would flow for Mozambique until they soaked the floor. At other times, there would be great praise and victory shouts that would ascend to Heaven.

Each time we gathered, we would reach another level with the Lord. I saw very clearly that we were severing the tentacles of some great octopus as we had to do on other occasions. The prayer and fasting convocations were interspersed with visits to Mozambique and preaching from village to village to encourage the people. I saw the horrors of the system in the slave labor camps, the villagers with missing limbs from mines deliberately planted in their villages at night, and churches burned to the ground with the congregations locked inside "to burn for Jesus."

I lived the horrors with the people and understood the indignation of the Lord. Of course, I understood, too, that the enemy was having his day and that he was using selfish and unscrupulous men who were willingly his tools. And, it was precisely on that issue that the Holy Spirit spoke to me one day whilst I was pouring out my heart to the Lord.

"I want the strongman of Mozambique bound and removed," He emphasized.

"I am doing everything that I know," I retorted.

"But you're missing the mark. Zero in on the real issues," He explained.

"Well," I questioned, "what are the issues?"

"Understand that the spiritual powers are supported by the natural powers and they give each other legitimacy. Knock out the both of them by dealing with the softer target."

I then operated a principle under the clear direction of the Holy Spirit, which causes many Christians great consternation because they do not understand the different facets of the nature of the Godhead. Yes, indeed, God is love, but He is also Judge and an all-consuming fire. Yes, indeed, we are in the Age of Grace, but the Lamb is also the Lion. Yes, indeed, there is a place where men overstep the bounds of God by willingly being a tool in the hands of the enemy. They will pay the supreme and eternal price for their crimes against God, for their crimes against His humanity and creation. Hitler, Mao, Stalin, Pol Pot, Machel, Belshazzar, Herod, Judas—all were agents of the evil one by their choice through their own selfish ambitions.

The strongman of Mozambique was that wicked Samora Machel. The Spirit directed one day as I was waiting upon Him, "Machel is not one of mine. He is reprobate. Do not pray for his salvation."

Instantly, the words of Esther rang in my ears, *"The adversary and enemy is this wicked Haman"* (Esther 7:6).

I knew that we had the enemy right there through Haman. Machel was going to hang on his own gallows, and tyranny in Mozambique would end. For almost 12 years, he had terrorized and ransacked the nation and slaughtered multitudes. Enough was enough. For many years I had been teaching RENAMO, as well as the churches, that men might fight in the natural, but unless the reigning powers of the enemy are overcome, even a physical victory would not count for very much. But it became very clear in the Mozambican case that a *natural* man needed to be removed—just as had happened in the days of Haman—*before* any conditions would change. Sometimes certain insights and privileges are given to intercessors for the express purpose of the battle that they are waging; and this was just such a case.

Thus began a cry for the removal of Machel from power. This cry, which continued for a couple of years for he was deeply entrenched, had brought us to the present "shut-in" with the Lord. The ten days began in anointing and power and ended with one of the mightiest explosions of God I have ever witnessed. Each day built upon the previous one, and I knew that we had the enemy on the run. There were 650 men of different tribes, languages, and races, but the Holy Spirit had molded us as one. A unified voice ascended to Heaven, not as at Babel but as at Pentecost.

One of the most powerful tools was a simple chorus in the Chichewa language of Malawi, which the Holy Spirit so anointed that even today it sends shivers down my spine and brings tears to my eyes and Mozambique instantly to my mind. The more that we sang the song, the more that we could feel, not our cry, but the cry of the Spirit ascending to God through us. True justice can be done to the chorus only by multitudes of African voices harmonizing as one:

Tumizani Mzimu Wanu Ambuye
Send Your Holy Spirit, Lord.
Tumizani Mzimu Wanu Ambuye (2)
Send Your Holy Spirit, Lord (2).
Tumizani Mzimuwo
Send Your Holy Spirit.

Ana anu afuna Inu Ambuye
We all need You, Lord.
Ana anu afuna Inu Ambuye (2)
We all need You, Lord (2).
Tumizani Mzimuwo
Send Your Holy Spirit.

Mozambik afuna Inu Ambuye
In Mozambique, they need You, Lord.
Mozambik afuna Inu Ambuye (2)
In Mozambique, they need You, Lord (2).
Tumizani Mzimuwo
Send Your Holy Spirit.

It is one of those rare, timeless songs, like the great hymns of the Church, which was penned in Heaven itself and given to men by the Divine Author for His own Glory. Often we would sing the song for several hours, and it became a mighty weapon in our hands and a delight to our own spirits.

That night of total victory is one I shall never forget. It simply has to be recorded in eternity as it was so powerful. What a culmination of five years of excruciating work for Mozambique! Men only see what is visible, but the eye of faith knows the inner workings. I was in complete control and felt what it must have been like for Churchill when news of Germany's ultimate surrender was signed. It was the last night of our prayer and fasting conference. I was leaving for Zimbabwe the very next day. Six hundred and fifty voices were blended in singing "Tumizani," and the song seemed to spiral up to Heaven, higher and higher, higher and higher. It was like a heat-seeking missile zooming in on its target.

The hall was electrified with the awesome presence of God. Intercession had found her mark, and I had no doubt that victory was assured. Tears poured from all eyes. I knew we were making history. There were no television crews, no newspaper reporters, and no magazine editors to capture the event. But there was a Scribe who was recording the Truth because He is the Author of Truth and He had engineered the battle plan that we were following.

Months of sighs, cries, and travail were coming together in one sweet savor to fill the nostrils of the Almighty and delight Him. The incense spoken of in Revelation, the prayers of the saints, reached Heaven and released the Father's hands for action and deliverance. Unlike the king who had smitten the ground but thrice, we had smitten and smitten again and again and again so that we had lost count of our smitings. But, in the process, we were assured that never more was such wickedness going to invade the land and stop the Gospel of God from going forth to that hungry nation. The root of wicked control was forever gone. I heard the sound of the many waters of Revelation and each voice blended and reverberated in worship and praise.

Then suddenly a shout went up from 650 voices, which shook the building. Far more important, it shook Machel and every demon and devil that had kept him in power. The different languages joined with one message to remove the man. Then the word came, "Bring him down; bring him down."

It caught a few of the men and spread like fire to the rest. Soon the whole room was reaching up and pulling down, reaching up and pulling down in a unison that was spellbinding. It was captivatingly stirring but also frightening. Something profound was happening. We did not need to know in the natural; we had the witness of the Spirit. Such shouting as would have made Joshua proud continued unabated for over an hour. I was exhausted but continued until I began to feel a great release somewhere far out in the heavenlies. It descended little by little like a huge blanket until it reached us and enveloped us. It was God's approval and release. The time was around ten in the evening. Just as a mighty whirlwind, which comes with so much activity and noise and departs leaving such silence, a complete calm descended upon the whole hall. It was over. Intercession had reached the Throne. I announced simply, "Mozambique is free. Yes, Mozambique is free *tonight*."

This was followed by shouts and cheers and whistling, which seemed as if it would never stop. Rejoicing continued with dancing and praising until the early hours of the morning. The natives really know how to celebrate appropriately. Oh what relief. Oh what freedom. The burden of Mozambique was gone. It had been a heavy one.

Blantyre, the commercial and industrial capital of Malawi, was like a military garrison the next morning. South African police were everywhere. The Zomba Air base was alive with South African fighter jets, and there were roadblocks and checks at all major highways. Something big had happened during the night. Just how big, we were soon to discover. There were rumors of invasion, but nobody was very clear about anything. A news blackout had been imposed, and the nation of Malawi was under a state of emergency.

Having finished last-minute business, I departed for Zimbabwe the following morning, Tuesday, at 4:00 a.m. The trip back to Harare was a grueling all-day affair at the best of times but seemed so much worse on that particular day. I felt as if the whole world was under suspicion, and the Mozambican military personnel looked at me with such hatred that I thought I had committed a major crime. Though I did not know it, to them I had! I could not wait to get out of their country and was relieved when I crossed into Zimbabwe.

As I arrived home, Roz, my beloved sister rushed out shouting, "Have you heard the news? Have you heard?"

"What? Quickly tell me what?" I demanded.

"Machel is dead! Machel is dead!" She declared.

I was stunned! Speechless! Amazed! "How?" I asked.

"His jet crashed on Sunday night in South Africa. Didn't you hear? The whole world is in an uproar, and South Africa is being blamed," Roz gushed in excitement.

"The world in an uproar for that tyrant? It just shows how sick men have become," I emphasized.

What incredible news and what swift judgment! The time of Machel's crash was the exact time that 650 men of God were pulling him out of the sky in Nsanje. Assuredly, the Haman of Mozambique had hung upon his own gallows. He was most certainly removed forever. He would never be a blight on the nation again.

The exact account emerged in the following days. Machel had attended a secret meeting of the leaders of the so-called "Frontline States" of Zimbabwe, Zambia, Tanzania, and Mozambique. This meeting was held at the Zambian Presidential Lodge in Luangwa Game Reserve. Originally planned as a holiday resort for foreigners, this lodge had become another "white elephant" on a "dark continent." An international airport had been built but never finished, so there were no refueling services. Machel had the longest distance to fly, and without the facilities to refuel, his pilot was cutting the situation very close.

The purpose of the secret meeting was for the planned overthrow of Dr. Banda, president of Malawi. By 1986 things had reached crisis proportions in southern Africa. Mozambique had completely fallen apart. Zimbabwe, neighbor and supporter of the communist government in Mozambique, had officially declared war on RENAMO and was committing thousands of troops to a futile guerrilla war. It was Vietnam on a miniature scale, eating up men, money, and machines. Machel, desperate for scapegoats for his own failure, accused Malawi of helping RENAMO. Those Marxist "Frontline" leaders flew to Blantyre to deliver an ultimatum to Dr. Banda.

"Stop supporting RENAMO and cease relations with South Africa, or we will cut off Malawi," they announced.

The problem was that Malawi is landlocked and surrounded by those neighbors. Caught up in their own self-importance and arrogance, the Marxist leaders were consequently blinded to the fact that they were actually opposing the Supreme Commander of the universe.

Dr. Banda's reply to the warmongers was, "Gentlemen, you may do what you like, but our God will deliver us out of your hands."

Having left the one-day summit in frustration and defeat, the leaders agreed on a meeting in Zambia to plan the overthrow of Dr. Banda and takeover of Malawi. Their diabolic strategy was to seek access through Malawi for their combined forces on the pretext of dealing with REN-AMO in eastern Mozambique. Once inside Malawi, they would back a *coup d'etat* and install their own puppet regime. The weekend of planning appeared to be a great success, and Machel carried the "blueprint" for the solution to Malawi. Having finished business, the leaders settled down to complete the weekend in revelry.

There was one major problem that those warmongers forgot. God in Heaven laughs to scorn the devices of evil men, and He was about to show His mighty hand in response to the persevering cry of His African intercessors.

Machel's Russian pilot had spent the weekend with the vodka bottles, so he was somewhat inebriated for the return flight to Maputo. To further add to the terrible predicament was the fact that the Russian jet was outdated and many of the gauges were malfunctioning. Low on fuel and unable to correctly judge his situation, the pilot panicked and thought himself to be farther south than he actually was. He radioed Maputo, the Mozambican capital, demanding they switch on the landing lights, only to be informed that they were on already. In his confusion, the pilot set a course west, thinking he had made a mistake by not having the lights visual.

The great problem was that the jet was flying low with its landing gear down in preparation for landing, and the new heading took the plane directly into the foothills of the Drakensburg Mountains of eastern South Africa. The plane hit a forest and instantly tore apart on impact. Machel and several of his ministers died immediately. Mozambique was set free from their Haman and his tyranny. The South African authorities arrived on the scene after three hours and found the blueprints for the takeover of their ally, Malawi. President Banda was immediately alerted, and he called in the South African armed forces and placed the nation under an emergency.

Yet again, through powerful intercession, God had intervened in international affairs to bring lasting changes. From the moment of

Machel's death, Mozambique began to turn, and the changes—which were long overdue—began to be implemented. Today, there is not only religious freedom in the land, but also a mighty move of God. Missionaries are hearing the call to Mozambique by the dozens, and churches are being established all across the land with freedom to evangelize and preach the glorious Gospel. Tyranny is forever dispelled and the Glory of the Lord revealed.

CHAPTER TWENTY-THREE

Rwanda: A Costly Lesson

INTERCESSION CAN never fail, for it is God's strategy in operation. Who *may* fail is the intercessor. Just as long as the eyes of the intercessor remain upon the Lord and he continues obediently, he will gain the place of intercession where victory is assured. The responsibility is a heavy one, for eternal destinies are weighed in the balance. There is no room for any complacency, for there are always new heights to be reached in intercession. So it was, that in the midst of the Rwandan genocide, the Holy Spirit quietly prompted me one day, "I want you to go to Rwanda and to the refugees."

"You've got to be joking!" was my instant reply. "Why me? I'm tired, Lord. Find somebody else."

"There *is* nobody else. Besides, you're experienced. I need you there," He persisted.

"I really don't want to go, and besides, I have no money for that kind of trip," I argued.

"I will deal with your heart and provide for you. Is there anything too hard for Me?" He questioned.

I knew that I was done. But I really did not want to go. The very next morning, Roz called from the United States.

"Guess what?" She chirped excitedly.

"What?" I questioned.

"Somebody has just sent a thousand dollars specifically for you to go to Rwanda."

My silence must have been deafening. I was stunned.

"It's the first time I didn't want a thousand dollars," I muttered to Roz.

"Do you see how quickly I work?" whispered the Holy Spirit. "I had it all previously planned."

"But who said I was even going to Rwanda?" I proffered.

"Well, I guess you are now," replied Roz.

"Yes, you *are*," reiterated the Spirit.

"Well, I don't have tires for my car, and those that I have are worn bald," I argued.

"Did the shoes and clothes of the children of Israel wear out in the wilderness?" He questioned. "No," He continued, "I kept them in all their ways. Well, I will take care of your tires all the way to Rwanda and back. They will not wear out, and they will give you no trouble."

I was defeated and I knew it.

The taxing trip across Tanzania cannot be adequately described. Day after day I crawled along at 8-12 miles per hour across horrific roads where there were no filling stations or services for hundreds of miles. At times the "road" degenerated into mere tracks through the wilderness, and there was no telling if I was headed in the right direction. Part of the route was through the hostile territory of the blood-drinking Masai tribe. It was too dangerous to sleep in those places at night; I did not fancy awaking—that's *if* I would awake at all—to a Masai raid or spear in my side.

There was one spot that was a tanker trailer graveyard where many had plunged over the cliffs after brake failure; others had jackknifed and overturned, and yet others had exploded. There were no hotels, and often, because of drought, there was little or no water available at wells or reservoirs. Conditions were very primitive, and I felt I could have been a David Livingstone. It was almost 3000 miles one way, and it certainly was wonderful to finally hit some tar (black top) again after many long days of grueling travel. It was then that I came over a hill one afternoon to be met by one of the most incredible sights I have ever seen, an entire tent city! As far as my eye could see, there were tents and makeshift homes for mile upon mile, sprawled out over a vast area of hills. A pall of smoke hung over the vicinity, and my first and immediate impression was, "This is how Israel must have looked encamped in the wilderness."

My heart was greatly disturbed at the appalling conditions, but even worse was the total lack of anybody preaching the Gospel to over half-a-million people forced to congregate in one spot by circumstance. Worst of all, was the suspicion in which everyone was held. The vast majority of the refugees were of the Hutu tribe, and since they were blamed for the genocide, they received little compassion and were all branded "killers" or "murderers." Certainly the United Nations personnel were leaders in the "name branding," and every kind of violation of human rights that they were supposed to uphold. Above all, from the outset, they adamantly opposed me in my desire to preach the Gospel. I realized that my greatest battle was going to be against this God-hating, ultra-liberal, New Age-controlled organization.

The Spirit expressly warned, "You are to take no sides, no matter what men might say. I want you to love these people and show them no prejudice. No prejudice, mind you."

"This is a vast work," I complained. "It needs an army of preachers."

"And I will raise them up," He declared. "I need your abiding."

My preliminary investigation left me, once again, overwhelmed with the plight of humanity and man's wickedness to his fellow man. It was not shortages in the natural that troubled me, for bodily needs seemed well addressed, but the major issue was of multitudes in the Valley of Decision with no shepherds and no direction. Such conditions were oppressing. I determined to return as soon as possible with equipment and a team to blitz the camps with the Gospel.

The journey back to Malawi went without mishap as the Holy Spirit had promised. Soon after my arrival back, a business friend saw my tires and declared, "Go immediately and get yourself a brand-new set of tires; they're on me." There was no need for the Spirit to say anything; I fully understood.

It was a few months, and I was back, much to the consternation of everyone. The general consensus was that we would be slaughtered by the Hutus. All of the UN staff and aid workers lived in relative luxury in the mountains of Ngara, some 20 miles from the camps. This was impractical for us, and to be isolated from the people we were attempting to reach was ludicrous. After all, we were identifying, and the price of that was going to be suffering. To pack, unpack, and transport our heavy sound equipment every day was altogether too time-consuming and would leave no room to reach the people whom the Spirit commanded we had to love. Consequently, I set up camp on the hill opposite the refugees, barely half-a-mile away.

Everybody proclaimed we would be slaughtered as we slept and all our goods and equipment stolen. We were "crazy," "irresponsible," and "playing with fire," according to most people. They feared they would suffer because of our foolishness. The woman official in charge of the UN did us much damage and instructed every organization not to assist us in any fashion and, in fact, to have nothing to do with us. Over 40 relief organizations complied with her dictates, and we found ourselves totally isolated in the midst of a sea of humanity, which, indeed, had become very hostile because of the way they were treated. But, despite the natural hardships, we were there as intercessors for the purpose of reconciliation and wasted little time in getting down to serious work.

It is very difficult to adequately describe the deprivation and conditions. Water had to be collected daily, generators broke down, a brand-new sound system gave problems, and above all, our campsite was not in the best position. The ablution facilities in the camps were pitiful to say the least, and consequently, flies bred at an alarming rate. As the wind changed we would experience a daily invasion of flies, which made us feel what it must have been like in Egypt during that plague. They settled everywhere and upon everything, even the sandwiches we were eating. However many flies I swallowed, I lost count.

Then there were the equatorial storms. The clouds would build up during the mornings and then release a torrential downpour so heavy that I could not see my hand in front of my face. Our camp would be blown in every direction, and everything was soaked. No matter how we battened down the equipment, the wind would whip it open and the daily deluge would demolish it. Dozens of children would drown in those downpours by being caught in culverts that instantly turned into swirling rivers.

Above all, people would simply not attend our crusades. The sound equipment was powerful enough to bombard the camps, which we did, but the people just would not come in large numbers and there *appeared* to be no good reason for that. What readers need to understand is that the refugees had time, and we were deliberately stationed right near the camps for the specific purpose of being in close proximity so that they would not have to travel any great distance. It didn't make sense. Later, however, I found out that there was a good reason for the meager attendance.

Another hardship came when a willful and disobedient young South African on the team took my Toyota Hilux and rolled it down the mountain, leaving us isolated and without transport except for my big truck. It certainly seemed that all hell was against us, and I knew that we were on to something very big. This was all part of gaining a place of intercession for not only the Hutus, but the entire Rwandan nation.

One day, the Holy Spirit expressly spoke, "I want you to carry the cross through the camp." Consequently, I divided everyone into four teams, and each day a team would carry the cross through the camp. That seemed to make no visible impression upon the people. I at least thought that such an event would bring people to the crusade meetings. They still did not come. I felt so bad on another count. My very special friends, Jerry and Marilyn O'Dell, had flown all the way from the United States to lead the crusades. They toted a new generator for us only to find that the crusades were pathetic; yet, there were 500,000 people not half a mile away.

I felt like such a fraud before them, having assured them of a great response, which did not materialize. It was another death. I died daily at crusade time as people came in their pitiful hundreds instead of tens of thousands. It seemed that all was in vain, yet the unseen hand of the Holy Spirit was moving in ways that I could never comprehend.

Our daily devotions—both morning and evening—were electrifying. The presence of God descended upon our camp and seeped into most hearts. The Lord gave us courage and hope and the strength to carry on despite all the outward problems. We really were "a city set upon a hill" in the midst of the darkness. Just as the Spirit had spoken, He began to touch each heart and infuse us with His love for those people, no matter their status, condition, or predicament. We were not concerned about the genocide; we were in the ministry of healing and reconciliation.

Two things very quickly emerged. Every refugee to whom I spoke described a supernatural phenomenon that they witnessed before the awful assassination of the Rwandan president as a prelude to the genocide. A large object had been seen in the sky and it could only be described as a "flying saucer." It was pulsating with a green translucent light and traveled across the whole nation. From village to city, poor to rich, ignorant to educated, everyone saw the spectacle and knew that it spelled something sinister. Personally, I have no doubt that it was demonic, a manifestation of the devil's power and his impending program to destabilize all of central Africa and create the very genocide that occurred.

The believers came to understand the nature and workings of the devil and how he can be defeated. Two of the greatest weapons he uses are fear and ignorance. Most Rwandans cannot explain how or why the events that followed took place. There was no planned genocide as the media and the UN have tried to interpret. It was simply a case where the nation "went crazy." Tutsis are equally guilty of genocide, which they continued to practice for months after the initial massacres against the Hutus.

I gathered believers of all persuasions for daily teaching and zeroed in upon the devil and his works. As we taught, we could see the veil of ignorance roll back from their minds. For the first time, they began to realize the nature of the true battle and how the devil hates mankind. I instructed them in intercession of which they also knew nothing.

We had a glorious opportunity to put our teachings into operation. The "witch of Ngara," as the head of the UN became known to all, was really a dictator. She imposed strong food and water rationing upon the refugees in order to "keep them subdued." We took her on in battle with her spirits and began to pray and intercede. It was wonderful teaching in a practical situation. As the days passed, the numbers to our teaching seminars swelled to hundreds. At the same time, our other activities of handing out tracts, carrying the cross, and holding crusades, continued. We had seven days of fasting to break the strongholds of the enemy and won a tremendous victory when the food and water supplies were increased to the required levels.

There was such rejoicing and triumph when all saw the reality of God's power working on their behalf. It was at that point that significant information came to me in one of the sessions. It was reported that the powerful Hutu leadership in the camp was actually preventing their people from attending the crusades for fear that they would get saved and join the army of the Lord. This, they knew, would spell the end of the army of Hutus they were raising and training to return to Rwanda to fight.

The presence of the Holy Spirit came upon me, and the anger of the Lord rose up inside of me. I openly challenged the leadership to a meeting, knowing that everything I declared would be reported directly to them—and it was! A few days later, I received an invitation to a secret meeting of the entire leadership. They instructed that I had 15 minutes to speak to them about "my" mission. I poured out my heart in love to them and powerfully preached the Gospel. Fifteen minutes became an hour, and the Holy Spirit had them captivated. When I finished, there was complete silence.

Finally, the chairman rose and said, "I have never heard an address like that in my entire life. We have been watching you people since you arrived here. I want to tell you that we regard you as our friends. Not only will we protect you from all danger, but we will ensure that our people attend your meetings. You are most welcome among us and feel free—our camps are open to you. You have not been like others who have come here, even Christians, and attacked us for being murderers. You are different."

What victory and how I rejoiced to hear those words! We had won the favor of a whole nation, and they had opened their doors to us in an incredible way. We could virtually do anything we wished because we had gained a place of intercession. What we needed was the support of the Body of Christ to establish the facilities for a Bible school, which was desperately required by the refugees. They distinctly told us, "We do not need food, clothes, and medicine, but the Word and teaching."

I specifically asked the spiritual leaders—those that were there—"If there is only one thing that I could provide, what would you have?"

"A Bible school," they chorused in unison.

We had lived with them, cried with them, and lifted them to the Lord in their plight. We had suffered with them and given several months to smash the yokes and chains, which held them captive. God heard our cry and answered in the most amazing way. At that point it seemed clear that phase one had ended and we geared up for phase two—the establishment of Bible training facilities. With high, lofty, and noble ideas I removed the camp to begin the next course of action. The tragedy was that I could find nobody to run my camp in my absence and was consequently forced to abandon it temporarily, or so I thought.

The greatest tragedy was, having won such victory for and with the refugees, very few outsiders were prepared to respond to the cry for help. From the 1,200 videotapes sent out across America, we received only two replies and 180 dollars. It was very hard to swallow the callousness of a church so indifferent to the spiritual plight of multitudes. The valuable time taken in a failed effort to mobilize the Church saw the terrible events of Zaire where Hutus were slaughtered by the hundreds of thousands as well as the dissolution of the camps and the forced repatriation of Hutus to a sure holocaust in Rwanda. Those who escaped were further scattered in the nations. The opportunity to powerfully impact a nation with God's Word was forever lost.

I learned the unforgettable lesson that men cannot be bothered, even when the cry of the Spirit is resounding in their ears. The church is too busy with programs. It is no wonder that the Spirit finds it so very difficult to mobilize people who will stand in the gap. Anyone who wishes to be an intercessor can never be bound by any program but His. He can sound the rally call at any moment and needs instant obedience, for when the Holy Spirit does call, the situation is critical.

Despite the victories that *were* obtained, I ultimately failed in Rwanda. My aim and vision, which came from the Divine Director, was to so teach a people about love and reconciliation—both Hutus and Tutsis—that forgiveness would reign and peace would be restored in the land. Instead, Rwanda remains divided and under the rule of bitterness, fear, and hatred. The devil has, indeed, fully established himself in the nation, and most still have no idea why they are controlled by such powerful emotions and from where they come.

The result is that untold numbers have been slaughtered in a second genocide for which the West must be held fully responsible. *Time Magazine*, in a rare admission of real truth, previously declared, "If we stand idly by and do nothing, God will hold us accountable."

How true. In the final analysis, when God balances His books, many will be in debt over Rwanda, including some of His own people. In retrospect, I should have held the ground I had fought so hard to gain and persevered without the help that I knew I needed so badly. Such a lesson in intercession may never be forgotten and neither will the Spirit ever let it be. The agony of seeing an incomplete work is great. Even worse is the knowledge that multitudes needlessly perished without Jesus. Failure is not the Spirit's nor that of intercession but it is because I did not press on through to total victory.

The greatest lesson I learned from Rwanda is that the universal Church needs to raise up a team of "Delta Force" Christians who will be ready at any moment with all the necessary equipment to blitz crisis areas and situations as they arise. I marveled at the operation of the UN as they swept in with their army of workers and their vast array of equipment and supplies. I realized that the Church has the means and wherewithal to mount similar strategies but lacks the vigor of cooperation because of fear and pride. Leaders are afraid that they will not be recognized and cannot individually seize the credit. The primary purpose of such a task force must essentially be to preach the Gospel and not get so totally caught up in the "social gospel" that they lose their focus.

Global crisis situations are multiplying annually and offer unprecedented opportunities to reach multitudes—who would never normally be reached—because they are thrown together by famine, war, or genocide. Above all, the Church must never disqualify itself by "taking sides." The love of Jesus is for all.

CHAPTER TWENTY-FOUR

Botswana

Missionaries and Christians in different nations are doing the work assigned them to the best of their understanding and ability. Most, however, know little to nothing about intercession—with the result being that they merely hold their own rather than making inroads into the enemy's territory. Only when the Church embarks on an aggressive offensive will she be triumphant, alive, and well. This is how the Lord purposed us to continuously operate. The Holy Spirit declared one day, "I want you to hold some crusades in Botswana. The land is going backwards spiritually, and it is a strategic nation."

This semi-desert and desert land has become exceptionally wealthy through diamonds, beef, and tourism. It has a very small population, which is relatively well-to-do, and finances are squandered by individuals on alcohol and other vices. The land was evangelized by Robert Moffat and his son-in-law David Livingstone, in powerful, sacrificial work—a legacy that the Holy Spirit never forgets.

As an intercessor, I firmly believe that Gospel crusades must be more than just a series of meetings. They must be the initial fire to establish an ongoing strategy for not only winning the lost but also establishing Kingdom living and principles. I believe in total *transformation* by the Gospel and the *order* that the Lord brings through it. This is of extreme importance in a continent like Africa where there are such roots of witchcraft, fear, and confusion. The Gospel must be seen to work in our whole *lives*, and I attest emphatically to its prosperous message. How could I not, having experienced and written of the mighty power and moves of God?

So, from Rwanda in central Africa, to Botswana in southern Africa, we again packed the truck for another African adventure under the direction of the Holy Spirit. I simply cannot undertake crusades or any other type of mission work just for the sake of doing something—He *must* be the Director. And when He is, there will be success. Success cannot be measured by man's standard, but by the Holy Spirit's criterion, which often is not seen by the natural eye.

The advance team met with instant opposition.

"Who are you?" the pastors of Gaborone, the capital city, questioned arrogantly. "We are accustomed to having Pastor So-and-So and Pastor So-and-So here. Last time Pastor So-and-So was here, he spent $60,000 on advertising alone. Five thousand people came. How much do you have?"

Very discouraged, the team was finally told, "We don't think that we really want you, as we already have our program."

But God had everything under control as always. Away in Molepolole, the largest village of Botswana, a small group had been praying for two years that someone would come and hold a crusade. There were a few struggling churches in the village. The chairman of the pastors group heard of the advance team and sent a representative to beg the team to travel there "for discussions." He pressed upon them the fact that never in the entire history of Molepolole had there ever been a crusade.

The Spirit was moving as only He is able and set in motion a crusade for the biggest village in Botswana, with over 60,000 people. Together with surrounding satellite villages, there were over 100,000 from whom to draw. People ridiculed that even when the president of Botswana visited Molepolole barely 2,000 people turned out to greet him; and they were mostly school children under obligation.

However, this was an altogether different situation, and it was not the president of Botswana but the King of Kings. I was very confident that we would enjoy success, as I was under a Divine Directive. The results were His. Furthermore, there had been continuous intercession for four months, specifically that the Lord would show His mighty hand with spectacular signs, wonders, and miracles. We had shaken the heavens and travailed for Botswana that the Lord would turn the land and stop the drunkenness and sin that had come with wealth.

Everything was set for the first night, and people flocked from every quarter. There were some significant factors that revealed the mighty hand of the Lord in operation. It was the first time in several years that there had been good rains. That meant bumper crops in a desert land. Also, it was the school holidays, and most children had gone home. Families were busy reaping and could spare little time to attend a crusade. Furthermore, the distance from the satellite villages is great so that people could afford to attend for only an evening or two at most.

Yet people came in response to the prompting of the blessed Holy Spirit. From the first night, there were over 5,000 in attendance and hundreds came to receive Jesus. Each night the Spirit focused on a specific area of healing, the first being eyes. Dozens of people came forward and received healing and wholeness for cataracts, blindness, shortsightedness, and other eye ailments. One elderly lady declared, "Once I was blind, but now I can see," and proceeded to point out landmarks way in the distance, beyond the stadium walls, and in the dark at that!

People rushed back to their villages to tell family and friends of the miracles, and each night the numbers swelled. People were saved, healed, and set free. They sang the crusade choruses as they worked in their fields, reaping their crops. One man attended in a wheelchair. He was totally bound and gnarled spiritually, mentally, and physically. The Word of the Lord was that if he would attend every night and come under the power of the anointed Word, God would deliver him and raise him from his chair. Each night as he faithfully attended, God worked a little more in his life to the extent that he received Jesus and was praising him with uplifted hands. A total transformation had taken place within, but when we were about to see him raised from his chair, he came no more and we heard nothing of him.

I prayed for a lady who was so crippled with elephantiasis that she could hardly walk. Three days later she bounced up to me declaring, "I'm healed! I'm healed!" Her legs and feet were normal. News began to pour in from all across the country that people wanted to come as they heard of the wonderful works of God.

Most spectacular of all was a young teenager who had been saved by the work of the pre-crusade team and who badly wanted to attend the crusade. She lived with her aunt on the far western border of Botswana across the Kalahari Desert. The aunt insisted that her niece return home to help reap crops; whereupon the girl nagged and nagged until her aunt agreed to take her to the crusade for two nights whilst she, herself, completed some business in the capital. Upon crossing the desert, the woman skidded, rolled, and totaled her pickup and ended in the hospital with multiple breaks and fractures. The girl was unscathed as the hand of the Lord was upon her and protected her. Having seen her aunt settled in hospital with a plaster cast from waist to ankles, the girl rushed to the crusade and came up for prayer. She did not declare the problem but quietly cried out to the Lord for a complete miracle for her aunt.

"I felt something like electric waves flow all over me as the man laid hands upon me and prayed," she later testified. "The presence of God was so real that I just knew He was touching my aunt. Next morning, I rushed to Gaborone to speak to her. She declared that she, too, had experienced similar waves flowing through her and felt totally healed."

Thereupon, the girl insisted that her aunt be cut from the plaster. After much persuasion, the doctor agreed. The woman leapt up and began rushing up and down, totally healed. As the Lord promised, He was confirming His Word with signs following. In fact, so wonderfully was the Spirit working that news reached the President about the events that were taking place.

A certain well-driller, whose work was famous because he always struck water after prayer, was called in to drill some wells on a ranch belonging to the president of Botswana. The men were old friends. Before commencing his work, he attended the crusade as the friend and guest of our Botswana host and witnessed the miracles firsthand. Later, whilst in the process of drilling, the President arrived for a weekend of hunting. Over dinner one evening, his excellency began to share how he had been receiving reports of "a certain crusade in Molepolole and amazing things that are happening there."

"Do you know anything, Roy?" he questioned.

"Well, what have you heard?" replied Roy.

"There have been many miracles and healings, and Molepolole is changing," declared the President.

"Yes, it's true," confirmed Roy. "I've been there and seen for myself. In fact, I have just come from there."

With that, Roy was able to share what God was doing and the tremendous impact it was having upon the village—where the police were suddenly out of work for the drastic drop in crime.

"That's what I want for this whole nation," summed up the President. "We need that. We must have more."

The testimonies spread like fire, and invitations poured in from every quarter of Botswana for me to hold crusades. The heavens had been opened.

"Never has Botswana seen such power and experienced such dramatic things," emphasized one leading pastor. "I have been to every crusade in the land and never has there been one such as this."

The Spirit was, once again, moving in response to the travail of His people and answering accordingly. Jesus was being exalted as Lord over the nation, and another strategy of the Lord was established in the spiritual realm as the devil was being conquered yet again.

CHAPTER TWENTY-FIVE

Slavery

S LAVERY WAS INSTITUTED by satan in the Garden of Eden and has woven a long and evil trail through the history of man. Spiritual bondage and slavery has always bred the natural counterpart. It is for this reason that people in different places of the world live under slavery one generation after another. Prince demons and fallen angels have manipulated and controlled whole areas and geographical regions for millennia, enslaving entire nations under tyrannies and wicked dictatorships, whose excesses have known no limits.

The Middle East, for instance, has been bound by the satanic princes of Persia from even before the illustrious Daniel—perhaps since the expulsion of satan from Eden. Those same princes continue to affect policy, and I believe, raise up leaders of *their* evil nature even today. Tyrants enslave the people at will, and the overthrow of one sees the rise of another more wicked.

Often, not even the Judeo-Christian teachings, which enjoin tolerance and respect for humanity created in the image of God, is sufficient to prevent the rise of evil men under the control of such manipulating spirits. The evidence of Hitler in a Protestant Germany is a clear example, and I have no doubt that the "beast" of Revelation is a nation, in fact, perhaps the nation of Germany. Out of the beast will come the antichrist himself and he, like Nimrod of so long ago, will both need and have the support of a worldwide religious system to give him legitimacy. That system is the false religion of another leader, the false prophet.

The very word *slavery* conjures up images of the Deep South in the pre-Civil War era of the United States, with all the guilt and mixed emotions that go with it. Such slavery is an abomination. Most people are totally ignorant of the history of that slavery. The perpetrators of it are the same perpetrators of a worldwide slavery that still flourishes today, the ugliness of which will emerge in all its fullness in the years ahead.

I am amazed that African-Americans are seduced by Islam and are joining its ranks in vast numbers, when it is a known fact that it was both black Africans and Moslems who enslaved their ancestors and sold them to America. Just as many slaves were shipped to the Middle and Far East as to the American South. The difference was that in America the slaves were allowed to live, whereas in the east, they were slaughtered after their usefulness had ended.

The Koran specifically encourages and blesses slavery, which it says should be practiced against all peoples except Moslems who "are the best peoples evolved for mankind…" (Surah 3:110).

According to biblical Law, God instituted slavery amongst the Israelites in Exodus 21:5-6, but that was a slavery altogether different than what I have been describing. *"And if the servant shall plainly say, I love my master, my wife, and my children; I will not go free: Then his master shall bring him unto the judges; he shall, also bring him to the door, or unto the door post; and his master shall bore his ear through with an aul; and he shall serve him for ever."* God's slavery is the "love slave," which is the type of relationship He purposes us to enjoy with Him.

In the volumes of hatred and criticism gushing forth against slavery and its evils, most have forgotten that there was a whole army of people who worked tirelessly against this blight on mankind. Perhaps one of the most powerful intercessions presented to God was for the abolition of the slave trade, and then, of slavery itself. There was the great philanthropist, William Wilberforce, and his mighty band of "Little Englanders" who gave themselves unceasingly for almost 50 years to the abolition of slavery. So great were their efforts that they purchased a suburb outside London so that they could live in a village community, thereby combining their forces to fight for the cause of the freedom of slaves first in the British Empire and then worldwide.

Most were powerful Christians spurred on by their love for the Lord and compassion for their fellow man. They were wealthy men, and each poured their own wealth into the cause of abolition year after year until victory was accomplished. In Africa, there was the notable work of David Livingstone who wrote describing the great evils of the system as he traveled throughout the mysterious "Dark Continent." With his powerful ally, Queen Victoria, Britain was steered into taking on responsibilities in Africa of which she never intended. This was done purely for the purpose of stamping out slavery and the horrid trade. General Charles Gordon of Khartoum was the most famous anti-slaver and did more to publicize and eradicate the trade in Africa especially by Moslems than anyone else. He is most noted for his brave stand in Sudan and ultimate death in Khartoum at the hands of Moslem extremists. Slavery acknowledges no color and neither is it a race matter; it is a sin issue.

One of the saddest things that faces the continent of Africa in *lieu* of the price paid to set Africa free, is a voluntary return to the slavery from which it has been freed. The reason for modern enslavement with all of its chains and whips just as before is because men have lost the initiative for freedom that their forefathers fought so hard to obtain. Today, in a case of "willing choice," it has become expedient to accept the bondage of slavery once again. Africans are selling themselves for a few pieces of silver, and *religion* has become their Judas.

Malawi, for instance, is termed a "Christian" country. And yet, this "Christian" country recently elected a Moslem president because of the promise of wealth and so-called freedom from the slavery of the "hated West." The economy of Malawi is completely in the hands of a mere 4,000 Moslem Asians whose business ethics are totally corrupt. Malawians, greedy for personal gain and riches, have sold themselves and their nation to the highest bidder.

Many years ago Malawi was annexed to Britain as part of its colonial Empire. There are no natural resources in the nation to have made it of any benefit to the British crown. However, Nyasaland, as it was then known, was a major focal point of the Arab slave trade for the entire interior of Central Africa. Slaves would be brought for shipment up or down Lake Nyasa and from there to the Indian Ocean. The reports of David Livingstone so stirred Queen Victoria that she pressured the British Government into annexing this portion of "no good real estate" to the Crown for the sole purpose of stamping out the Arab slave trade. Later, the same thing was to happen in Sudan. Today, we find yet again, that Malawians are once more slaves of the Moslems in a well-orchestrated plan of satan to enslave the whole world through Islamic *jihad*.

Oh, the price to set men free from every area of slavery has been enormous. The travail and agony of some intercessors, who captured the heartbeat of God and saw through the eye of the Spirit the desire of the Almighty for men to live free so as to worship Him, has been costly. Jesus, Himself, the greatest intercessor, paid the ultimate price to set the entire human race free from the tyranny of sin and the shackles of the devil who hates men. And still, men love to return to the chains and prisons of that slavery, which is so torturous and robs them of their dignity.

Perhaps the worst form of slavery is *religion*, which makes false promises and presents false hopes to men who are manipulated by its systems, seduced by its vain ritual and captivated by its myths and mysteries. Religion is the greatest robber of relationship with God. This is precisely what the enemy of our souls desires and what he purposes to use in these last days as he seeks to establish a worldwide ecumenical movement, which will embrace all persuasions in one great brotherhood similar to that which defied God on the plains of Shinar so long ago. It is this affront to the Lord, Himself, which will finally bring down His ultimate wrath on rebellious man.

This is slavery, most arrogant and rebellious, when men defy the living God and choose the prison of darkness rather than the freedom of His glorious light. All religious forms are slavery, whether bowing to an idol in India in the hope of pleasing some grotesque deity, prostrating in fear before Allah in a Moslem mosque, or the burden of penance from some priest when confession to *Christ* brings forgiveness. By the testimony of Islam's own Koran, Allah is portrayed as a deceiver, murderer, and torturer and is unjust and unfair. He gives no assurance of any eternal destination in paradise *except* if a Moslem dies a martyr's death fighting any non-Moslem in Allah's cause. What slavery! In the same way, a Roman Catholic spends much of his life seeking to please God and living in fear of excommunication and purgatory. What slavery too! There is no difference in any of these three examples.

We know that the devil is going around *as* a roaring lion seeking who he may devour, for he knows he has a short time to live. The world is about to see the greatest expression of slavery since time began. If ever there is a need for intercession to open the eyes of men to that which is coming, this is the hour before the worldwide holocaust descends and sweeps literally billions into deeper slavery. Freedom is only in Jesus for He declared, *"If the Son therefore shall make you free, ye shall be free indeed"* (John 8:36).

The world is on the verge of religious and physical slavery, the likes of which has never been seen. Nothing can stop what is coming, but intercession will prepare a remnant of uncompromising martyrs who will raise the standard of the Lord and give hope and courage to the faint of heart who will find it difficult to stand. Men everywhere are selling themselves for money and to get rich quickly. At the same time, because man is a spiritual creature, albeit a rebellious one, he will seek comfort in a religious system that *demands conformity*, for in conformity there is unity. The slavery of the next system that is going to sweep this planet is absolutely diabolic and will impact every person on earth in one way or another. The stage is set, and the players are in the wings ready for their cue.

CHAPTER TWENTY-SIX

The Islamic Advance

A S THE SANDS OF THIS dispensation finally run out in the hour-glass, the most sinister and diabolic system of all time has already been launched by the devil, though it is not yet recognized by most men. Very few Christians, too, have realized that which is taking place on a global expanse. This system will cause communism to fade into nothingness by comparison. Its evils are much greater because it embraces all the wicked characteristics of every other "ism" and, being a religious movement, is far more fanatical.

This last Machiavellian move by satan is going to require for its defeat the greatest number of Christian martyrs ever to have marched. Global spiritual warfare is about to be launched on an unprecedented scale. What is needed is the largest army of intercessors ever to have been mobilized. From secret meetings in their jaded palaces of Saudi Arabia to the frenzied verbal attacks by Imams at Friday prayers in their mosques in London, from the secret brotherhood of fundamentalist Moslems seeking to restore order in South Africa to the excesses of the fanatical Hizballah in Lebanon and Iran, from the ranting of presiden-tial maniacs in Sudan, Libya, and Iraq to the combined consciousness of the millions gathered in Mecca for the hajj, their one objective is to overthrow and annihilate the terrible infidel. For the infidel, the only escape is to convert and say the Shahada (testimony) or suffer imprison-ment, beatings, torture, and final beheading or crucifixion—all of which are required by the Koran.

The greatest threat to Christendom in 2,000 years is going to prove the manifestation of her greatest Glory, culminating in the coming of the King of Glory. The victory, whilst assured, will not come without unprecedented suffering and carnage that will make the Emperor Nero look as if he were playing games. The concentrated hatred and anger of such vast multitudes is the sinister operation of the devil in his last ditch attempt to wrest this planet from God. He knows this to be an impossibility hence the fury of his rage, but at the same time, the exposure of His designs.

Islam has the oil wealth, the infrastructure, and the fanaticism to take on the world and win. The Islamic invasion has begun with the objective of converting the West to Islam. What most people do not realize is that to accept Islam in any form is to accept the controlling devils of the system. Those spirits are the strongest of the Middle Eastern princes of darkness. They have ruled for millennia through the kingdoms of Persia and Babylon with all their accompanying wicked excesses typically characteristic of satan. Allah is not God but, precisely, is one of those wicked Princes.

It is providential that the last arena of battle will be a complete circle back to the site of Eden. Moslems are required to follow the patterns that Allah has revealed in the Koran thereby making them deceivers, murderers, and torturers of non-Moslems. They are encouraged to be unjust and unfair without the slightest sense of guilt; and any Moslem who believes in Jesus must be persecuted, tortured, and killed in the most brutal way.

The five pillars of Islam are a pathetic attempt to copy the Old Testament Law but without the accompanying atonement. Every Moslem must declare the Shahada, pray five times a day, fast the month of Ramadan, give alms (called *Zakaht*), and undertake the pilgrimage (*hajj*) to Mecca. The Koran contradicts every teaching of Christ thereby making it impossible for Allah to be God. Christ is God in the flesh. Moslems are absolutely forbidden to befriend Jews or Christians on the penalty of death. How ludicrous, then, for the West to spend so much effort, time, and finances fighting for countries such as Kuwait except there be ulterior motives.

Islam is the fastest growing religion on planet earth today. With petrodollars and international financing, the Moslem states are able and willing to fund their cause for international Islamic control. In December 1982, the Iranian president, Ali Khamenei spelled out the *modus operandi* for a spiritually cleansing worldwide Islamic "crusade," when he instructed Imams from 40 Moslem countries to turn their mosques into "prayer, political, cultural, and *military* bases" and to "prepare the ground for the creation of Islamic governments in *all* countries."

There is no doubt that the northern confederacy of Ezekiel 38 and 39 against Israel is the ultimate *jihad* of Islamic fundamentalism and Russian Orthodox traditionalism, which also hates the Jews. That such hatred in Russia is so strong that Orthodoxy would go as far as to form an alliance with Islam for the annihilation of Israel is amazing yet true.

With its mysticism, discipline, and fear, Islam is attracting unprecedented numbers of converts. Moslems, too, believing in the concept of four wives, are encouraged to procreate for Allah to the extent that they have the fastest growing population in the world. In less than 50 years, Iran alone is boasting of over a billion people. Because of the nature of the ruling spirits, Moslems, especially their men, have the strongest seducing demons, which they use to entice, capture, and enslave particularly Western women. The conquest of such women is thought to be of particular honor to Allah. Young Moslem men are infiltrating Western universities, leading captive "silly" Western girls and spoiling them or enslaving them as wives forever.

The Koran teaches that men are superior to women, who receive only half the inheritance of their male counterparts. Women are unclean beings and are considered chattels of men who may divorce them by mere declaration. It is believed that women should be beaten, and their testimony in court is only half that of a man. From such wicked bondage, Christ came to set us free.

In a book on intercession, it is not my intention to fully describe the evils of Islam, for it would take an entire volume alone. The West, however, is asleep, is drunk on the opiate of the devil's strongest draft of seduction and is complacent and uncaring. The great wars to keep Islam out of Europe have been relegated to history textbooks, and now, Christendom has thrown wide her doors and embraced multitudes who are enslaved to the evil and are working day and night to enslave others.

The only answer to this final move of satan is intercession—intercession that will touch Heaven and open the eyes of man, even Moslems, to the truth of this diabolic religion, intercession that will manifest the Glorified Christ, and intercession that will raise up true harvesters for the Moslem fields that are white for reaping. Never have there been such opportunities to do such great things for God as the times in which we live. The battle is fully on earth, and the enemy has pulled out all the stops. It is time for the Church to rise up and begin to march against what I believe is the last onslaught. To conscript, train, and motivate an army of believers is going to require hard, very hard intercession, for those same princes of Persia are going to stand in the way of every development as they did to Daniel. Nevertheless, we will ultimately win.

It is time for us all to be discerning the season in God's calendar. It simply cannot be "business as usual," for the Spirit has sounded the trumpet for the beginning of a new season, perhaps the last in this dispensation.

The angel of Revelation 14:18 is commanded to *"thrust in thy sickle and reap: for the time is come for thee to reap; for the harvest of the earth is ripe."*

Argentine missionary, Luis Bush coined the phrase "10/40 Window" because between the 10th and 40th latitudes are the concentrated masses of almost every major non-Christian religion with some 95 percent of the world's unreached peoples. Since we are commanded to reach the lost and the lost lie concentrated in this area of particularly strong demonic powers, it means that the warfare is going to be intense because the enemy aims to maintain his territorial control over such a vast population. There is a divine strategy for assailing satan's Jericho, and it is imperative to ascertain that strategy and to operate in it. Frighteningly only *one percent* of the entire global mission force—or less than 3,000 workers—were dedicated to that area at the beginning of 1990. If we are serious about the Great Commission to "every creature," then there needs to be a re-deployment of personnel, energies, efforts, and finances.

The needs are enormous, but attitudes must change. We are living in the most momentous times of change and the season of ultimate fruitfulness. We need, as the tribe of Issachar of old, to be men who have *"understanding of the **times** to know what Israel ought to do"* (1 Chron. 12:32). The word "times" means to "advance, pass on or continue to the fullness of fruiting." The Hebrew is similar to the Greek *kairos*, which is "the fullness of ripening."

Isaiah's watchmen simply must be discerners of the seasons. A season in Scripture is the time taken for the fullness of the ripening of the fruit, and God's calendar, both natural and prophetic, is made up of seasons. We are in the season of the fullness of ripening, and it is time for men to listen to mature intercessors who are well able to tell the Church of what is going to happen because they have been on the rooftop and watched.

"Watchman, what of the night?" (Isa. 21:11), declares the prophet. The answer is tremendously victorious: *"Babylon is fallen!"* (Isa. 21:9). What a powerfully prophetic word for this hour when maniacs like Saddam Hussein are rebuilding the city that is an affront to God and planning to reinstitute the complete Babylonian system. The system is more than the city, for the system was brought down to earth and introduced to men by the fallen lucifer. It is contrary to everything that God has ever purposed for man especially in their relationship with Him.

The Babylonian system is the basis for all civil, military, and religious forms of government and adopts the "pyramid pattern" or "papal-type" structure with its authoritarian headship through which all decision-making must pass. God developed the hierarchy for His angels, not man, whom He ordained to enjoy an immensely personal *relationship* with Himself without a third party being involved. The Babylonian system is ultimate manipulation and control, which breeds fear and indecision. It was effectively used by Nimrod, but we know God's verdict on the matter when it culminated in the babbling of men. What a judgment on that which He did not approve, yet men in their consistent rebellion still return to that Babylonian system.

Babylon is fallen and though there will be a holocaust before its ultimate demise, the eye of faith looks upon the great victory parade of all time. The coming of Jesus, the true Lion King, in the clouds of Glory so that every eye shall see Him and every tongue shall confess Him as Lord and every knee shall bow to Him alone, will be the introduction of the rule of the Lord across the whole earth.

I have embarked in serious intercession for this last, end-time assault on the planet. First, an awakening and an awareness is required amongst God's people as to what is really taking place. I believe that there is ruling fear that causes people to ignore the truth because they cannot face the problem. Like the proverbial ostrich, men would rather bury their heads in the sand and pretend that there is no issue than deal with it. The cry and desire for revival that is beginning to touch the Church will bear no fruit until there is a *wail of repentance*. Only then will men be truly equipped to take on this last of giants. We can fill volumes with statistics to prove our point that the Church is expanding, but the ultimate standard is the fruit we see on the ground. I see that fruit as pathetically sparse at this time. It will change in both size and quality.

Second, there needs to be great compassion for those who are already enslaved in bondage. All too often, we become emotionally stirred against the people rather than the ruling principalities.

Finally, circumstances demand a concerted onslaught be launched against the powers of darkness for the release of those who wish to change but *are* enslaved. The cry of the Spirit is the same as His cry for Israel in their Egyptian bondage, *"Let My people go, that they may serve Me"* (Exod. 8:1).

There were also many Egyptians who wanted freedom from the enslavement that they had imposed upon themselves too, and Moses' confrontation with Pharaoh spelled *their* release. The cry of "let My people go" is going to grow louder and louder as it gains momentum and reverberates around the world until it becomes one voice so loud that Heaven must take note and intervene. It will be at that time that the voice from Heaven will declare, "Come up here…" and the snatching away will occur so that we will meet the returning Lord in the air whilst His wrath is being poured out upon the rebellious earth.

The battle is already intense, and the devil bombards with volley upon volley of missiles directed against both men and equipment. We are assailed from without and attacked from within. He seeks to divide and rule through the weaknesses of the flesh and the greed and ambition of people. Since embarking on this greatest assignment of intercession, equipment has broken down, vehicles have stopped running, and some staff have acted irrationally. The enemy has robbed us, raised up voices against us, and sought to change our attention and focus thereby making us ineffective. But, above every tactic of the enemy, there remains the cry of the slaves of this world who long to be free. Their sigh and travail *must* be flavored with our intercessions and carried to the Throne of His deliverance so that they might be liberated.

I will never forget sitting at Cairo Airport when a Moslem family came and sat beside me. The woman was totally covered with a veil and even wore gloves so that her hands were not exposed. Her husband bought her a drink, which she took beneath her veil and began to sip with obvious difficulty. The anger and indignation of the Lord rose up inside me. I felt like tearing that veil from her face and declaring her free. Naturally, such an act would have been foolish and landed me in prison, but the Holy Spirit impacted me that moment and impressed upon me the wickedness of the slavery perpetrated against His creation. Such an indelible mark was made that I determined to crusade with the Spirit to end such a violation of freedom. Even today, my blood boils when I see such a veil for it symbolizes ultimate bondage for which Christ died to liberate every woman. The fight is tough, but I will not give up until victory is assured no matter how high the price. And victory is as sure as Christ rising from the dead to live forever.

Intercession has now become a true issue of international strategy for the freedom to evangelize not only the *10/40 window* but all the world in accordance with the Great Commission. Doors are rapidly closing in nation after nation, as they have done in Russia and will elsewhere, as the devil inspires men to oppose the Gospel. One of the major focuses of intercession is to ensure that the enemy does not precipitate world events before their time, thereby, frustrating the great harvest that is to come. The reason that God has chosen to work in partnership with men remains a mystery, but nevertheless is true. The power of the devil in men who have chosen to be his instruments is in direct conflict with the power of the Holy Spirit especially as He is working through His intercessors.

CHAPTER TWENTY-SEVEN

School of Intercession

INTERCESSORS, LIKE MISSIONARIES, are not born but they are *made*. As I carefully analyze the ministry of the Lord Jesus to His disciples, I realize that during three-and-a-half years of intensive training, He was molding them into a band of mighty intercessors in his "mobile" school. They loved Jesus, respected Him, and feared Him as He rooted out, broke down, built up, and established their lives once again but on a totally different standard with totally different goals and visions. Perhaps the greatest work Jesus was achieving in His disciples was the death of selfishness as He formed a team of men whose only purpose was *His* purpose and the only Kingdom they desired to build was the Kingdom of Heaven. Even then, one of them was a failure. Judas failed because he would not let go of his personal ambition and everything that went with it. Actually, in the eyes of the world today, they all would be failures, though in actual fact, they are the most successful band of men who has ever been joined together.

The Holy Spirit spoke to me expressly concerning the training of men and women for the ministry of intercession. "I want you," He emphasized, "to raise up and train a company of real intercessors who will carry My burdens and allow Me to live My life through them."

I was up against what I thought to be a big problem and one with which I needed to deal. Under the culture and traditions of Africa and the propensity of the natives to be manipulated and controlled by public opinion, how was the Holy Spirit going to take lives and change them? Even whilst I thought on the issue, He spoke and declared, *"Am*

I not big enough? Was it not I who inspired, 'There is neither Jew nor Greek' (Gal. 3:28). "If I am able to change a Jew or a Greek, can I not change anyone?"

"I suppose You can," I mumbled, yet again amazed at how He read my thoughts.

"Well then, you do your part, and I will take care of the rest. I am already working through *you* to touch many, and I will work through you to touch them too."

I saw the necessity of an "attack force," not simply for the ministry with which I was involved, but to make national and international impact. I would be taking raw people who knew nothing of either the ways of the Spirit or even the ways of the devil and training them into a well-equipped fighting team. For many years, I have seen that one of the greatest failures of most Bible colleges is that the students never get an opportunity to see Christ "lived out" on a daily basis in the staff. Most staff members merely teach during the morning at their respective schools, and that's all the student sees, yet Jesus was with His disciples 24 hours a day, 365 days a year, for three-and-a-half years. If Jesus insisted on such intensive training, how do we think that we can get by with any less?

The purpose of such a team was to be for warfare, taking on any issue anywhere that was preventing the glorious message of salvation from going forth. The entire lives of both staff and students was to be totally surrendered and lived for "every creature" and not self. Tribalism, regionalism, and nationalism, which are so strong in Africa, had to be broken down and a people "created" who would stand for identity with the King alone. The Holy Spirit had wonderfully worked much deliverance and freedom in me, and I knew He would do the same for others. I little knew just how tough it was going to be and just how high the failure rate was going to prove. I guess that, once again, I would never have started had I known such things from the beginning.

Perhaps the greatest problem that wreaked havoc in the school from almost the outset was precisely the issue of tribalism. This strong force in Africa is very central to everyone, and it seeped into every area of life at the school. I saw just how the enemy was going to use such a thing to destroy the purposes of the Holy Spirit. If I could not get a team together on the home front, however was I going to prepare a platoon to take on the enemy nationally and internationally?

I appealed to every noble sentiment in the students but to absolutely no avail. Actually, it was very frightening to see just how stubborn people can become once their flesh is really touched, and it was touched by a myriad of things on a daily basis, from food to sleeping arrangements to seating positions to blessings. Even when staff would praise a student, it would be carnalized into "tribal preference." The enemy threw every dirty tactic into the fray, and I saw that a victory for him was a defeat for the Great Commission and the salvation of multitudes to the ends of the earth.

It was a matter for real intercession, and I was reminded again how the enemy used sin from within to defeat Israel so many times. The situation I faced in the school was a definite case of "sin from within," and I saw that it would only be a visitation from the Holy Spirit Himself that would be the turning point. He alone would bring the deeply needed conviction of self that would break the stronghold of tribalism and set the captives free. I fasted and prayed and, together with the staff, took the matter before the Throne. Relating the details of the problems would not glorify the Lord, but suffice it to say that He brought the whole school to a major breaking point after almost 15 months of strong crying out to Him.

It was a decidedly tough battle, and I saw that the enemy did not want to lose an inch of territory. Some of the students even stirred up their local pastors until there was a case of false charges before the government. The victory of the enemy in the matter would have meant instant expulsion from the country. It was time for serious fasting yet again as we were called to answer before the highest authorities in the land. The fight was intense and continued day after day. It seemed as if the enemy had won when a missionary couple who had been with me for 14 years went over to the devil's camp and allowed themselves to be used by him. What was particularly disturbing was that they knew the most intimate details of the ministry and used such knowledge against both me and the work. Things looked very bleak and actually turned bleaker with each succeeding day. There seemed no respite.

The enemy fired volley after volley against us as I continued to take my stand against him. I was actually fighting for something much larger than I realized, namely a force that could move through Africa. With the support of the defected missionaries, the militant faction of students who had taken matters into their own hands thought that they had fired the winning shots. During those months I saw small victories that gave the assurance that, indeed, the Holy Spirit was working. Individuals would come under deep conviction followed by repentance, but I sought for the complete work that would touch the whole school and transform it.

One point that needs mentioning is that there was also division and jealousy between the employed native staff and the students. This is significant, for the real intercessors were to be found amongst the former. Though not students, most began to hunger for the deeper things of the Lord as they availed themselves of opportunities to attend teachings and daily prayers. Many began to change, but again, it was the general transformation for which I travailed. The enemy was not going to win. I was not going to let him gain any territory, and I stood on the promises of the Holy Spirit that He would move. And, move He did.

I decided to throw the devil into disarray and went on the offensive, as I had nothing to hide. Instead of dealing with any minor official, we went directly to the top and presented the case before the secretary to the President. The whole situation was laid bare upon the table. One thing about the devil is that he cannot work in the light and truth. The moment he was unable to cloud issues and bring confusion, he was exposed. There was nothing to hide as we presented all the relative evidence. The devil wanted me out of the land and knew that if he could sever the head, the body, too, would die. The secretary was an absolute gentleman and saw the real issues immediately. Far from being commanded to leave the country, the Holy Spirit turned evil to good and defeat to victory as the secretary promised to present the case to the President himself and to recommend that we receive an official status *of our own* by being incorporated. This would be an incredible miracle as no incorporation was permitted by Presidential decree. This meant that the President himself would have to circumvent his own decree. It was a test case of whether the Holy Spirit could change the hand of an Ahasuerus for it was definitely a situation of the law of the "Medes and Persians."

"Is there anything too hard for Me?" He challenged.

"Not at all," I agreed as He spoke clearly one day.

"Well, the battle will continue to be fierce and that, for quite some time."

"Oh, no!" I groaned. "I don't know how much more I can take."

"Paul was buffeted by some strong spirits all his life," He proffered, "and he came through. I was with him, and Jesus was sufficient for him."

"And You'll be with me too?"

"I'm here 'til Jesus returns," I heard Him distinctly chuckle as He interrupted. "I will never leave you and will be beside you to direct you."

Continued fasting and intercession went on for many months, during which time the enemy attempted time and again to assail our fortress. Africa is very fluid, and changes tomorrow can derail every plan. A secretary can be out of favor instantly at the whim of a president with the result that a case ends up dormant. A president himself might be overthrown, and policies and people change instantly. The power of intercession, however, kept the secretary in his seat and the President upon his throne. The news of great victory came when a certificate of incorporation, signed by the President himself, was awarded us. This certificate is really awarded by the Holy Spirit Himself in answer to concerted intercession for the greater purpose of Heaven.

It took three years before the hand of Ahasuerus was prevailed upon to change his own decree for a brief moment so that Heaven would be assured another victory. I will never know all of the natural events that went into granting the incorporation. But, one thing is certain. Yet again, man had to bow to the sovereignty of God, and natural law had to submit to the higher authority of a greater Kingdom. Four years later, the very missionaries who had conspired against the work of the Holy Spirit through us, were themselves expelled from the country together with others who had joined league with them. What a vindication and victory over the enemy. His routing was total, and after years of intense battle, victory was very sweet though we can never rejoice in the misfortune of others.

Above all, the greatest victory was the visitation of the Holy Ghost. He did not come all at once, for to have done so would have been too much for most. He came initially in great convicting power and so totally broke the hearts of the students that they were changed. Some staff had begun to see the situation as "hopeless" and often quoted the lepers outside of the gates of Jerusalem, *"Why sit we here until we die?"* (2 Kings 7:3).

Well, that is precisely what the Spirit intended. It was a morning I shall not forget. Each day at the mission is started with corporate devotions and prayers. There was nothing out of the ordinary that particular morning. We had gathered for only a short while when the conviction of the Holy Spirit fell heavily upon one of the young male students. There was a sudden electrification of the atmosphere, and without warning, the young man leapt up and began a wail that sent shivers down my back. I instantly recognized the situation for what it was. That was no mere emotional outburst but the very real dealing of the Spirit with a life that was not in tune.

The young man was in a great agony of soul and wailed for quite some time before he collapsed on the ground. His wailing subsided into moaning and weeping. The floor was bathed with his tears. Other students also came under conviction and began to weep and moan. There was great distress amongst many, and the situation continued for several hours. Eventually, the original young man was in such agony that we carried him to a room and laid him upon a bed. Most assuredly the Holy Spirit was at work in the student.

After several hours we adjourned to return later for normal classes. The presence of the Spirit was so awesome and near that I was unable to teach. I simply declared, "The Holy Spirit has not yet finished…"

That's all I was able to get out, for in an instant, the same young man who had then been sitting quietly at the back literally leapt into the air and collapsed on the floor once again. The Holy Spirit felt tangible and came upon one and all, both staff and students. Many of the students were being delivered, and as the work continued, the Holy Spirit drew in the other native staff like a vacuum sucking in the air. Everyone was being affected and a great cleansing was taking place. The Holy Spirit was so real and had assuredly come to fulfill His task of convicting of sin, righteousness, and judgment. What He was wanting were vessels through which He could both live and work to reach the multitudes of lost. We had often spoken and taught of demon possession, but this was an issue of Holy Spirit *possession*. He cannot dwell within unless He fully possesses and that dwelling is all upon His terms.

After His initial dealings, we were simply prostrate before Him. I found people literally walking tiptoe across the campus for fear of offending Him. A holy hush descended upon the place, and days were spent quietly meditating or in isolation. There could be no normal program under the circumstances. This was the enormous event for which I had sought the Lord and poured out my own heart.

The Spirit showed that there were going to be years of intense battle and what He required of each and everyone was *absolute* commitment to Him. Some were really not willing to make that commitment after weighing the price. With time, they moved on to other fields as the Holy Spirit sifted their hearts. It was very clear that the Spirit was seeking to build a dedicated, committed team. It was only about ten days that His visitation lasted but everything and everyone was affected by His abiding. Nobody would ever be the same again. He is greater than all our perceptions and understandings of Him. He transcends all things because He is the glorious Third Person of the Godhead. When we truly understand Him, we can only weep in repentance for having limited Him and quenched Him so many times before. He had come with Holy Fire to set a people both apart and ablaze for Him. He had sealed a corps of African intercessors for the main purpose of the Great Commission.

Most are simple men with simple understandings. Many are totally uneducated and cannot even sign their names, but with such things, the Holy Spirit is unconcerned. Some might build megachurches with tens of thousands, but the Holy Spirit was building a band, knitted together in love and passion and transparency. Of this team, I am also able to quote the high priest who, *"when they saw the boldness of Peter and John, and perceived that they were unlearned and ignorant men, they marveled; and they took knowledge of them, that they had been with Jesus"* (Acts 4:13).

Mechanics, cooks, gardeners, teachers, or general laborers amongst others are all called as part of the Holy Spirit's attack team to bind up the nobles and princes with fetters of iron so that the Gospel might go forth to the ends of the earth. There is no place on the face of the earth that is too tough for us to handle, for the battle is, indeed, the Lord's. The *greatest* battle, though, is that of yielding to the dictates of the Holy Spirit, for His commands are always contrary to both the understanding and desires of the flesh. The Spirit has called and commissioned a people whose lives are not their own but who have been willing to surrender personal ambition and even calling to His higher purpose.

In His call for total surrender, the Spirit has made individual demands that each has had to pay a personal price to answer. For some, it has been celibacy, for others the surrender of a career or even calling, whilst yet others have had to give up family and nation and comfort to fulfill His call. The rewards are immeasurable—above all is the stamp of His approval and the sure knowledge that I can make an impact upon this planet for time and eternity by being a yielded vessel for the Holy Spirit.

CHAPTER TWENTY-EIGHT

Sudan

I WANT YOU TO GO to Sudan," said the Holy Spirit. "I have a work for you there."

"Another war zone! That's the other end of Africa," I protested.

"Yes, correct. Look what I have done. If natural men can blaze a trail of Glory for wealth and power, then you can blaze a trail for the Kingdom," He revealed.

I immediately thought of Cecil Rhodes who had vowed to spread the British Empire from Cape Town to Cairo. He lived to see his dream realized as Britain swallowed up a string of colonies in a perfect line from south to north. I saw how prophetic it was that we had been interceding for Africa all the way, country by country, from south to north, and had actually traveled the whole length of it. At that time Sudan was the only nation on that route to which I had not been and where I had not preached the Gospel.

"Sudan is a gateway to the South," He revealed, "and it is all very well for men to fight in the natural, but it is the real enemy that must be defeated. Unless there is someone who will teach them, they will never be able to stand. Remember Rwanda?"

"Shall I ever forget!" I interjected.

Once again, He is the Spirit of Truth and nothing can be hid from Him.

"Of the *few* Christians who *are* going, most are seeking adventure," the Spirit revealed. "But I am looking for commitment without which I am able to do nothing. Prepare yourself," He concluded.

I was on the point of departure for ministry in the United States and thought that I could conveniently forget what the Holy Spirit had challenged, for a while, anyway. He has a way, however, of convicting and always reminding us of those things to which He has called us. Whilst ministering in Minneapolis, at the church of a dear friend, another precious pastor and his special wife arrived at the meeting. The Holy Ghost fell in all of His awesome presence as the meeting proceeded. Without even thinking about my conversation with the Holy Spirit, I walked over to the visiting couple and declared, "God wants you to go to Sudan!"

Those friends began to weep because the Spirit had been speaking to them about the matter. At the same time He did not even need to remind me about my unspoken promise. Together, we could feel the cry of a disheartened nation and a people who were reaching out for moral and spiritual support more than anything else. Jan and Tonnie Bosman covenanted to come to Sudan and admirably prepared for the journey, which would be a drive halfway up Africa. God was bringing them and using them to provoke me into action.

I was ready to go, but there was so much other ministry I had planned, including preparing for another major crusade in Botswana. It seemed that there would just never be time to go to Sudan. Jan and Tonnie decided to come to Africa anyway and willingly surrendered the nation into the Father's hands, knowing that He had called them and would make a way. The Spirit had everything under control. He was moving because all of a sudden the workload simply seemed to disappear, leaving time for a hectic trip some 6,000 miles up Africa and back.

Sudan is mentioned variously in the Bible as Cush, Ethiopia, or Nubia. In the prophecy of Isaiah 18, the land *"beyond the rivers of Ethiopia"* (Isa. 18:1) may well refer to southern Sudan, which has always been important for its slaves. Zephaniah declares, *"From beyond the rivers of Ethiopia My suppliants* [worshippers], *even the daughters of My dispersed, shall bring My offering"* (Zeph. 3:10). The Ethiopian eunuch in Acts was returning to the court of Queen Candace at Meroe from whence the Sudanese Kingdom of Cush was ruled. The conversion of that treasurer began the Church of Sudan way back in a.d. 37 whilst Islam came by the sword only 1,200 years later.

Modern Sudan is a travesty of colonialism, for it is really two nations in every sense. The south is equatorial rain forests whilst the north is essentially Sahara Desert. The people of the south are typically African in color, custom, and culture compared to those from Khartoum who are Arab. The official language of the south is English versus Arabic in the north. Finally, the religion of the south is Christian and Animist whilst in the north it is Islamic.

The untapped wealth of Sudan, including vast oil reserves, arc in the south, thereby, making it very difficult for any serious discussions on the independence of the south. More importantly, the introduction of *Shari'a,* or Islamic Law, to Sudan in 1983 legalizes the accompanying *jihad,* or holy war, against the Christians of the South. Such is nothing less than *genocide* on a grand scale, which goes on unchecked by the West for fear of offending the Arab nations who control oil, thus manipulating and ransoming the world with their petrodollar investments in international financing. The Northern Moslems have pillaged the South for centuries but particularly since independence in 1954. Consequently, the civil war that now rages and costs the Sudanese Government billions of dollars each year is a fight for the very survival of the South.

The gateway to Moslem North Africa is a road strewn with slavery and death, persecution and corruption, torture and deprivation. My introduction to it was crawling along a "road" at a pitiful speed of nine miles per hour while I breathed air so heavy with the putrefaction of human flesh that I was heaving. Dead bodies in various stages of decay lay strewn everywhere as witness of the bloody and cruel war that has raged relentlessly since the declaration upon Sudan of *Shari'a* in 1983. This country, Africa's largest and covering almost 8 percent of the continent, has a population counted variously between 26 and 28 million people of whom roughly 70 percent are Moslems, 20 percent Christians, and 10 percent Animist.

In the longest recorded war in Africa, Sudan has seen the slaughter of millions of its people through civil war, the displacement of over 5 million refugees, and the literal enslavement of hundreds of thousands. In the mid-1870s the Moslems argued, "It might be wrong to enslave people but the economics of Sudan require a constant flow of fresh slaves and can any reasonable man deny that the life of a Negro, as a slave in Egypt, Turkey or Syria, is infinitely preferable to his life in Equatoria (a province of Southern Sudan) or the Congo where life is poor, nasty, brutish and short?" During that period, almost 80 percent of the Sudanese population were slaves. Every Moslem, even the poorest, owned a slave.

Nothing has really changed today where hundreds of thousands of black Africans are on sale in Moslem Sudan at the price of $100 (U.S. dollars) a human being! The only escape from slavery and death is to convert to Islam. Sudan, in one of the worst travesties of modern humanity, is engrossed on "systematically destroying the fabric of society in the South and the Nuba Mountains by means of terror and hunger. In short, the Government of Sudan is committing genocide." This report from Christian Solidarity International goes virtually ignored while human rights are ruthlessly violated on a daily basis.

One of the quickest ways for the sigh and cry of any peoples to reach God is through the oppression of slavery. The Holy Spirit assured me that the Lord has heard the sigh of the southern Sudanese and is sending a mighty deliverance. It is not the power of carnal weapons nor even the concerted prayer of multitudes of Christians that will set Sudan free, but the travail and intercession of vessels who really know how to pour out their hearts to Him. Prayer has largely failed; now it is time to intercede.

Southern Sudan is strategic in Africa. It is the gateway for the Islamic advance south and should, therefore, also be the door and launching pad of the Christian crusade north. The military principle of the "best form of defense is a good offense" is very appropriate in the Sudanese context.

"All too often," the Spirit spoke, "My people are simply too willing to sit back and accept what comes. It is absolutely required that you fight no less in the war in intercession than a natural soldier does on the battlefront. My people, however, are reluctant to expend the energy. You are going to Sudan not to tell the world of horrors and war but to conduct one of the strongest battles ever fought on African soil. It is a war for the very survival of the whole continent. You are against the powers of the prince of Persia who has come down with his evil system. It is the same spirit that inspired Pharaoh."

Commander Thomas Cirillo, of the Sudanese Peoples Liberation Army (SPLA) was a former officer in the artillery corps of the Moslem army. He describes how the Sudanese Moslem army would take whole families into the Sahara Desert and make parents bury their children up to their necks in the sand. Thereafter, they would place a bottle of water in front of the face of each child with the parents lined up and looking on, the soldiers standing in between. As long as the parents were prepared to bow to Allah and declare the Shahada they could give their children water and dig them from the sand. If they refused, the children were left to bake to death whilst the parents were crucified nearby and left for the vultures to pick.

The same commander read and translated a letter taken from the corpse of a young Arab Moslem who had been killed the day before my arrival. In that letter written home to his mother, the young man had declared, "Mother, do not cry for me when I die in this *jihad* (holy war) for I know that I am going to paradise. Be sure that you send my two younger brothers here to take my place, that they too, may have the honor of dying and also going to paradise.

Commander Thomas himself has openly declared:

> The Moslems cannot defeat us. We stand firm as Christians and we will die for our faith. Our struggle is not against Islam or against Moslems, but is against a regime that wants to destroy our African heritage. It is discouraging to see that the Islamic dictatorship in Khartoum receives material and moral support from other Islamic countries, while we receive no support from the Christian world. But we will continue our struggle for freedom even if we are forsaken by Christendom. We will die for our faith and we will die as Christians.

The initial trips to "spy out the land" produced good reports despite the land mines, the bombing, and the death and destruction we encountered everywhere we went. It is obvious that the Moslems are very serious about their war and have no intention of releasing southern Sudan spiritually or physically. I was sincerely requested by both military and civilian administrations to open a Bible school and train a corps of chaplains, whilst being greatly encouraged by the authorities in the vision of holding crusades across the liberated zones. Such receptivity has already launched the devil on a concerted attack not only to slow, but completely derail the initiative. He has thrown every tactic and force into the battle before we have even moved north. Defections to the enemy have taken place as our own familiar friends have risen up and conspired against us. Every conceivable thing that possibly could go wrong, technically, has done so. From the outset of my being commissioned for Sudan by the Holy Spirit, the fight has been fierce. He has attempted to divide the core of the ministry but, happily, has not succeeded. I have seen him seek to rob and plunder us, confuse and derail the mission, and close doors to us.

Supplies and equipment have had to be trucked from Durban in South Africa through the customs of 9 separate nations, involving 18 different transactions in all. Clearing agents have failed to do their jobs correctly, documents have mysteriously disappeared, and the enemy has confused the airways regarding orders and instructions. We have fought in intercession each step of the way and have ultimately prevailed, but it has been tough, very tough. This incredibly prophetic journey is for the purpose of establishing a permanent base in southern Sudan where there are no supplies of any description. Because of drought, there is limited food. Consequently, all of our personal supplies have had to be transported from southern Africa. Multitudes of refugees are pouring into Uganda from southern Sudan mostly from drought-related starvation rather than the fighting.

As we dedicated the team for Sudan, the Holy Spirit declared, "Sudan is a virgin land. Though some have had the Word, they have never experienced the fire. Your main purpose as you set up battle against the enemy is to bring My fire into the land. I want intercessors, but they must be only those who fulfill these conditions. If a man would really be *prepared* to take his family—his wife, his children, his relatives, and his goods—and move to Sudan to live, then he may intercede for the land. If a man does not have My fire, he may not intercede. If a man is a gossip or backbiter, he may not intercede. I must have purity coming out of pure vessels. There must be no opportunity for the enemy to blaspheme and therefore have occasion against you so that you are unable to complete the task. Remember, Sudan is to you as a virgin land. She has never had the fire and is one of those lands that prevents the coming of the King."

Am I ready to pour out my heart for Sudan as if it were my own land? Am I ready to cry out and travail for a stranger who faces death and loss of home and loved ones as if they were mine? Am I willing to spend and be spent for a people who do not know me or the power of intercession or the God of that power so that they might go free at my expense? Am I truly prepared not to fight any less hard for Sudan in giving, going, and interceding than I would for myself?

"How would you feel," said the Holy Spirit, "if you came home and found your wife beaten, raped, and dead whilst your children had been taken into slavery? How would you feel if you reached your mother's home and found her crucified because she loves the Lord? That's how I want you to pray—as if such criminal acts were being perpetrated against your very own."

The Holy Spirit fell on another of those simple African songs that is more anointed the longer it is sung. The song carries a distinct cry of the Holy Spirit to sacrifice in the fight so that He is able to undertake:

Ndidalira, Ndidalira, Ndidalira Ine
I depend, depend, depend on You.

One: Inu Mbuye (x3)
You Lord (x3)

All: Ndidalira Ine (x3)
I depend on You.

One: Pamavuto
In troubles

All: Ndidalira Ine
I depend on You.

One: Ku Sudan
In Sudan

All: Ndidalira, Ndidalira, Ndidalira Ine
I depend, depend, depend on You.

How shall I do any less than give my all and be ready for any sacrifice for Jesus because He paid the ultimate sacrifice for me? Moslems often tell me, "The problem with you Christians is that you are not prepared to die for what you believe, whereas we Moslems are."

I declare that not only are we not ready to die for Jesus, most are not willing to even *live* for Him. I was reminded of the great hymn, "So Send I You," which is seldom sung and perhaps even known today. It is one of those timeless, true missionary songs. As I thought about the words, the Holy Spirit whispered, "Yes, I inspired it, and the words are Mine."

> "So send I you, by grace made strong to triumph
> O'er hosts of hell, o'er darkness, death and sin,
> My name to bear, and in that name to conquer
> So send I you, My victory to win.
>
> So send I you, to take to souls in bondage
> The word of truth that sets the captive free,
> To break the bonds of sin, to loose death's fetters -
> So send I you, to bring the lost to Me.
>
> So send I you My strength to know in weakness,
> My joy in grief, My perfect peace in pain,
> To prove My power, My grace, My promised presence
> So send I you, eternal fruit to gain.
>
> So send I you to bear My cross with patience,
> And then one day with joy to lay it down,
> To hear My voice,
> "Well done, My faithful servant
> Come, share My throne, My Kingdom, and My crown."

The strongman over Sudan is being bound. As this is done in the spirit, so there will be great change in the natural. I fully expect the Khartoum regime to be overthrown. God heard our cries for Mozambique and He will do the same for Sudan. The regime has defied the Living God and usurped Glory due His name. Enough is enough, and those who have exalted themselves must be abased.

Khartoum has touched the Holy Vessels, and the regime is weighed and found wanting. They will be overthrown in one night. Nothing must stop the Gospel from going forth. Because of obedience to God's Word to take *fire* into Sudan, I am able to claim God's protection from the enemy. When any fight against us, they are fighting against the Lord; He becomes my Shield and my exceeding great Reward. We are praying confusion and anarchy in Khartoum. The Spirit said, "Remember the word of the Lord to Isaiah on behalf of Hezekiah?"

"Yes," I eagerly acknowledged. "It is in Chapter 37."

"I will send a blast upon him, and he shall hear a rumor, and return to his own land; and I will cause him to fall by the sword in his own land" (Isa. 37:7), repeated the Holy Spirit.

"I want you to pray that Khartoum will hear a *rumor* and that there will be an overthrow of the system and freedom again," said the Spirit.

I took up the charge and immediately felt the prompting of the Spirit to pray for offense between Libya and the Khartoum government and that the already existent offense between Egypt, Eritrea, and Ethiopia against the Khartoum government will explode into a major issue, which will cause a withdrawal of all forces from the South. Since the Lord clearly said, "Prayer has failed, only intercession will succeed," we have been locked in mortal combat that will continue until we break through to the very Throne where we will be assured of victory.

CHAPTER TWENTY-NINE

The Apple of His Eye

G OD DEFINITELY HAS favorites, and they are those who are obedient to do His will. At the same time, to him who is given much, is much required. It is very sobering working with the Holy Spirit. He allows the intercessor no license, for His ministry is serious, very serious indeed. Without Him, nobody is able to come to Jesus. There is no such an issue of, "I gave my heart..." as is commonly declared in Christian circles. The Holy Spirit makes very clear through the Word, *"Ye have not chosen Me, but I have chosen you, and ordained you, that ye should go and bring forth fruit..."* (John 15:16).

Without the Godhead, I am nothing and can do nothing. Without the blessed Holy Spirit, it is impossible to be convicted of sin, righteousness, and judgment or to enjoy any kind of fellowship with the Lord. In God's order of things, there is "The Price of Disobedience" whilst at the same time, there is "The Reward of Obedience." Perhaps like nobody else, the intercessor enjoys an intimacy with the Lord and a knowledge of the inner chamber that makes him, *"The apple of God's eye"* (see Deut. 32:10).

When God ordains a mission for the intercessor, the latter has the right then to expect God's divine protection and provision. Similarly, those who come against the intercessor in the natural are coming against God, for the intercessor is on divine appointment. Because the great commission to reach *every creature* with the Gospel is so very important to the Lord, it is therefore reasonable to assume that any interference in that agenda is a direct violation of that which is dear to

God's heart. Opposing God, especially when His Spirit is moving, will bring down His wrath even in this "Age of Grace."

I well recall my earlier days when I was really battling financially. The presence and blessings of the Lord was stamped upon everything. There just never seemed to be enough money to do all that I not only needed, but also wanted to do. I was having a conversation with the Lord about the matter and complaining to Him of the situation. Without warning, the Holy Spirit quickly challenged, "Should you wish for one million dollars right now, I will give it to you."

Suddenly, my grumbling ended as I was face to face with His divine person and all the bravado was gone. This was reality, and my breath was completely taken away as my mind raced to give an appropriate reply. In the light of His presence and eternity, my complaint was paltry and even a million dollars was not attractive. Of course in those days, a million was an awfully large amount of money. I was afraid to say anything for I knew just how serious the Spirit was.

"Come on," He prompted. "I'm offering you all that money. What's your reply?" He questioned.

Suddenly, I felt all the passion of the Holy Spirit Himself pour through me. *His* choice was all that mattered. I blurted out, "Give me a million souls," and it seemed that the deed was done right away.

I have seen over the years the Lord raise and train an army of men and women in Africa who have gone through the nations and won multitudes of souls because His *modus operandi* is multiplication through fire-filled vessels according to the principles of the Acts of the Holy Spirit. The great commission is "the apple of His eye," and the moment that anyone becomes truly jealous for "every creature," they instantly merit the favor of the Almighty. At the same time, God has faithfully provided as we have poured our life into the work of winning the lost, sometimes under the most difficult of circumstances.

There are times when the enemy has directly sought my annihilation and that which he purposes for evil, God turns around for good. I had traveled to a remote tip of southern Malawi for ministry and also to visit a school where fees had to be paid for some orphans. I parked the vehicle in the shade of a large baobab tree and was instantly surrounded by hundreds of children. It is generally my habit to play with them. I was engrossed in some activity with children running in all directions laughing, shouting, and falling on the ground when all of a sudden, the headmaster appeared from his office at a distance. He was shouting and running towards me waving his arms crazily. With the distance and the noise of the children, I was unable to follow what he was trying to communicate. Without warning, the children broke into pandemonium and ran in all directions. Some of the smaller ones were bowled over and stampeded, but they in turn were up and off in a frenzied rush.

I was thinking that the headmaster was of the opinion that the children were annoying me and he had come to discipline them. Halfway through his advance the man leapt into the air, completed a double turn and fled back to his office. The whole scene looked so comical and happened so quickly that all I could do was collapse into laughter. I was in the greatest of mirth when, from behind, the first wave descended upon me without warning. They were a swarm of African killer bees.

The whole event happened so swiftly that I barely had time to even think. All I could feel was the pain as literally hundreds of bees stung me with still more descending. They were up my nose, in my mouth, down my chest, and lodged in every part of my clothing. I was quickly numbed by the huge amount of poison being pumped into my body and was rapidly going into shock. Usually allergic to any bee sting, only one was enough to send me into unconsciousness. I had been accompanied by two little girls and one of my native pastors. The girls had sat quietly in the vehicle with the pastor. When the second wave began to hit me, I knew that I had to get the girls away. I leapt into the car and closed the window, instructing them to do likewise and to lie flat on the floor and try not to beat off any bees that might begin to buzz around them.

In the meantime, I was already crying out to the Lord, "I'm ready to go home, but there is still so much to do."

Instantly the peace and calm of the Holy Spirit descended upon me, and I felt His presence round about. I was not anxious and not in the least concerned about death though I felt like a walking corpse. In minutes, my entire body had swollen to double its size and my eyes were almost shut. My ears were ringing, and if ever I might have felt like I had experienced an overdose of heroin from the descriptions I had read, then I was hallucinating from something very similar. I concentrated all my efforts upon getting the vehicle with the little girls out of the killing zone. In the process of leaping into the car and waving off the bees, I had accidentally knocked off my spectacles. There was no time to retrieve them and far too many bees to even consider such an attempt. The entire swarm had surrounded the car and were frantically attempting to get at us. I drove the vehicle well clear of the bees. There were still hundreds inside the vehicle and I kept praying for the Holy Spirit to cover the children who lay quietly on the floor and never moved.

As soon as we were well away, I pulled the little ones out and left them in the safe keeping of a villager whilst I went to retrieve my spectacles. Miraculously, the children were not stung once. When I reached the spot again, the entire swarm had descended upon those glasses, having picked up my scent. They were very angry bees. I later discovered that the older boys had been stoning the hive to deliberately anger the creatures and create just such an incident.

By that stage my fingers were the size of sausages. I sat in the heat and dizziness and numbness, my mind racing against time. In the natural, I should already have been past being dead. My throat and chest had constricted, and I was gulping for breath. I quickly thought that by revving the exhaust fumes on to the bees, they would disperse at least sufficiently for me to snatch my glasses into the car. As soon as the diesel fumes began to pour upon them, the bees scattered in an angry cloud. I instructed the pastor who had accompanied me back to the scene that he open the door quickly and grab the glasses. Terror overcame him as he watched thousands of bees swarming the car. He froze to his seat. Quickly I jumped over him opened the door only sufficiently to slip out my hand and grab my spectacles before the bees swarmed me again. I do not even know if I was stung again. At least thereafter, I was able to see.

As I sat pondering my options, I saw a crippled man making his way toward the car. He had a withered leg and leaned heavily on a cane. I was amazed and instantly thought him to be, perhaps, the witch doctor who owned and controlled the bees by his magic. This is very common in Africa. The cripple seemed completely oblivious to what was happening. I jumped up and down trying to gain his attention so that I might warn him, but to no avail. Despite my discomfort, impending death and the heat inside the vehicle, I sat transfixed by what was about to happen. The man was not a witch doctor. Suddenly, he hobbled into the "killing zone" and was instantly attacked. What happened next, I shall never forget. I witnessed an instant miracle! The man threw away his cane, threw up his hands and fled. That withered leg pumped into action, and he took off running like the wind.

I was four hours from the nearest facility where I might obtain medical assistance. I gathered several local pastors to pray for me. A simple prayer of faith turned the situation. The calm assurance that all was fine grew stronger as we departed for Blantyre. By the time we arrived in the city, I was back to normal. There was not a single indication of how seriously ill I had been. I never even bothered to see a doctor. The Divine Physician had already intervened. I felt quite a fraud. To date, I am no longer allergic to any bee sting! The enemy had sought to get rid of me but He had set charge over me and delivered me from the snare of the fowler.

The intercessor must never wage a personal battle. The weapons of war are not carnal, but mighty to the pulling down of strongholds. My first test case was during the war years in Rhodesia. Everyone was part of the military and carried a rifle. As a pastor living in a remote rural community, I spent most of my days either in intercession or visiting and encouraging the local farmers and villagers. I had been given a handsome rifle but was not really committed to carrying one. The rifle lay in the trunk of my car and the magazine elsewhere.

One day, the Holy Spirit spoke concerning that weapon, "Michael, just as long as you have that rifle, you are going to fight your own battles because the matter is in your hands. Imagine what will happen if the terrorists should stop you and find that weapon. If, however, you get rid of that weapon and trust Me, then the battle becomes Mine, and I will fight for you."

The matter could not have been clearer, and as an intercessor, I would far rather have the Lord fight for me than try to solve the problems myself. Consequently, I surrendered the weapon and trusted the Lord. From that moment He truly became my shield whether driving through the war zones of Rhodesia or flying through the MiGs and radar of Mozambique. God has been my protector, whether driving the land-mined roads of southern Sudan or facing the anti-personnel mines on the village paths. Through bullets and roadblocks manned by trigger-happy youths toting AK-47 rifles, God has been my protector and shield. In the words of the wonderful hymn:

"Cast care aside, lean on Thy Guide

His boundless mercy will provide

Trust and thy trusting souls shall prove

That Christ is all in all to thee."

Through all the trials and persecutions, I have learned that He is sufficient and He will see me through. When the enemy comes against me as His intercessor, he is coming against the Lord. In the order of things, the spiritual enemy inspires his natural counterpart who becomes the tool and medium to wipe out God's people and frustrate God's program for the preaching of the Gospel to every creature. Just as long as we turn the tables and recognize that the battle is directly against the "apple of God's eye," then victory is assured. God will fight. Of course I know that we are living in the Age of Grace and that God is merciful. But, I am also a pragmatist and realist. Some people deliberately line up with the enemy and, in so doing, make a choice of being used by him. They must bear their own responsibilities and carry their own burdens. God is as much in the judging business today as He ever has been. He will remove the tyrant who stops the Word from reaching every creature, *even* in this Age of Grace.

So many times, not only have I seen the Lord miraculously protect and deliver Me, but He has also been there to comfort and undertake for me in periods of sickness and bodily affliction. There have been times of sickness because of a direct attack of the devil often through the magic of a witch doctor. The Bible is very clear that if we *"resist the devil he must flee"* (see James 4:7).

At other times, there has been sickness and disease because of water, food, or general conditions. At such times there is the practice of anointing with oil and the prayer of faith as prescribed by James in his Epistle (see James 5:15). It works every time and my oil has variously been engine oil, kerosene, or cooking oil. Sometimes, it is necessary to take up a position of abiding so as to overcome, but victory is as assured as Jesus' arising from the dead.

There have been times when I was so delirious that I thought I would never live to see another day. In such moments, the power of anointing with oil and the accompanying deliverance has been mighty, and I have instantly arisen on many occasions completely whole.

CHAPTER THIRTY

The Vials of Odors

NOBODY MAY EITHER doubt or argue that there are *three* major developments in the Book of Revelation that are dramatically associated with the "prayers of the saints." That God in His providential dealings should have chosen to use and rely upon fickle men never ceases to amaze me. Yet, the truth faces us in stark reality directly from the pages of His Word as well as personal testimonies, both past and present. Today, as ever, God needs an Esther, a Daniel, an Ezra, as well as a Peter, James, and John to achieve His purposes for man in this age. His greatest and most important purpose is for the Gospel to go to *"the ends of the earth."*

In the Old Testament Tabernacle of Moses, the prominent item of furniture in the Holy place was the golden altar of incense. It stood directly in front of the Ark on this side of the curtain indicating that it was the last and most important act to be performed before access into the Holy of Holies. The priests were to burn incense thereon morning and evening so that a rich fragrance filled the room continually. The bread on the Table of Shewbread was to be saturated with that fragrance as it stood for the whole week before being eaten by the priests. Very powerfully, the incense was made of four main ingredients, all of which had very strong prophetic significance. According to Exodus 30:34 the Lord commanded, *"Take unto thee sweet spices, stacte, and onycha and galbanum; these sweet spices with pure frankincense; of each shall there be a like weight."*

The stacte was a sap from a desert thorn that would ooze and distill forth from the tree. It was collected and dried and beaten into fine powder. Significantly, each of the ingredients was nothing on its own, but once combined together made such a fragrance that God had to warn Israel that they should not use it or make anything like the incense for a perfume. The distilling of the stacte speaks of the *prophetic* word oozing forth from the anointed vessel.

Onycha was an ocean shell with a pungent, unpleasant odor. Gathered, dried, and ground into fine powder, it was an important ingredient, for the Hebrew word *onycha* means to roar as a lion. There are times when the intercessor must roar as a lion. When the African lion roars, the whole jungle goes absolutely silent and still for all beasts know that the king of the jungle has spoken. There comes then, that time, when only the *roar* will make the enemy take note. It has nothing to do with loudness, but all to do with authority.

The galbanum was a white, fatty gum gathered from a desert shrub. The word in Hebrew means to oil or grease and speaks of prayer, which "oils" our Christian lives.

Finally, the most important and fragrant ingredient is the frankincense. This most costly of products could be afforded only by the very rich and was given to Jesus as a gift at His birth. The word in the Hebrew means white, *white* speaking of absolute purity, and points to the highest offering in the incense—that of worship. Jesus' life was a continual fragrance to the Father, and without worship, there can be no true intercession.

Daily, as the incense ascended to the Lord, the ingredients were a sweet aroma and signified their prophetic role. Isaiah, in his "redemption" chapters, reveals the heart of God and declares that the day was coming that whosoever offered incense anymore would be as if he blessed an idol. There is something far greater to God and of infinitely more fragrance than even the costly incense made according to His own perfect recipe. The sweeter aroma is that which comes forth from the deepest, inner part of a separated vessel and flows forth in a fluent stream to the Lord. God no longer wants a smoke from ingredients on an altar, but He wants the smoke of the anointed word, prayers, intercessions or roar, praise and worship and tears from the living altar of a New Testament saint. It is for this reason that we are called *"lively stones"* or *"kings and priests,"* and are supposed *"to show forth the praises of Him who has called* [us] *out of darkness into His marvelous light"* (1 Pet. 2:9).

Revelation 19:10 summarizes two key themes woven through the Book of Revelation. These themes are worship and "the testimony of Jesus is the spirit of prophecy." The latter cannot exist without the former and is dependent upon it. Without worship, there can be no anointed word coming from any vessel or "priest."

What then does the testimony of Jesus and spirit of prophecy have in common? Precisely this: The anointed word is that word distilled and stirred by the Holy Spirit who has taken up His residence in a separated vessel. The word that such a vessel speaks is not his own. The whole ministry of the Holy Spirit is to glorify Jesus; therefore the ministry of that separated vessel is to glorify Jesus too. Only those who really have the authority of the Lord are able to speak the truly anointed or prophetic word.

The more that I worship, the stronger becomes the testimony of Jesus, and therefore, the mightier is the spirit of prophecy. After John eats the book in chapter 10, he is commanded to prophesy to "many peoples, and nations, and tongues, and kings." This is of exceptional importance since we are clearly told that the book is sweet in the mouth but bitter in the belly.

Ezekiel was commanded to eat the scroll with the same results. This is a perfect prophetic picture of the *intercessor*. The revelation of the word is sweet to the mouth but once it gets down into the inner being or seat of the Spirit the responsibility of that word is heavy and enormous. The intercessor is obliged to "take action," and this is the bitterness in the belly. The ministry of that word and of the intercessor is to *prophesy* or declare the wonderful Gospel to *every creature* to the ends of the earth, to every people and kindred and tribe and tongue.

Now, the three major developments involving the "prayers of the saints" includes the opening of the book, the Judgment of God, and the cry of the martyrs. In Revelation 6, with the opening of the fifth seal, the martyrs are revealed with the specific description that they were *"slain for the word of God, and for the testimony which they held"* (Rev. 6:9). Once again, the Spirit presents us with the picture of the testimony of Jesus being the Spirit of prophesy in the death of the martyrs whose company is far from complete as described in verse 11.

It seems clear that the cry of the martyrs paves the way for the opening of the sixth seal. Such is the power and importance of intercession.

The sixth seal brings such terror upon the earth that all the inhabitants flee and seek to hide from the face of God's wrath, so terrible it is. Before it happens, however, the Company of Martyrs must be completed. The blood of those slain for "the testimony of Jesus" cries out to God from the ground for vengeance. Just as Abel's blood cried out, so does the blood of everyone who has been murdered, including the multitudes of aborted. God is bound to avenge abortion against every nation. In the same way, He will avenge the blood of every martyr.

There is a call going forth today for that Company to be completed. The Church is going to see the greatest number of martyrs, perhaps for her entire age, consummated in this hour in which we live. Such terrifies most Christians, but it is nevertheless true.

In Revelation 5, it is very clear that there is a direct relationship between Jesus receiving the book, breaking the seals, and opening it, and the intercession of the saints whose incense has been collected in golden vials. This is called, *"odors, which are the prayers of saints"* (Rev. 5:8).

May I suggest that the word goes so far as to reveal that Jesus is assisted in the opening of the book by these very odors. Indeed, no man is worthy to take the book and break the seals except Jesus, but He has given the saints the privilege to be a part of this tremendous event. Once again, the harps speak of worship, which chapter 5 goes on to describe in detail. The opening of the book is accompanied by the singing of a *new song* or the song of Heaven which is the song of the Lamb notably "Thou art Worthy...."

Remembering that Moses sang the song of Moses and of the Lamb at the Red Sea reveals the significance of high praises in intercession. In Revelation 15, they sing the song of the Lamb and of Moses. I am not saying it is the only earthly song sung in Heaven, but it is the only one that I have found to be recorded. The prayers of the saints have been collected over the centuries. These are not the simple, selfish prayers of so many people for their own desires, but the intercessions of those who have made themselves available to the Holy Spirit to be used for earth-shattering change. Such intercession culminates in the judgment of God.

Everyone who has ever carried the burden of the Holy Spirit in his bosom and cried out for the lost, or for God to be glorified in the earth, or wept and travailed for those imprisoned, or agonized for the martyrs, or angered against the blasphemy of man towards God will have had their cries and tears and prayers and sighs captured and placed into a bottle. Such are odors are sweeter than the beautiful fragrance that the priests offered on the Altar of Incense. It is for this reason that God does not want literal incense anymore. He has found something far sweeter; it is the prayers of the saints who assist in the opening of the book. Such a tremendous event must absolutely stir us to intercession like never before. For eternity, your tears and cries and sighs are going to be poured on the altar before His throne to offer the sweetest smell to God that has ever been produced. No wonder we are commanded to work whilst there is yet time.

Finally, in Revelation chapter 8, the seventh seal is broken preparing the way for the sounding of the seven trumpets. The significance here is that there is silence for the space of half an hour. Silence speaks of judgment and the Lord used silence at Jericho to judge that city before the walls even fell. The silence of Revelation will be a silence of the entire universe and will bring a reigning terror to all of creation except those who are under the blood of the Lamb. In verse 3, an angel has a censer full of incense, which is clearly revealed as the prayers of the saints. Those are not common prayers but the true intercessions of such as who have been jealous for God and His creation. These intercessions are the prayers that have been directed by the Holy Spirit Himself who *"helpeth our infirmities: for we know not what we should pray for as we ought...because He maketh intercession for the saints according to the will of God"* (Rom. 8:26-27).

Once again, the incense is poured out upon the grand Golden Altar before the throne. Such incense is true intercession that ascends up to God. And still once again, there is a direct relationship between these intercessions of the saints and the release of the next series of events in God's order of judgment. Part of that judgment is the vindication of God Himself against all the wickedness perpetrated by man.

Anyone at all, then, who feels that intercession is over is missing the greatest opportunity to have his cries as part of that Holy Incense delighting the nostrils of the Lord for all eternity. The intercessor is, indeed, the watchman on the walls, and his job will never be completed until his call home. It is not insignificant, either, that following the eating of the book by John in chapter 10, comes the intercession and prophecies of the two witnesses, culminating in the catching away.

Chapter 11 of revelation significantly opens with the measurement of the temple of God and the altar and the true worshippers. Again, the Word reveals the interwoven themes of worship, prophesy, the testimony of Jesus, and intercession. Of particular importance is the fact that God does not work sovereignly but in concert with His people: those who are willing and obedient. It is for this reason that Daniel declared, *"But the people that do know their God shall be strong, and do exploits"* (Dan. 11:32).

This declaration follows Daniel's three-whole-weeks fast. This fast enabled the angel of the Lord to break through the ranks of the prince of Persia and reveal mysteries and secrets concerning the last days. It is apparent that without Daniel's fast it would have been impossible for the messenger to have reached the prophet. God has chosen to work in close conjunction with His people through intercession, the cry of which will always reach the ears of the Lord.

Other books by Michael Howard

RECKLESSLY ABANDONED is a true story about the war years in Zimbabwe and of how an ordinary young man believed in and obeyed his extraordinary God.

LOVE CONSTRAINED, the sequel to *Recklessly Abandoned*, is about missions work in war-torn Mozambique and how God used ordinary people through intercession to change the destiny of a nation.

THE ONLY GOOD ONE IS A DEAD ONE. Real stories of African snakes and how alike they are in character to the devil. An unusual look at breaking soul ties.

THE PRICE OF DISOBEDIENCE is a study on the price paid by a person, church, or nation when they do not obey God's Word.

WHAT IS YOUR DESTINY? is a powerful exhortation to the Body of Christ today to line up with the Word of God and carry out His destiny for you.

THE PERVERTED GOSPEL is an end-time book that reveals how the Church has taken different aspects of the Word and made them into Gospel thus perverting the only Gospel.

Contact the Author

For further information regarding the work of this ministry please contact us at any of the following:

KALIBU MINISTRIES

P.O. Box 124

Escourt 3310

South Africa

Tel: 011-27-363-335399

Fax: 011-27-363-335399

KALIBU MINISTRIES

P.O. Box 1473,

Blantyre, Malawi, Africa

Tel: 011-265-633187

Email: Kalibu@malawi.net

KALIBU MINISTRIES

P.O. BOX 55

Banket, Zimbabwe

011-263-67-26293

Email: rozhoward@mango.zw

SHEKINAH MINISTRIES
P.O. Box 34685
Kansas City, MO 64116
United States of America
Tel: (816) 734-0493
Fax: (816) 734-0218
Email: Shekmin@aol.com

SHEKINAH MINISTRIES
P.O. Box 186, Station A
Etobicoke M9C 1C0
+1-416-626-1543

SHEKINAH MINISTRIES
17 Wayside
Weston-super-Mare
England BS22 9BL
011-44-1934-629785
JandH@wint829.fsnet.co.uk

OUT OF AFRICA
Päivölänrinne 1 E
FI-04220 Kerava
Finland
358 404 13 22 00
andreas@outofafrica.fi

Books to help you grow strong in Jesus

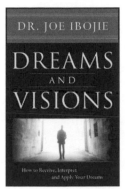

DREAMS AND VISIONS: HOW TO RECEIVE, INTERPRET AND APPLY YOUR DREAMS

By Joe Ibojie

Dreams and Visions presents sound scriptural principles and practical instructions to help us understand dreams and visions. It seeks to equip believers in the revelatory realm of dreams, their interpretation and usefulness in our everyday living. The book provides readers with the necessary understanding to approach dreams and visions by the Holy Spirit, through biblical illustrations, understanding of the meaning of dreams and prophetic symbolism, and by exploring the art of dream interpretation according to ancient methods of the Bible.

ISBN: 88-89127-13-9

THE ILLUSTRATED BIBLE-BASED DICTIONARY OF DREAM SYMBOLS

By Joe Ibojie

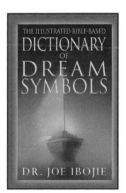

The Illustrated Bible-Based Dictionary of Dream Symbols is the companion book to *Dreams and Visions: How to Receive, Interpret and Apply Your Dreams*. This book will help today's believers to understand the images and meanings of what they see in their dreams. When used through the Holy Spirit, it can take away the frustration of not knowing what your dreams mean and avoid the dangers of misinterpretation.

ISBN: 88-89127-14-7

Order Now from Destiny Image Europe
Telephone: +39 085 4716623- Fax +39 085 4716622
E-mail: ordini@eurodestinyimage.com

Internet: www.eurodestinyimage.com

HOW TO LIVE THE SUPERNATURAL LIFE IN THE HERE AND NOW

By Joe Ibojie

This book teaches you how to bring the Natural and the Supernatural to a place of balance in your life. Despite the tendency to live life in compartments, Dr. Ibojie believes that all of life is spiritual! The book will show you how to blend the Supernatural and the Natural, allowing you to function in harmony in all aspects of your life!

ISBN: 88-89127-16-3

COVENANT: G-D'S PLAN FOR ISRAEL IN THE LAST DAYS

By Baruch Battelstein

Are you ready for the great and awesome Day of the Lord? Do you know and recognize with understanding how the horrendous events that will take place shortly on this earth are going to impact your life and those around you? Perhaps you are one watching from afar thinking it will not come near me? No one will be able to escape. Are you ready? Like a tsunami racing across the ocean, events are taking place today that in our minds only a few short years ago we could not, in fact would not even dare conceive, yet they have come to pass; Events and changes that are happening seemingly in the blink of an eye. This book has been written with a pen of a ready writer. The author has brought forth in clarity, G-d's plan for the spiritual and physical redemption of His people, His land, and Jerusalem. His plan as revealed in the Tanach (Bible) is unfolding right before our very eyes.

ISBN: 88-89127-18-X

Order Now from Destiny Image Europe

Telephone: +39 085 4716623- Fax +39 085 4716622
E-mail: ordini@eurodestinyimage.com

Internet: www.eurodestinyimage.com

CONFESSIONS OF A FASTING HOUSEWIFE

By Catherine Brown

This books is more than a spiritual guide to fasting—it is a practical primer on the "dos and don'ts" of fasting. Within these pages, Catherine Brown shares her experience in fasting in a 21st century world. Her humor, insight, and missteps during her sojourn will make you laugh—and empathize—with her plight as she discovers the emotional ups-and-downs of fasting. Spirituality and practically meet head-on in *Confessions of a Fasting Housewife*. Get ready to learn everything your pastor never told you about fasting! Then…fast!

ISBN: 88-89127-10-4

Order Now from Destiny Image Europe

Telephone: +39 085 4716623- Fax +39 085 4716622
E-mail: ordini@eurodestinyimage.com

Internet: www.eurodestinyimage.com

Additional copies of this book and other
book titles from
DESTINY IMAGE EUROPE
are available at your local bookstore.

We are adding new titles every month!

To view our complete catalog on-line, visit us at:

www.eurodestinyimage.com

Send a request for a catalog to:

Via Maiella, 1
66020 S. Giovanni Teatino (Ch) - ITALY
Tel. +39 085 4716623 - Fax +39 085 4716622

✳ ✳ ✳ ✳ ✳ ✳ ✳ ✳ ✳ ✳ ✳ ✳ ✳ ✳ ✳ ✳ ✳ ✳ ✳

Are you an author?

Do you have a "today" God-given message?

CONTACT US

We will be happy to review your manuscript for
a possible publishing.

publisher@eurodestinyimage.com